New Media for a New China

Edited by

James F. Scotton and
William A. Hachten

WILEY-BLACKWELL

A John Wiley & Sons, Ltd., Publication

Registered Office
John Wiley & Sons Ltd, The Atrium, Southern Gate, Chichester, West Sussex,
PO19 8SQ, United Kingdom

Editorial Offices
350 Main Street, Malden, MA 02148-5020, USA
9600 Garsington Road, Oxford, OX4 2DQ, UK
The Atrium, Southern Gate, Chichester, West Sussex, PO19 8SQ, UK

For details of our global editorial offices, for customer services, and for
information about how to apply for permission to reuse the copyright
material in this book please see our website at www.wiley.com/wiley-blackwell.

Library of Congress Cataloging-in-Publication Data

New media for a new China / edited by James F. Scotton and William A. Hachten.
   p. cm.
  Includes bibliographical references and index.
  ISBN 978-1-4051-8797-8 (alk. paper) – ISBN 978-1-4051-8796-1 (pbk. : alk. paper)
1. Mass media and culture–China. 2. Mass media–Political aspects–China.
3. China–Politics and government. I. Scotton, James Francis, 1932- II. Hachten,
William A.
  P94.65.C6N49 2010
  302.230951–dc22

                                      2009045871

A catalogue record for this book is available from the British Library.

Set in 10.5/13pt Minion by Graphicraft Limited, Hong Kong
Printed and bound in Malaysia by Vivar Printing Sdn Bhd

1   2010

New Media for a New China

For Christine and to the memory of Harva

Contents

Notes on Contributors   vii
Preface   ix

Introduction   1

1   2008: New Challenges to China's Media   11
     William A. Hachten and James F. Scotton

2   Development and Theory of the Media   19
     William A. Hachten

3   The Impact of New Media   28
     James F. Scotton

4   Newspapers: Changing Roles   43
     Guo Ke

5   Magazines: An Industry in Transition   61
     Chen Peiqin

6   Radio Broadcasting: Deregulation and Development   74
     Chen Peiqin and Haigui Liu

7   Television: Entertainment   83
     Anne Cooper-Chen with Yu Leon Liang

8   Television: News   98
     Anne Cooper-Chen and James F. Scotton

9   Xinhua: The Voice of the Party   115
     James F. Scotton

10 Advertising: Wings for the Media   128
     Hong Cheng

11   Public Relations   141
     Yan Jin

12   Film: An Industry versus Independents   163
     Yong Liu

13   English-Language Media in China   183
     Guo Ke

14   Overseas Media Serve Chinese Diaspora   198
     William A. Hachten

15   Conclusion   207
     William A. Hachten and James F. Scotton

Notes   213
Bibliography   238
Index   241

Notes on Contributors

Hong Cheng is an Associate Professor at the E.W. Scripps School of Journalism at Ohio University. He is co-editor of *Advertising and Chinese Society: Impacts and Issues* and *Social Marketing for Public Health: Global Trends and Success Stories*. In 2008–9 he was head of the Advertising Division of the Association for Education in Journalism and Mass Communication (AEJMC). He holds a PhD from Pennsylvania State University.

Anne Cooper-Chen is a Professor at the E.W. Scripps School of Journalism at Ohio University. She was founding director of the Institute for International Journalism at Ohio University and Director of the Ohio-Shandong (China) Center. She is the author or editor of four books. She was a Fulbright Senior Research Scholar in Japan in 1992–3 and was on research leave in China in 2008–9. She holds a PhD from the University of North Carolina-Chapel Hill.

William A. Hachten is Professor Emeritus at the University of Wisconsin-Madison. He is the author of *The World News Prism*, *The Growth of Media in the Third World*, and *The Troubles of Journalism*.

Yan Jin is an Assistant Professor at the School of Mass Communication at Virginia Commonwealth University. She has authored book chapters and numerous articles in the *Journal of Public Relations Research*, *Public Relations Review*, *Journal of Contingencies and Crisis Management* and other publications. She holds a PhD from the University of Missouri-Columbia.

Guo Ke is a Professor at the College of Journalism and Communication and Director of the Center for Global Public Opinion of China at Shanghai International Studies University. He holds an MS degree in Journalism from Kansas State University and a PhD in Mass Communication from Fudan University.

Yu "Leon" Liang is currently working towards dual master's degrees in Journalism and Communication and Development Studies at Ohio University. He is interested in the impact of new media on multicultural societies. He completed a master's degree in Linguistics at Shanghai's Jiao Tong University. He worked as a journalist with *China Daily*, as an editor with the *Observer Star*, and as a commercial assistant with Sun Media Investment Holdings in China.

Haigui Liu is a Professor at the Journalism School of Fudan University. He is the author of 10 books, including *News Psychology, Best News Writing: A Reader*, and *Reporting Strategies of Development for Chinese Newspapers*.

Yong Liu is a Lecturer at the School of Journalism at Fudan University. He is the author of *Television and Film Production Theories in a Digital Age*. He has also produced several short films and the feature film *The Lake* (2008). He holds an MFA degree in Cinema from San Francisco State University.

Chen Peiqin is an Associate Professor at the College of Journalism and Communication at Shanghai International Studies University. In 2006–7 she was a Fulbright Visiting Research Scholar at the Graduate School of Journalism, Columbia University in New York. She holds a PhD from Fudan University, Shanghai.

James F. Scotton is an Associate Professor at the John and Mary Diedrich College of Communication at Marquette University. He has been a Visiting Fulbright Professor at Shanghai International Studies University and Fudan University. He is co-author of *World News Prism* (6th and 7th editions). He holds a PhD from the University of Wisconsin-Madison.

Wynne Wang covers China's financial markets for Dow Jones Newswires in Shanghai and is a photographer. Wynne holds a bachelor's degree in broadcasting at Fudan University. She is married to Robin Xiong. They have a big family with two cats and two dogs.

Preface

During recent years, and particularly in 2008, the eyes of the world have been on China. Several extraordinary news events occurred in that year – a revolt in Tibet, a devastating earthquake in Sichuan, and the spectacular and dramatic Olympic Games in Beijing.

News coverage of these news events – more properly news processes – provided insights into the ways the Chinese media function as well as how the controlling Communist Party reacted to and tried to shape both Chinese and worldwide perceptions of these events. And then, during the early months of 2009, China was wracked by the same global recession that hit the rest of the world.

These events provide the prism through which we have in part studied China's vast media system and how it relates to authority and society.

Both Professors Scotton and Hachten have had a long interest in China and have taught about Chinese mass communication in their journalism and communication classes. In 2001–3, Scotton spent 18 months in China as a visiting Fulbright professor at two universities. In 2007, he was a visiting research associate at Fudan University in Shanghai. On one trip he worked as an editor at the *Shanghai Daily*.

In the early planning for this textbook the authors realized that for such a broad subject it was desirable to include contributions from scholars active in Chinese communication education. So, drawing on his contacts, Scotton recruited several Chinese professors who are affiliated with Chinese or American universities. We are pleased that they have joined our efforts and believe their contributions were essential to this study.

This book is intended to be a textbook for students and scholars who wish to know more about Chinese mass communication. We hope the book will introduce students to the fascinating and complex ways that China's media interact with the nation's 1.3 billion inhabitants – the world's largest media audience. The Chinese people not only receive much information from their government-controlled media (and sometimes from foreign sources), but they often share information with others and initiate communications via cell phones and personal computers. Daily, Chinese news enters the international news flow and much foreign news finds its way into China. Increasingly the world realizes that China is too large and too important to be ignored in global communication. We hope, too, that this book is of interest to the many Chinese who read English.

We have tried to make this text as current and as topical as possible. After all, the news media are mainly concerned with what happens today and tomorrow.

For much of modern history, China has been remote, xenophobic, and self contained with little interest or involvement with Western nations and their affairs. All of that, of course, has changed. With a vibrant economy and spectacular growth and modernization, China has become thoroughly integrated in globalization becoming a major player in world trade and finance. Throughout this dramatic rising up, China has been aided and abetted by modern mass communication.

(Editors note: Some of the chapter notes do not have page numbers. This usually means the material was retrieved from the Internet. No web addresses are given since the material can be obtained from the Internet via a search engine. Also, if no retrieval date is given the material was available, via a search engine, at the time of writing.)

Introduction

The social and economic juggernaut of today's China has exploded onto the stage of our globalized world, and with it has appeared an expanded and vast system of modern communications that enhances and facilitates – but also threatens – the new and self confident nation of over 1.3 billion inhabitants.

The earlier or "old China" utilized the traditional media – newspapers, magazines, radio and even television – all tightly controlled and in fact owned by the ruling Communist Party. By the 1970s, these traditional media expanded after China's leader Deng Xiaoping told party members that making money was acceptable . . . even desirable. His successor Jiang Zemin went further and told the party that if some media could not make a profit in this new market place then those media would close.

These expanding media became part of a rapid economic revolution changing from Marxist communism to authoritarian capitalism (see Figure I.1). Concurrently, the Chinese joined the digital revolution and became conversant with communication satellites, computers, the Internet, email, cell phones, CDs, DVDs and all that went with them, including numerous and uncontrolled blogs. So China now has a modernized, Westernized multimedia society that has been caged within an authoritarian political system that is having difficulty maintaining control over it.

This book will analyze the diverse roles and interactions that China's media play to its vast audience – more TV viewers, more cell phone users, more readers, and more computers sending more e-mails than in any nation in the world. This flood of content enhances as well as threatens the existing political order.

Rapid economic growth has created myriad problems for China – widespread pollution, social stresses, and widening disparities between the newly rich urbanites and poverty ridden peasants in over 500,000 villages.

Figure I.1   Shanghai's Pudong District, which was farmland just 25 years ago. The central areas of China's commercial capital are ablaze with lights every night. The Oriental Pearl Tower sends radio and television signals to 16 million people in the Shanghai area. In the foreground a tourist boat navigates the Huangpo River.
Source: Wynne Wang

With social and economic transformation in the burgeoning great cities have come some civil unrest and a rising yearning for greater civil liberties and human rights. Still controlled and restricted by an authoritarian Communist Party, the media are seeking greater freedom and autonomy. The nation faces a growing struggle between an autocratic government trying to perpetuate itself and a restive urban population – better educated, more affluent and tuned-in to the outside Western world. How will China deal with its vast social problems – harshly or democratically? How China evolves has important implications for the rest of the world. And China's media are right in the middle of this struggle.

Moreover, media in China are major players in the global communication system. They send out news and entertainment and receive both from the West. But many Chinese have long avoided paying for the pirated movies, music CDs, cell phones and computer programs that flow in from abroad. Many believe that China must change its ways and become a full and responsible participant and partner in international communication flows.

From another perspective, the media in China are leading a new revolution. At what some see as "breakneck speed" the media, including Internet blogs and cell phones, are pushing political and social institutions toward change – and openness. This revolution is fueled by a fierce nationalism. Most urban Chinese are proud of their new China and deeply resent criticism from abroad.

Those foreign critics are sometimes unaware or unappreciative of how much the media are changing in China and tend to measure the Chinese media by Western standards. In an attempt to counter this there are many chapters in this book written by Chinese authors. Westerners, particularly Americans, also have a fundamentally different view of government and its role in society. As an article co-written by an American and Chinese author has noted, people in China tend to respect government as a wise parent; Americans distrust government as an always threatening and obtrusive agency.[1]

Although government owned, China's media are as varied as you would expect in any country the size of the United States with four times the population (1.3 billion). The sheer size and reach of media is mind boggling. For example, in 2008 China had 250 million Internet users, 350 million cell phones and perhaps 300 million blogs and countless bloggers building an "all to all" communication network.[2] China Central Television (CCTV) has 16 national channels including one predominantly in English (CCTV-9) that attempts to compete with CNN and the BBC. There are six national radio channels including one aimed at Taiwan. Provinces and cities have their own TV and radio stations, many grouped for better management and financial support. There are hundreds of daily and weekly newspapers and thousands of magazines and journals on every conceivable topic. For example, Fudan University's Journalism Department library in Shanghai makes available 87 Chinese magazines and journals on the subject of communication.

The Chinese government tries to control all media including the Internet and cell phone communications but that is a nearly impossible task. Bloggers, many of them young, are especially likely to challenge authority (as they say, "go under the firewall.") In 2007, bloggers led the way in exposing corrupt officials who let mine and brick kiln owners kidnap and enslave child workers in Shanxi province. A local television picked up the story and it became a national and international scandal. With cell phones, citizens in Xiamen spread photos of protests against a proposed chemical plant in that scenic seaside city. Government officials were forced to cancel the project. Such citizen-led protests clearly upset government officials but even the government's official English-language newspaper, *China Daily*, saw benefits. After the Shanxi scandal one of its columnists called for more investigative journalism.[3]

The media in China by some measures are as free and vigorous – within limits – as most media in the world. Perceptive editors and broadcast news directors know which stories are acceptable and which are not. A leading financial magazine, "Caijing," can expose stock market manipulations and even corrupt public officials but its editors know "where the line is."[4] Thousands of talk radio show callers can harangue local officials about potholed roads and poor health services but program hosts are careful to steer clear of sensitive political issues.

As elsewhere, most media content tends to be entertainment. Young people spend little time following political, economic, and social issues. Surveys show their media time is mostly spent keeping up with music, sports, lifestyle information, and social interaction. A small portion is interested in the "news" and they tend to look at weekly digests in such-scandal focused publications as *Southern Weekend*.[5] Also popular are China's afternoon tabloid newspapers with their diet of sex and crime plus some stories on private or even local government corruption.

But entertainment, especially the reality television shows, attracts huge audiences. The annual CCTV New Year's gala attracted 800 million viewers in 2007 with even a brief appearance catapulting some performers to national stardom. One hugely popular reality show put on by a provincial station, "The Mongolian Cow Sour Yoghurt Super Girl Contest," drew huge national audiences away from the national TV channels. Millions decided the best singer by cell-phone voting. A "cultural journal" which lost its government subsidy attracted a new paying audience with photos of seminude models and celebrity interviews.

Government officials are not always happy with these developments but find it increasingly difficult to restrict the media. Almost all government subsidies have disappeared. Editors and program managers have to pay their bills with circulation and advertising revenue, so they have great leeway in developing popular fare. China's major media have been reconstructed economically but their social functions are now less clear.[6]

The government goes to great lengths to monitor the new media. A reported 50,000 government agents monitor the Internet for signs of dissension. Foreign journalists in China find it difficult to get access to officials and some report outright harassment. Foreign media trying to get established in China find the rules changing suddenly. After years of negotiating his own entry into China's booming media market, media mogul Rupert Murdoch said Chinese officials seem "paranoid" about what gets through media channels.[7]

Chinese media policies seem unpredictable. Reports of more liberal policies and then more stringent controls have appeared in the same week.[8] Chinese regulations regarding media access sometimes seem to go unenforced. Satellite TV receivers officially require licenses in China and are supposed to be strictly limited. Yet, hundreds of satellite dishes are visible on roof tops and balconies in cities such as Shanghai.

Our first chapter considers three major news events in China in 2008 – the worst protests in years against Chinese rule in Tibet in March, a devastating earthquake in Sichuan province in May, and the 2008 Olympic Games in Beijing in August. Hachten and Scotton collaborated in reporting how China's journalists rose to unprecedented heights of professionalism in reporting these events in both the old and the new media. It also records how the Chinese government censors worked to control and censor this news.

Chapter 2, by Hachten, traces the development of media in China and tries to fit the Chinese media experience into one or more of the theories that scholars use in an attempt to explain how the media work. He notes that the most successful Chinese editors have learned to gauge the rivalries in Beijing so they know what is and is not permissible to present to the public. All the time these editors must balance the political sensitivities of China's government leaders with the demands of readers, listeners, viewers, and advertisers.

Scotton's contribution in Chapter 3 shows the enormous impact – not always positive and not always welcomed by the Chinese government or even the Chinese public – that the new media are having on Chinese society. Computers, cell phones, iPods, and other electronic devices are giving the Chinese people new ways to communicate with each other and with people all over the world despite rules and laws that are supposed to limit or prohibit this.

Newspapers remain strong in China with hundreds of millions of readers. In Chapter 4 Guo Ke examines how they are increasingly breaking away to follow independent news sources and controversial stories. Chinese newspaper editors have become expert in discerning the underlying goals and even the moods of Communist Party officials and are quick to move into controversial topics and just as quick to back away when they feel goals and moods are changing. How one Beijing newspaper reports the world to its audience is seen in an excerpt from Michael Meyer's book, *The Last Days of Old Beijing*.

In Chapter 5 Chen Peiqin describes the magazine industry in China which is, as she notes, "an industry in transition." International conglomerates have moved, with Chinese partners, into fashion, sports, and business magazines, areas which the government sees as non-political and therefore open to foreigners. Foreign partners are also welcome to invest in more politically sensitive areas as long as editorial control remains in Chinese hands. But, as Chen suggests, financial influence inevitably translates into editorial influence.

Radio has developed rapidly in China especially in recent years following the government's authorization that allowed stations to develop their own programs. Authors Chen Peiqin and Haigui Liu show in Chapter 6 how talk programs, call-in programs and music programs have grown with some hosts becoming personalities in their own right in the station's city and province. As more prosperous urban Chinese drive to work in private cars, morning and evening drive-time programs have prospered. Computers, a new outlet for radio in China, have brought rapid development of digital radio.

In Chapter 7, on television entertainment, Anne Cooper-Chen rightly points out that most television in China, as elsewhere in the world, consists of entertainment shows. This entertainment includes the same movie reruns you find on TV networks everywhere, but Central China Television (CCTV) has developed its own entertainment shows that capture enormous audiences during Chinese holidays. Lately, however, provincial and even city TV stations have come up with programs that can steal away huge parts of this national audience and foreign satellite channels are constantly seeking a route to these Chinese viewers.

In Chapter 8 Cooper-Chen and Scotton describe how CCTV is trying to remake itself in order to keep the audience its national news programs have attracted for decades. CCTV tries to reach overseas audiences with English, French, and Spanish channels. It has ambitious plans to launch an international 24-hour news channel in English to compete with CNN and the BBC in an effort to win friends for China and to have more influence in the world.

Scotton, in Chapter 9, examines Xinhua, the giant state news agency that can control the content of much of China's media when it wants to exert its authority. It is the voice of China's government and can insist that the Chinese media report only its version of the news. Xinhua faces the problem of all media operations in China. It wants to expand its reach and influence in the world but it relies on government subsidies, which make it unlikely that it will break away from government control.

According to Hong Cheng in Chapter 10 if the media in China are becoming more independent of direct government control, the growth in advertising must be given major credit. He points out that China's media get at least 80 percent of their revenue from advertising, a big change from the days of heavy government subsidies. Advertising has grown in the traditional media, including radio as advertisers try to reach those urban commuters in their new cars. It has also grown on the Internet and advertisements are common in subways, buses and taxis as well as on many billboards and as neon signs on the sides of buildings (see Figure I.2).

In Yan Jin's Chapter 11 on public relations she reports that even the Chinese government has embraced public relations campaigns. Government officials find these campaigns can be more effective in persuading citizens than the old straight propaganda approach. Meanwhile public relations professionals try to define public relations in the Chinese

Figure I.2 Huge neon advertisements are found on buildings in Chinese cities.
Source: Wynne Wang

context, seeking a moral and ethical basis for their work. The profession is growing rapidly and is finding a place in the curriculum of more Chinese universities.

China's film industry has been suffering from too much success with its own blockbuster films like *The Warlords*. One result, Yong Liu reports in Chapter 12, has been the freezing out of independent film makers and even medium-budget movies. Investors see a high-budget film with lots of name stars as a safer bet. Chinese film makers have their own battles with the censors, often over sex scenes rather than political themes. They have also increased their own demands for a crackdown on DVD pirates since they are biting into their own revenues.

China has had some English-language media for many years, the earliest served small settlements of foreigners in coastal cities. China also used English language print and broadcast materials to reach the outside world. There were blatant propaganda broadcasts and publications in the years dominated by Mao Zedong but these became increasingly sophisticated after the reforms of Deng Xiaoping in the 1980s. Guo Ke points out in Chapter 13 that the demand for English-language learning material also supports many publications and broadcasts in English. English has been seen by both citizens and government as China's vehicle for entry into the global communication village.

There are Chinese-language media outside China that serve the huge audience of Chinese who have migrated to and settled in other countries. These are examined by Hachten in Chapter 14. By far the greatest proportion of this Chinese audience lives in Southeast Asia where they often form an affluent and influential part of the society, but many live elsewhere, particularly in Canada and the United States. They have had their own media, of course, especially in the early years after emigration as they struggled to adapt to their new societies. The Chinese government also tries to reach them with its own messages, trying to keep them as a supportive audience even as they learn to live in their new countries.

This, then, is China and its media at the start of the 21st century. China has a booming economy that produces huge trade surpluses amid some of the most modern and populous cities in the world. Prosperous urban Chinese struggle with such Western problems as traffic-clogged freeways, water shortages, and deadly air and river pollution. But Chinese in the less prosperous areas often lose jobs and benefits as old state-run factories collapse.

The media in China must live by new rules as government subsidies drop off and advertising and circulation revenues leap ahead. Media bosses thus have the incentives and budgets to develop more challenging content to attract larger audiences. A central problem for the media is to find a balance between satisfying their audiences and satisfying (or at least placating or not antagonizing) government officials. So far, the government retains firm if sometimes erratic control of all media from the most obscure journal and smallest provincial newspaper to the most popular Shanghai TV station. Even faculty members in the journalism and mass media programs that are now popular in hundreds of Chinese universities meet regularly to study government policies on news and information.

This book reports and analyzes the current state of media in China. It will include newspapers, magazines, radio and television – long standing media that are being used in ways that are not traditional, at least in China. The "new media" of the Internet, cell phones, and blogs will be highlighted because of their impact; they are rapidly changing the economic, political, and social landscape of China. The book will also include material on Hong Kong, Taiwan, and Singapore as well as Chinese language media outside of mainland China. Hong Kong and Taiwan, which China has always argued are part of China, have greatly influenced media inside China. Chinese officials at first tried to block media influences from Taiwan and Hong Kong but everything from rock music to news and political discussions seeped around and under the barriers, often by way of widely available pirated CDs and DVDs.

As noted earlier, in order to minimize what some could consider a Western bias in this text, we have included major contributions by some highly qualified Chinese scholars, some teaching in China and some currently at universities in the United States. As will be seen, the contributions of Guo Ke, Peiqin Chen, Hong Cheng, Yan Jin, Yong Liu, Anne Cooper-Chen, Haigui Liu, and Yu "Leon" Liang have been substantial. Wynne Wang provided most of the supporting photographs.

Editors Scotton and Hachten believe the book realizes an important balance through their contributions. Any attempts at balance, however, are not meant to exclude differing points of view and opinions. The purpose of this book is to stimulate scholars and students and to contribute to the debate and discussion of a major region of the world's journalism and communication.

For their translation and interpretation assistance, the editors wish to thank Dr. Rasha Abdulla of The American University in Cairo, Siwen

Wang of Marquette University, Xiao Wenjuan, formerly of Shanghai International Studies University, and Dr. Zheng Yang of the State University of New York at Buffalo and formerly of Cornell University.

The authors wish to thank the J. William and Mary Diederich College of Communication of Marquette University and Kappa Tau Alpha National Honor Society for Journalism and Mass Communication for financial support.

1

2008

New Challenges to China's Media

Three events in China caught the eyes of the world in 2008. They were the violent protests against Chinese rule in Tibet that erupted in March, the tragic earthquake in Sichuan in May that killed an estimated 70,000 people including thousands of school children who were trapped in buildings that some said collapsed because of shoddy corruption, and the Beijing Olympics in August where the performances and the Olympic city itself dazzled a huge worldwide audience. Journalists in China and throughout the world rushed to cover these events, sometimes blocked, sometimes assisted, but always closely watched by Chinese authorities. Media reporting of these major stories and the government's reactions to them tell us much about media-government relationships in China today.

Protests in Tibet

In mid-March, Tibetan rioters attacked Han Chinese in Lhasa. For weeks, Chinese security forces tried in vain to extinguish the continuing protests. Chinese officials and state news media blasted the foreign media as biased against China, castigated the Dalai Lama as a terrorist "jackal," and called for a "people's war" to fight separatism in Tibet. The Communist Party seemed concerned with rallying domestic opinion by appealing to the deep strain of nationalism in Chinese society. Playing to national pride and national insecurity, the party used censorship and propaganda to position itself as defender of the motherland and at the same time block any examination of Tibetan grievances or its own performance in the crisis. Most vocal Chinese and the domestic media supported the government's stance.

US journalist Nicholas Kristof said it would be convenient if we could denounce the crackdown in Tibet as the unpopular action of a dictatorial government. But it wasn't. It was the popular action of a dictatorial government and many ordinary Chinese think the government acted too wimpishly, showing too much restraint toward "thugs" and "rioters." China and the United States, Kristof said, clash mostly because of competing narratives. "To Americans, Tibet fits neatly in a framework of human rights and colonialism. To Chinese steeped in 150 years of 'guochi' or national humiliation by foreigners, the current episode is one more effort by imperialistic foreigners to tear China apart or hold it back."[1] Even Chinese students overseas and some non-Chinese supported the government's stand in Tibet and accused the Western media of exaggerating and distorting the Tibetan situation.[2] The Chinese state media had inundated the public with many reports from Lhasa about the suffering of Han Chinese merchants and the brutal deaths of Chinese at the hands of rioters. The Tibetan crisis touched the raw nerve of separatism at the core of Chinese nationalism and China failed to provide an even-handed report abroad about Tibet. C.-C. Lee points out the Party leaders will use the media to rally Chinese nationalism against any perceived challenge to China's national sovereignty or international status and that this is standard practice for China's media.[3]

Nevertheless, even the media coverage of the sensitive Tibet situation suggests that there is there is more media freedom in China today than in the old days of Mao Zedong. Even Xinhua, the tightly controlled official Chinese news agency, admitted in its reports that despite police efforts the riots had spread to Tibetan-inhabited areas in China outside Tibet.[4] Personal freedom to criticize the government has also grown considerably. Chinese people can express opinions that diverge from the party line and even something as sensitive as the Tibet policy in private conversations. However, the Communist Party, which maintains a monopoly of power, makes it clear that certain views cannot be publicly expressed. Views questioning the official policy on Tibet certainly fall into that category.

Earthquake in Sichuan

Chinese authorities were simply unable to control media coverage of the Sichuan earthquake in contrast with its tight control of media reports of the riots in Tibet just two months earlier. Within 3 hours of the Sichuan earthquake the Central Propaganda Department in Beijing ordered news-papers not to send reporters to the quake areas. Some papers, including the *Oriental Morning Post* of Shanghai, simply ignored the order and by next morning had front-page earthquake coverage from Sichuan includ-ing photographs. Reporters from other newspapers soon joined in to fully report the earthquake.[5] Bloggers were also sending photos and information from all over the earthquake area, ignoring any restrictions. One com-plicating fact was that only on May 1 the government had put forth new rules that required authorities to make public any information involving the "vital interests of citizens."[6] The Propaganda Department withdrew its restrictive order within a day. Originally apprehensive reporters soon found that they were free to move around and write whatever they believed was important.

One reason government authorities eased off media controls was that media reports were almost universal in their praise for the speed and efficiency of government rescue efforts.[7] The media had been faster and certainly provided major coverage of the earthquake, but their content reflected government policy. It focused on the relief efforts and did not go into criticisms of local officials and school construction. Shi Hong, network news coordinator for the Shanghai Media group, explained, "The executives have instructed us to go deep into the front line and send back vivid images of Shanghai people participating in the damage relief up there."[8]

One thing the Sichuan earthquake did was at least temporarily silence critics of China's human rights record. The deaths of nearly 70,000 people from the earthquake brought a wave of sympathy for China from overseas and forced some critics of the Beijing government's policies, including its Tibet policies, to think twice about their tactics.[9]

Among the images that showed a new face of China were media photos of Premier Wen Jiabao visiting earthquake sites within a day of the disaster. Television, newspapers, and even video blogs showed "Grandpa Wen" directing aid workers and comforting parents and victims.[10] The Chinese government used the media to channel the emotions of the after-math of the earthquake into grief rather than into the anger that had been shown earlier because of what many parents saw as the shoddy school construction that contributed to the deaths of their children. Later buses carried advertisements about the earthquake to further support the victims (see Figure 1.1).

However, angry parents could not be ignored by the Chinese media. A dramatic photograph of a senior official on his knees begging parents

Figure 1.1   A bus advertisement reminds people to "Remember the Sichuan Earthquake," Campaigns like this raised huge amounts for the victims.
Source: Wynne Wang

to trust the government to investigate the school collapses was published in *Southern Metropolis Daily*. The confrontation was quickly picked up by many blogs in China, which spread the photograph and the parents' anger throughout the nation. *Southern Weekend* in Guangzhou, a newspaper that frequently investigates claims of corruption or serious government errors, ran an interview with a Sichuan education official who said that the earthquake alone could not be the cause of all the school collapses. *Caijing*, a business journal noted for its own tough investigations of private and official corruption, also called for a government probe into shoddy school construction. Even Xinhua, the official government news agency, said an investigation should move forward. Shortly after that Beijing sent a notice to all media to cut back on such coverage.[11]

A month after the earthquake local officials were trying to block foreign reporters from visiting quake areas and to prevent parents of victims from talking to journalists.[12] Officials told citizens not to talk to the media and to portray China in a positive light. The Government also moved to shut down their most vocal critics, including Huang Qi, a human rights campaigner. He was arrested while he was advising parents who lost children in collapsed schools how to pursue legal action against local governments. He also wrote about it on his website. Huang had already spent 5 years in prison for campaigning on behalf of parents who lost children in the 1989 government crackdown on the Tiananmen Square demonstrations. Another activist, Liu Shaokun, was also detained and sentenced to a year of re-education in a labor camp for "seriously disturbing social order." Liu had posted Internet pictures of collapsed schools and had visited parents who had lost children in the earthquake and told them they should protest at government offices.[13]

A year later on the anniversary of the earthquake officials including President Hu Jintao held a memorial service in Sichuan. Chinese media covered the service and the anniversary but emphasis was clearly on government efforts to get people prepared for China's next earthquake. "Are we better prepared for another disaster?" asked one guest columnist in *China Daily*.[14] Another Xinhua article reported government efforts to check the safety of school buildings across the country, only in the last paragraph of the article was there a mention of parents' complaints about school construction in the earthquake area. No one has ever been charged as a result of those complaints.[15] Clearly the government does not want to emphasize the toll and parents of the 5,335 students whom the government officially acknowledges died were told not to hold their own memorials under threat of jail sentences. One government official did say that there was need of some investigation, but otherwise officials met questioners with a "wall of silence."[16]

But one prominent Chinese citizen is speaking out about how the government has handled the Sichuan tragedy. Ai Weiwei, an artist who helped design the Olympic National Stadium known as "The Bird's Nest," posted numerous criticisms on his popular blog. Ai is the son of one of modern China's most famous poets and from a very famous intellectual family which is why many believe his blog has not been censored. Ai is a provocative figure in China and even though he helped design the Olympic stadium he refused to attend the opening session because, he said, he believed in freedom, not autocracy. Ai and his supporters are working on a documentary about the Sichuan earthquake and have been interviewing parents of children who were killed in the tragedy. He has also been trying to get official records from local officials, who claim they have been as cooperative as the law allows. "He's totally crazy, he kept asking questions again and again," said one Sichuan province official who chose to remain unidentified.[17]

The Beijing Olympics

Many people including Western journalists commented on the "dazzling management" of Beijing's 2008 Olympic games. Huge crowds, a spectacular 4-hour opening ceremony and impressive Chinese athletes were all part of an Olympiad that will be hard to match.[18] A University of Maryland study of 68 newspapers in 29 countries across the globe found overwhelmingly positive (45 percent) or neutral (40 percent) stories which focused on the games and not politics. Only 15 percent of the stories in the study, which only covered the first week of the games, were negative in tone.[19]

China did try to downplay the cost of the games (estimated at $42 billion) after the Sichuan earthquake devastation only 3 months earlier. Official efforts to control the media coverage of the games and everything else were very clear at times.[20] Indicating the caution and thoroughness of the Chinese approach to the media was the suspension, 2 months before the games opened, of a tourist publication *Time Out Beijing*. When censors spotted a photograph of some wounded victims of the 1989 Tiananmen Square protests, the *Beijing News* was ordered off the newsstands and its website censored.[21] Most public protests were blocked before they got started, but a British TV journalist was seized by police and detained when he witnessed a pro-Tibet demonstration on the Olympic green.[22] He was released when Chinese authorities verified he was an accredited journalist. Foreign journalists protested themselves when they arrived in Beijing and found that many websites were blocked. They had been promised that websites would be open to them. To mollify them President Hu Jintao held the first press conference he had ever given for foreign journalists and promised the websites would be open to them. A few days before the games some, but not all, blocked websites were opened. Amnesty International became accessible but not the Human Rights in China site. The Chinese authorities restored some of the blocks in December, arguing that some websites were violating Chinese law.[23]

Some public protests were officially allowed at the Olympics but Chinese authorities required a permit application 5 days in advance. Some Americans without permits who tried to protest about Tibet were arrested and deported. A few received short jail terms for "disturbing public order." Chinese who wished to protest about even non-political issues such as land compensation in their home cities found their attempts to get a protest permit effectively blocked.[24]

One embarrassing incident that caused a media reaction in much of the world was the arrest of two elderly women who came to Beijing and tried five times to get a permit to protest about eviction from their home in a distant city. The women were first sentenced to a year in a labor camp for "re-education" but the sentence was later dropped.[25]

Olympic Committee President Jacques Rogge pointed out that political protests have been banned at Olympic Games for more than 50 years.[26] China also had its own violent terrorists to worry about during the Olympics. Their actions had been largely confined to far western China although a bus bombing in Shanghai in May 2008 killing three people was blamed by many on western Uighur separatists. Just before and during the Olympics attacks in western China killed police and security guards. Chinese security officials also claimed to have uncovered a plot to kidnap journalists and others during the Olympics.[27]

If the media had some controls to worry about during the Olympics, for Central China Television (CCTV) the games were a spectacular success. Watching the opening ceremonies were 840 million Chinese, with an estimated 97 percent of TV sets in China tuned in. In the United States, NBC counted a mere 29 million viewers. CCTV renamed its Sports Channel the "Olympic Channel," but at one time or another was broadcasting Olympic events on 18 TV channels. Women's table tennis had 330 million viewers, more than the US population.[28]

The long-range influence of the Olympic Games on China's media is unpredictable. Even before the games started Liu Jingmin, Beijing deputy mayor in charge of the Olympics, said the long-range effects of the games would be good for democracy in China. "If people have a target like the Olympics to strive for, it will help us establish a more just and harmonious society (a phrase frequently used by China's President Hu Jintao), a more democratic society, and help integrate China into the world."[29]

Nicholas Kristof, a *New York Times* correspondent in Beijing, tried unsuccessfully to get through the official barriers to get a protest permit during the Olympics. He said he wanted to protest about the failure of authorities to do enough to preserve Beijing's old neighborhoods. He was unsuccessful but also believes some democratic changes are coming to China. "My hunch is that in the coming months, perhaps after the Olympics, we will see some approvals granted. China is changing; it is no democracy but it's no longer a totalitarian state."[30]

Since the Olympics the Chinese Government's attitude toward the media has been decidedly mixed. In March 2009 the official *China Daily* felt free to criticize abuses at local jails but the Government also started requiring critics on major Internet portals such as Sina, Sohu, and Netease to post their real names. Another indication of the mixed Chinese view was its 2009 government requirement that all computers install the "Green Dam Youth Escort" filtering software on new computers. After numerous protests the Government "delayed" the requirement.[31]

An Olympic Toll on Journalists

In 2000, China established November 8 as Journalists' Day to honor the nation's 1 million news people. The day had particular irony in 2008 due to the toll that the Olympics and Paralympics took on many in the profession, such as the journalist who had 1 day off from late July to mid September.[32] A TV reporter said he knew his career choice would probably mean sacrificing his health and a normal life. For one thing, journalists everywhere in China spend more than 4 hours a day at their computers and have to deal with an ever-watchful political system as well as the usual deadline and other stresses. A report based on 23,640 journalists' physical exams found 97.5 percent of news people to be "sub healthy."[33]

2

Development and Theory of the Media

China has long been one of the oldest and most culturally developed nations. Yet, in recent times, the world has judged and criticized China for the turmoil and disarray of the twentieth century even though it was just a brief episode in the long history of a great and illustrious civilization.

In large nations the early development of media is very much influenced by physical geography. China is slightly larger than the United States – China has 3,691,000 square miles compared to 3,623,000 square miles. However, the United States has more than 5 acres of farmland per citizen, whereas the Chinese have about one-third of an acre of farmland per citizen, according to Robert Bishop.[1] Further, one-third of China is mountainous with the world's largest and highest plateau. Mountains also divide China into almost autonomous areas.

Rivers have always been crucial for China. For traveling from east to west rivers have long been the easiest means. China's rivers have not helped in centralizing power since governmental lines of authority run north to south.

With easy access to the sea, it could be expected that the Chinese should be seafarers. However, China has developed as a self-sufficient feudal agricultural state with an ambition for international commerce.

Except in the mountainous regions, most Chinese live in tightly knit villages of about 500 to 700 people. The total number of such villages has been set as high as 500,000.[2] A larger market town serves 20 to 30 villages. China's traditional weakness in sea power made the country vulnerable to invasion and colonization by European sea powers. Foreigners congregated at Hong Kong, Guangzhou, and Shanghai and their influence extended up nearby rivers. Later, railroads provided the main route for Western and Japanese influence. Today, these three cities are at the heart of China's economic revolution.

As is the case in most nations, journalism and mass communications that developed in China were transplanted from the West by way of the "old media" of printed newspapers and broadcasting. Historians believe that some form of journalism appeared much earlier. Scribes probably sent news to provincial subscribers during the Han dynasty, 206 BC to 220 AD, as did the Romans during the same period.[3] During the Tang dynasty, 616 to 906 AD, formal court gazettes began to appear. Even though moveable type originated in China in the eleventh century, the gazettes were still hand-carved from one block per page. Another form of communication with a long history is the Tatzebao or big character posters. Posters, written secretly, were a traditional outlet for grievances against local officials. In the hands of the Maoist Communists the Tatzabao were a powerful means of communication during the 1960s and 1970s. Modern journalism arrived with Protestant missionaries in the early 1800s. The first Chinese language monthly magazine was first published by William Milne, a British missionary, in 1815.

In the tumultuous twentieth century printed and broadcast words were heavily involved with China's revolutionary leaders from Sun Yat Sen to Chiang Kai-shek to Mao Zedong. It should be noted that during this period the Chinese language press had rarely if ever known freedom of the press – that is independent expression free from the controls of government authority.

According to the World Press Encyclopedia (2003), it was not until the 1890s that newspapers were introduced in China and at first they were run by foreigners, particularly missionaries and businessmen. Before long, progressive young Chinese were introduced to newspapers from the West and along with them the principles of objective journalism. The May Fourth Movement in 1919 saw the publication of books in Chinese on news reporting as well as the first financially and politically independent newspapers in Chinese.

The burgeoning Chinese media were, however, suffocated by Nationalist censorship in the 1930s. Soon after the Kuomintang (KMT) took control of China in 1927, it launched a media policy aimed at enforcing strict censorship and intimidating the press to follow KMT doctrine. Despite brutal enforcement, the KMT had no organized way to control the press and when times were good it was fairly tolerant toward the media. The KMT stressed ideology less than the Communist Party and therefore newspapers were allowed greater freedom. The press at this time was clearly operating under the Authoritarian Theory of the Press.

Chinese journalism under the Communists (CCP) has developed in four phases. The first phase began in 1949 after Communist forces took control of mainland China and lasted until 1966 when the Cultural Revolution began. At this time private ownership of newspapers was abolished and the media gradually turned into party organs. Central manipulation of the media intensified during the Utopian "Great Leap Forward" movement when excessive emphasis was placed on class positions and the denunciation of objectivity produced distortions of reality. Millions of Chinese peasants starved to death while the media reported exaggerated crop production. In the second phase, from 1966 to 1978 journalism in China suffered even greater damage. During the Cultural Revolution almost all newspapers ceased publication except for 43 party organs. All of the provincial party papers tried to emulate the page makeup of the *People's Daily*. The papers just copied the lead and secondary stories, the total number of stories and even the type face. After this experience many Chinese people considered most news reporting false, exaggerated, and empty.

The third phase began in December 1978 when the Third Plenary session of the Eleventh Central Committee of the CCP convened. The open door policies of Deng Xiaoping brought about nationwide reforms that nurtured an unprecedented boom in media development. Among the most important media reforms were a crusade for freedom of the press, a call for the press to represent all of the people, the making of journalistic laws, and even the emergence of some independent newspapers. In those heady days, there were cuts in state subsidies of the press and the rise of advertising and other forms of financing. This pointed the way for greater economic independence which in turn had the effect of promoting editorial autonomy.

The student uprising and suppression at Tiananmen Square in Beijing in 1989 marked the beginning of the fourth and latest phase. After the student movement was crushed by the army, political freedom of journalists suffered crippling setbacks. The central leadership accused the press of bourgeois activities, of reflecting public opinion, providing false information, and putting too much focus on entertainment. Press freedom was abolished and the door closed on political freedom. Furthermore, the post-Tiananmen era witnessed the dramatic turn toward economic incentives allowing media commercialization to flourish while restricting freedom of political coverage. This produced a mix of Party logic and market logic that is the defining feature of media in China today.

Theory of the Press and Public Communication

In brief, the ruling Chinese Communist Party has tried to retain its orthodox Leninist theory while changing its relations with media to let them prosper and be financially independent. Media enjoy economic freedom but little political freedom, i.e., the right to talk politics.

Despite its Leninist beginnings China is today controlled by a system of Authoritarian Capitalism – certainly with regard to the press – the largest and most successful example of this concept in the world today. Philip Pan in *Out of Mao's Shadow* pointed out that

> the government engaged in the largest and perhaps most successful experiment in authoritarianism in the world. The West assumed that capitalism must lead to democracy that free markets inevitably result in free societies. But by embracing market reforms while continuing to restrict political freedom, China's Communist leaders have presided over an economic revolution without surrendering political power. Prosperity allowed the government to reinvent itself to win friends and buy allies, and to forestall demands for democratic change. It was a remarkable feat, "all the more so because the regime had inflicted so much misery on the nation over the past half century."[4]

> The theoretical framework for the media of China has evolved and changed as political conditions and the media themselves have gone through transformation since 1949 when Mao took complete control of the mainland. The Mao regime brought in the Leninist concept of the press which required that all newspapers and broadcasters become arms of the government to serve the aims and goals of the state. Private ownership as well as the autonomy of journalists was abolished as in the Soviet Union, giving the state a monopoly over both news and communications broadly. Yet today, the people enjoy greater prosperity but also more personal freedom and access to information than ever before under any Communist rule. By almost any measure, the country's last twenty five years have been the best in China's five thousand year history.[5]

As China slowly began its spectacular economic development, government subsidies were removed from the proliferating media. They were told by Supreme Leader Deng that making money was a good thing because it facilitated economic and media growth. Although the media were still state owned and forbidden "to talk politics," the Communists began to lose their monopoly and control over public communication at large.

"Authoritarian Capitalism"

The new China was more accurately described as "authoritarian capitalism." The main reasons for this were the explosive new media coming in from the West – the Internet, satellite television, cell phones and digital DVDs, all of which enabled much greater access to information and entertainment including news and views often critical of China's control of ideas and information. Further, people could communicate among themselves and dissidents could now organize and resist government policies. Despite extensive and expensive efforts to block and censor the vast information flows from inside China and the world at large, these "new media" have reshaped public opinion in China.

So China has become a kind of global oddity – a nation with a robust economy and rapidly modernizing but still under authoritarian political controls that forbid democratic elections, an independent judiciary or even serious public discussion of public affairs. The totalitarian socialist state that Mao had built is no more. In its place is a more cynical, stable, and nimble bureaucracy, one that values self preservation above all else and relies on an often corrupt and predatory form of capitalism to survive.[6]

Experts are divided on whether these changes in China indicate it is heading toward democracy. Political stability in this century may depend on which way the new China matures.

The Communist government can no longer completely suppress most unflattering news. On July 8, 1976, a great earthquake in Tangshan killed 240,000 people – the news was not reported in China and did not reach the outside world until later. However, another devastating earthquake hit the Sichuan province in May 2008 killing about 70,000 people. That disaster was fully reported in China and throughout the world despite official efforts at first to downplay the story. Chinese journalists themselves insisted on reporting the story with the help of millions of Chinese who, using cell phones and computers, rapidly spread the news to a vast Chinese public eager for all the details. Nonetheless government officials refused for months to permit reporting of protests over shoddy school construction which potentially caused the deaths of thousands of young students. After the Olympics, the government conceded that faulty construction may have contributed to the student deaths.

Under such authoritarian controls, media editors, as usual, know how far they can go to avoid government intervention. The government has suppressed and moved against political activities that would seem to threaten its authority. Hence regular suppression of dissidents protesting for a free Tibet or greater autonomy for the far western provinces of Gansu and Xinjiang inhabited by Muslims take place regularly. Even the mild activities of the popular Falun Gong are regularly harassed.

Cultural Differences

Some of the contradictions that Westerners see in relations between their media and government and those in China spring from cultural differences. Studies have shown that Western businessmen, for example, tend to accept confrontation as a step toward settling differences. Their Chinese counterparts see confrontations as poisoning relationships and expect parties to continue to negotiate even after an agreement – seen by the Chinese as more or less temporary – is reached.[7] Westerners, particularly Americans, see government as an obtrusive agent that is not to be trusted. Chinese see government as a wise parent that guides them. After a food poisoning event, Western journalists wanted to know casualty figures – how many died? How many seriously ill? Chinese journalists were more likely to agree with the government views that the most important information for the public was what was being done to prevent future similar tragedies.

In today's global economy, Chinese manufacturing and trade are so important to the world that Chinese authorities must often deal with the overseas Western press which is quick to report and criticize defective Chinese products such as poisonous medical products, dangerous toys, etc. Hence, Western journalists operating in and out of China act as a kind of a surrogate Chinese press, performing such basic news functions as exposing news stories that the Chinese media have been barred from reporting. In such ways important news reaches the Chinese public via routes never dreamed of in the original Communist press theory. Thus the Leninist theory has become a hollow shell and is no longer a useful guide to understanding mass communication in today's China.

However, the Chinese government owns and controls all the media in China, and appoints all editors and managers. The *People's Daily* (in Chinese) and *China Daily* (in English) plus hundreds of other official newspapers, magazines, books, (government owns all the publishing houses, too) still provide the Communist Party's official views of the world, especially to the Chinese population. CCTV's main 7 p.m. news program, for example, plows through reports of official meetings just about every evening. Still, journalists must pay close attention to what is and what is not acceptable to authorities to present. Editors can be praised for exposing corruption but they can also be fired for misreading the political signs and getting involved with material that party officials view as threatening the government.

Some editors reportedly misread these signs and found themselves prosecuted on charges of "embezzlement." In reality, however, government controls become more and more difficult to impose in the new era of "market socialism." An editor at a Shanghai English-language daily one morning chose Hollywood's Academy Awards as the main story, ignoring a Communist Party announcement on agricultural policy that was the main story in China's official papers. (The agricultural story showed up the next day in the Shanghai paper.)

Another Shanghai editor said he does not read messages from the Ministry of Information in Beijing because he finds most of them irrelevant as he tries to gauge what will attract readers and help boost circulation. Another editor in Guangdong, a thousand miles further south of the capital, reports he rarely read them since he is so busy meeting editing demands. Within the government itself there are other stresses that make media control difficult. Provincial governments are constantly testing their own independence from Beijing and local media follow their lead.

Monitoring Government Rivalries

Editors constantly monitor central and local government rivalries to find out which issues can be presented safely. Chinese nationalism rather than Communist ideology would seem to justify and explain much of the continuing friction between the press and authority. The CCP has no hesitation to censor or suppress any news that reflects badly on China or the leadership of the party. Suppression of dissent is seen as protecting the nation's image or reputation.

Yet the basic function of the media is to communicate – to convey ideas and information whether as public information (news), as entertainment, or diversion. The media's vastly expanded ability to speak out clashes frequently with party leadership and that leads to confrontation. As the government blocks so much news that it considers inappropriate or worse, the Chinese people or its elites are unable to freely discuss or argue about real or imagined issues of public affairs. China has a long tradition that

Figure 2.1   An advertisement in Hangzhou's West Lake District urging visitors to stay longer. The West Lake District was the favorite vacation retreat for Chinese emperors and now attracts tourist from around the world. At night, the advertisement lights up in many colors.
Source: Wynne Wang

"the emperor knows best" and many Chinese accept that and often do not think for themselves. Today, millions of Chinese are better educated and more affluent than at any time in their history and want to think for themselves and choose their own leaders.

And yet, buoyed by extraordinary economic growth, the Chinese people hold strikingly positive views of their national economy and the direction their country is taking. China ranked first in two measures of 24 nations in a 2008 poll by the Pew Research Center. Some 86 percent of Chinese said they were content with the nation's direction, up from 48 percent in 2002 and 82 percent of Chinese were satisfied with their economy, up from 52 percent. By comparison only 23 percent of people measured in the United States said they were satisfied with their nation's direction and only 20 percent said the American economy was good.[8] The reality of media communication in China today is that even though the government owns the media, modern communication, e.g., newspapers and broadcasting plus the Internet, emails, cell phones, communication satellites, prevent the government from effectively controlling the vast flow of information and diversion coursing through the heads (and hearts) of over 1 billion Chinese citizens. No one can be sure of the direction the communication juggernaut is headed – toward a more open and democratic society as in Europe and North America or to a more repressive, autocratic society reminiscent of earlier dynasties. Even holiday destinations once considered suitable only for Chinese emperors are now advertised and attract citizens to visit (see Figure 2.1).

The year 2008 presented great challenges to China – protests and violence in Tibet, a massive earthquake in Sichuan province killing over 70,000, and the glory and frictions of the Beijing Olympics. How the media dealt with these challenges provided clues and insights to the future of China.

3

The Impact of New Media

Michael Anti (Zhao Jing), at one time perhaps the most famous political blogger on China's Internet, was the keynote speaker at the Fourth Annual China Bloggers Convention in mid-November 2008. Estimates of how many bloggers there are in China vary widely usually ranging from 500,000 upward.[1] There are clearly a considerable number among the 1.3 billion Chinese, but some say there is no way of knowing and no point in counting. Anti agrees, lamenting "The End of the Golden Age of Blogs in China." Anti sees that as the short period, that began with the 2003 sex column by Mu Zimei and ended in December 2005 when Microsoft shut down his political blog.[2]

Anti may be right. At about the same time bloggers were meeting in Guangzhou, the closing of Bokee (Chinese for Blog) was announced. Bokee was, a few years ago, the biggest blog site in China with a staff of 200 managing two million blog accounts and an advertising clientele that included IBM. Founder Fang Xingdong kept the authorities at bay with a staff of 10 guarding day and night against "sensitive content."[3] Clearly things are changing rapidly with China's new media.

The 2008 conference was clearly not focused on political topics. The two days of talks and panels were heavy on technology, copyright and how to make money with a blog. Alibaba, which claims to be China's largest online marketplace, is trying to organize individual bloggers so they can develop a reliable revenue stream from advertisers. Perhaps a sign of the increased interest in business by bloggers is the fact that Wang Xiao, which calls itself the number one blog in the world, focuses on stock market reports and other economic news. Shaun Rein, an Internet columnist for China Stocks, claims that bloggers represent a great business opportunity since at one time or another 50 million Chinese are either creating or reading blogs.[4] China's Internet bloggers include some who attack local corruption and at some risk criticize government officials. In general, however, China's bloggers as a group are following the path of traditional media to "commercialization without independence."[5] Even in the 1990s, at the outset of China's Internet boom, Zhao warned against equating "reform with commercialization."[6]

The Internet, just like all other media in China, is tightly controlled by the government. One reason for the decline in blogger interest in politically "sensitive" topics may be the gradually tightening of laws governing the Internet.

Wanted: "Healthy, Civilized News"

The government's two main targets seem to be politics and pornography. In order to control blogging of sensitive topics the Government introduced, in 2005, a blogger register that requires a blogger to present an ID card to prove who they are. The Ministry of Information Industry (MII) wants only "healthy, civilized news and information beneficial to the nation."[7] How much sex is considered healthy is unclear since the censors allowed the notorious blog by Mu Zimei on Sina.com where she described her multiple affairs, sometimes with more than one man at a time. Sina.com promoted the blog heavily and claimed Mu Zimei (real name, Li Li) attracted 10 million visitors a day. Li Li, who started out as a feature writer at a fashion magazine, said she became a sex columnist because, "I think my private life is very interesting." The censors finally moved in and banned her diary (*Ashes of Love*), which had huge preorders.[8]

The Ministry and several other government agencies have an elaborate system to keep unwanted topics off the Internet in China. An estimated 30,000 to 50,000 monitors constantly look for pornography and references to such taboo topics as democracy or freedom or Falun Gong (the banned religious group seen as a threat to order in China). Another concern of the authorities is the increasing sign of web-based gambling addiction. In recent years Chinese authorities have reported shutting down thousands of Internet sex and gambling websites but new ones keep emerging. In 2004 the Government closed down 47,000 Internet cafes for too much sex and gambling. In early 2007 the government decided 113,000 Internet cafes were enough and said no new ones would be licensed because of too much gambling.[9] The Ministry of Information says 90 percent of the pornographic sites originate overseas.[10]

There are also numerous websites clearly offering illegal materials including "date rape" drugs. One site claims that they can, for a fee, improve your grades in the national education database. Many of these sites temporarily disappear with the six-monthly government sweep. However, the Internet has grown so big so quickly in China that the government cannot keep ahead of all the illegal sites.[11]

The Chinese public is also concerned with what it sees as the spread of Internet fraud and immorality. A man named "Freezing Blade" on the Internet discovered an online relationship between his wife, "Quiet Moon," and college student "Bronze Mustache." He posted a letter denouncing the student and revealed his real name. A bulletin board posted the details and called on the public to denounce the student and the university to expel him. He had to drop out of school to avoid the taunting mobs and then barricade himself in his house. Even "Freezing Blade" asked people to drop the harassment campaign, which had caused a huge traffic spike on Tianya, which claims to be the world's largest Internet bulletin board. "If it is a personal attack on someone, we delete it," said a Tianya webmaster, "but it is very difficult given that we have 10 million users."[12]

Even among some university students there is a sense that the Internet culture is encouraging too much harmful material. At one Shanghai university a corps of student monitors watch student bulletin boards for what they consider harmful comments that would hurt the school's reputation. "A bulletin board is like a family," said one student, "and in a family I want my room to be clean and well-lighted without dirty or dangerous things in it."[13] Most young Chinese are generally very defensive about anything they see as critical of their nation and even the government's protective policies.

China's Great Firewall

The government, however, is primarily interested in tracking down Internet users who persist in sending forbidden material and less concerned with personal problems and the casual violator. Foreign journalists in China occasionally try to test the Internet censors by posting provocative words or phrases. They report the censor's response is sporadic but do not know whether this shows that the censor is inefficient or just not very interested in their activities.

The effectiveness of this "Great Firewall of China," called the "Kung Fu Net" by Chinese bloggers, in blocking messages is open to debate. Chinese citizens connect quite freely to the Internet within China although they realize that their activity and messages may be monitored by the government. However, some researchers inside China say the government is very effective in keeping foreign information out.[14] Andrew Chadwick, who studies the politics of the Internet, believes the Chinese government can block access to outside sites rather easily since all international traffic must pass through a small number of state controlled backbone networks.[15] The government also has the technology in place that blocks web pages and cancels links that would lead to unacceptable sites ranging from pornography to international news.

Other researchers believe that Chinese Internet controls can easily be evaded. Benjamin Bates, who studied digital networking in China, stated that to those who want it foreign content is "always available" via the Internet.[16] Students reported that they gained access to websites in Taiwan using proxy servers.

As the censors work in China to limit access to Internet sites, overseas individuals and teams work to thwart them. One of the leaders is Ron Deibert of the University of Toronto. He and a team from Harvard and Oxford universities developed encoded software (psiphon) that evades the Internet firewalls in China and elsewhere. Knowing that any software code can be broken, Deibert discreetly distributes his software only to trusted citizens in firewall countries including China.[17] This may work for a time, but some Chinese researchers say it is simply impossible to hide on the Internet because of social pressures as well as technology.[18] Some suggest that one problem for the censors is that there is not any clear policy about what is banned from the Internet except for "the double T" (Taiwan and Tibet). One author says that the growth of monitoring agencies has moved control of China's media from the ideological areas to structural rules less connected to political policies, making the guidelines less clear to both the controllers and the controlled.[19]

The speed of communication via the new media certainly makes it more difficult for the Chinese government to control information. Shortly after the Sichuan earthquake in May 2008 the propaganda ministry issued directives to journalists on what they could and could not report. However, the public was already getting information about the disaster via the Internet and cell phones. Many journalists ignored the directives, citing their "civic duty" to report on the situation. The directives were soon withdrawn under public pressure. Also, because the Internet quickly disclosed the extent of the damage and casualties, the official media had no choice but to repeat them even if government officials wanted to minimize the tragedy.

An obvious problem that the Chinese authorities have in controlling the Internet is its vast size. In mid-2008 the China Internet Network Information Center (CNNIC) reported that China had 250 million Internet users, surpassing the 190 million in the United States. This is a rise from just 33 million Chinese online only 5 years earlier. There were also an estimated 2 million websites. The number of Internet users in China may well be higher since they often share accounts. The reported figure of 250 million represents only 19 percent of the Chinese population so there is likely to be continued Internet growth. Cost is not a major factor as the average monthly cost for a family to connect to the Internet in 2007 was less than $10. Demographically, 60 percent of Internet users in China are aged less than 25 and 80 percent of these young users live in the cities. About 60 million students use the Internet, averaging 11.6 hours per week.

The CNNIC also reported that a slightly higher percentage of men (20 percent) than women (18 percent) use the Internet regularly. About 22 percent of city residents in China had access to the Internet at the beginning of 2007 compared to 5 percent of rural dwellers. Internet development is very uneven throughout China, even from city to city, and, of course, between cities and rural areas as the CNNIC report showed. In the long run, however, some Chinese researchers believe the media, especially the new media, may have the strongest impact in the rural areas of China.[20]

Entertainment, not Politics

CNNIC also found that the Internet is the source of information for more people (85 percent) than television (66 percent) or newspapers (61 percent). For 47 percent of those with access to the Internet it is their primary information source. Although young Chinese are by far the biggest Internet users, they seem to use it for school assignments and for entertainment and have little interest in politics. When 800 students in South China were asked about their "heroes" in a 2000 survey, only one political figure showed up on a list of more than 100. Most "heroes" were singers, artists, and pop culture icons. Material pursuits and not political ideas were found to be the main interest of China's youth.[21]

Although the Ministry of Information Industry (MII), the State Council Information Office (SCIO), and the State Administration of Radio, Film and Television (SARFT) control the Internet and other media there are many other agencies keeping watch – some known and some probably hidden. SARFT keeps a close watch on the content of major websites and has ruled that none can generate their own news. Since news can come only from official news sources, most websites just copy freely from Xinhua, the official government news agency, or available newspapers. This has led to increasing complaints from newspapers that see not only their news but also their readers and advertising revenue flowing to the web. In 2006 newspaper editors said they would no longer tolerate commercial websites taking their stories without payment. No real change has been worked out as websites are banned from developing their own news.[22]

Websites in China get about 80 percent of their revenue from advertising. Attempts to charge membership fees have generally been unsuccessful, especially among young people. Only websites offering movies for a fee have been able to build up a substantial revenue flow from their viewers. The top websites in China are constantly changing but those on top in a 2008 survey by Nielsen and likely to stay near the top for a while are: Baidu; TenCent QQ; Sina; Google (China); and NetEase (163).

- Baidu is considered to be the Chinese Google and started in 2000. It is the leading Chinese language search engine, being used by an estimated 70 percent of Internet search engine users in China and has also branched out into Japan. Baidu is facing a legal challenge under China's new anti-monopoly law.[23] It was listed on New York's NASDAQ exchange in 2007. It is trying to attract more young people through its Baidu Post Bar, an online community it calls "the water cooler" for Internet users.

  Baidu also seems to be taking the lead in video sharing sites. It has been censored by Chinese authorities for excessive sexual content on its website but it continues to increase its audience with a daily poll to find the 10 most beautiful women in China. In 2008 Viacom decided to use Baidu in an attempt to get more US music and TV programs onto the Chinese market. Only a small amount of US programming gets onto China's tightly-controlled main TV channels. Baidu, like Google in the United States, has replaced the library as a research site for student papers. When a research paper is assigned, Chinese students "Baidu it" to get the information they want.

- TenCent QQ is the most popular chatting tool in China, especially for young people. Any news young people find interesting moves with extraordinary speed via the QQ network which extends to student groups overseas. Chinese students studying overseas report chatting with family back home and sending them videos on a regular and even daily basis via QQ. The site also provides instant news and entertainment. Its elaborate membership system remained free into 2008 after an unsuccessful attempt to set some fees. QQ decided it was better to keep as many young people as possible coming to the site rather than lose some because of a fee system.
- Sina is the leading news center with news, comments and photos. Its blog, by the actress Xu Jinglei, has been ranked the most popular in China. It does not generate any of its news itself, but must rely on the Xinhua news agency or other official sources.
- Google (China) has struggled to gain an audience since the Chinese have preferred their own websites. In 2008 Google introduced a special version of its powerful search engine without email or the ability to create blogs. Google said it hoped its search engine limits would enable it to avoid legal problems with the Chinese government.
- NetEase (163) claims to be the largest Internet community. It specializes in online games.

One reason these websites stay on top, of course, is that they are careful not to challenge the censors.[24]

Another popular website is taobao.com, which means "hunting the treasure" in Chinese. It is the most popular shopping site. Over 63 million Chinese have shopped on line. Tudou.com, a popular site for podcasters, is similar to YouTube in content.

Google and Yahoo tried to enter the Chinese market with limited success until 2008 when the modified Google (China) service showed up on Nielsen's list of top Chinese websites. Both Google and Yahoo have cooperated with the Chinese government in tracking down dissidents who used their service to violate censorship rules. In 2004 Yahoo turned over to the government the email address of Shi Tao, a Chinese dissident who wound up in prison. Yahoo now stores data offshore so local employees cannot provide it even if ordered to do so by government officials.[25]

Young Chinese make up more than half the Internet users and drive many of the Internet sites. For young Chinese the hottest online tool is xiaonei.com, the Chinese version of Facebook. Most university students get some space on xiaonei and then upload their journals, photos, and general comments online. They can also buy an e-pet and send e-gifts for holidays and birthdays. If you are unhappy, you can leave a message on your space and hope that friends will be calling online to cheer you up. The goal of xiaonei, of course, is to keep these students connected as they grow older and more affluent and thus even more attractive to advertisers.

Many overseas Chinese use the Skype online text and phone service which links up computers for low-cost talk and text messaging. A Canadian research group reported in October 2008 that these messages too, are monitored by Chinese censors with thousands being archived if they contain sensitive words such as Taiwan or democracy. The Canadian researchers pointed out that the monitoring system is very similar to that used by the US government since the terrorist attacks in September 2001.[26] The ability of Chinese censors to track overseas Chinese through their Internet use was suggested when the Internet user "Mainland Facing the Sky" returned from studying in the United States and was arrested because he reportedly was paid for spreading false rumors about China.[27] Watching TV shows via youku.com, the Chinese version of YouTube, is also a favorite online pastime for young Chinese. Playing games via the Internet is also popular. "Fighting the Landlord" (Dou Dizhu) is one of the most popular poker games played on line by Chinese students. The latest online activity for young people in China is the "Human meat search." In this a video clip showing an individual doing something socially unacceptable is posted and then an Internet search is carried on until the perpetrator is found.

Webcasting, basically online broadcasting, is growing in China. The top webcasters are those with a traditional media base. These include CCTV, China's national television network, Xinhua, China National Radio, and China Radio International.[28] Most webcast news programs come from Xinhua, the national news agency, but newspapers are increasingly providing video and audio along with their Internet text and still picture reports. Online movies were growing faster than any other type of webcast programming. A Beijing bookstore started an audio-book reading site and there are also video and audio stock-market reports. Sports contests show up regularly on the web. Webcasting, like much of the Internet, is regulated by SARFT, but there are many pirates providing unlicensed programming. A 2004 study found 70 percent of webcasters were operating without a government license.

Cell Phones: Bi-directional Messaging

Cell phones are the most bi-directional of the new media, meaning that the source and receiver of the message can switch places instantly by a voice or text signal. Cell phones are ubiquitous in China, especially in the cities and among young people. CNNIC reports about 60 percent are used by individuals below age 25 and 80 percent of users live in cities although as Figure 3.1 illustrates cell phones can be used in rural areas. One estimate was that by 2005 there were 350 million cell phones in China, many of them with cameras. It is close to impossible for the Chinese authorities to monitor all the individual cell phone messages even if they include banned text, photos or videos. A 2008 report on "Chinese Internet Utilization" said 30 percent of Internet users use a cell phone to link to it.

Again young people are at the leading edge in adapting this new communication tool, putting their own answering theme on the phone depending on their mood. The most widespread way of using a cell phone in China is not to make phone calls but to send text messages. China Mobile

Figure 3.1   Keeping in touch with the world via cell phone from a quiet lake in central China.
Source: Wynne Wang

and China Unicom have short message services that can save a lot in phone tolls for individuals who have an educated thumb. China telecom now has a second PHS (Personal Handy-Phone System) phone that it markets to people who have a phone for texting but want a simpler and separate phone for old-fashioned phone calls, but also want to use photos and videos.

One texting phenomenon that is growing rapidly in China is Twitter that allows short text messages and can be used with Flickr, which sends photos via cell phones. Also growing rapidly is video sharing. There were 250 video-sharing sites at the start of 2007, up from just 30 a year earlier.[29] The younger generations can be expected to be using this for sending all kinds of information that the censors may or may not like.

Cell phones are becoming a mass medium. In early 2007 the *People's Daily*, the major government newspaper in Beijing, began sending reports to mobile phones. During the Olympics the Beijing government alerted citizens to traffic jams via cell phones. Malls in China alert cell phone users in their area to sales.

Young people are, of course, very adept at avoiding the censor when they want to. While a few will check out commentary from sites in Taiwan "out of curiosity," most are interested in seeing movies and Japanese cartoons that are blocked by the censors. Viacom in 2008 signed agreements with China Mobile and China Unicorn in hopes of reaching this market with US entertainment programming. Students who want to reach forbidden sites quickly learn to use a proxy server for access so there is no record of their visits. Numerous Internet articles are available on how to use proxy servers and students were able to access a video clip on this at tudou.com. "Verycd," also called "electric donkey," provided almost all blocked movies which people can then download and view. Students also feel free to post messages complaining about censorship of films. While a few topics such as the 1989 Tiananmen Square student protests are recognized by students as dangerous to discuss publicly, they find ways to get information about them. Of eight students interviewed at Peking University, all but one had downloaded and viewed a banned video on the Tiananmen protests.[30]

Chinese groups use cell phones and the Internet to mobilize quickly, even if only online. This can be a problem for Chinese authorities even if the group supports the government. During the Olympics, for example, the government discouraged student groups that planned demonstrations supporting Beijing's policy in Tibet.[31] Patriotic groups can be very useful to Chinese authorities but while the government promotes "patriotic education" it worries that even Internet demonstrations will get out of control. In April 2001 a cyber war broke out between China and the United States after a US spy plane and a Chinese jet collided off Hainan Island. Expert US and Chinese Internet users hacked hundreds of websites. A particularly aggressive Chinese group was the Honker Union of China, led by a 22-year-old whose campaign was widely supported by the public. This added to the difficulties of US and Chinese negotiaters.[32]

Satires and Protests

Chinese authorities have also had a difficult time balancing Internet policies where satire is concerned. A short video by amateur film director Hu Ge entitled "A Murder Caused by a Bun" shot him to instant fame in 2006. The video was a spoof of "The Promise," one of the most expensive movies ever made in China. The film, about an orphan girl, won numerous foreign film awards. Chen Kaige, director of "The Promise" and other famous and successful Chinese films, was upset enough to threaten to sue Hu Ge although he finally did not. Hu Ge produced a number of these increasingly popular video parodies including "The Legend of Suppressing Mt. Birdcage Bandits," which satirized the US war on Iraq. At first the government saw no problems and *China Daily* even suggested the satires provided good relaxation for hard-working Chinese. Inevitably though, the parodies by Hu Ge's imitators began to move into the political arena and various officials and offices targeted raised protests. In addition, a large number of so-called video parodies appeared almost overnight on the web and went to extremes to attract an audience. Nude scenes and disgusting eating scenes were among those that brought many public protests. SARFT finally ruled that all videos must be registered (and approved) before they can be shown on the Internet.[33]

The Internet in China, like the Internet everywhere, contains huge amounts of useful information and the censors do not want to block all public protests. A check found these complaints among the blogs:

- public officials get too expensive cars;
- education degrees and certificates are for sale;
- high price of housing;
- low pay for teachers;
- need for anti-discrimination laws for workers;
- need for more holiday time;
- environmental pollution;

- unruly students;
- mistreated farmers; and
- fake journalists demanding bribes.

Such complaints may not bother the national censors, but local officials who are their targets are often aroused. These officials find it increasingly difficult to deal with the "new media" – the Internet, blogs, and cell phones. Citizens using the new media are making it very difficult for Chinese authorities to block information about serious public controversies. The information is not spread by well-known dissidents who can be kept under watch, but by individual citizens who are simply disturbed and technically knowledgeable enough to spread information before the authorities are able to control it.

One of these citizens is Zhou Shugang, who goes by the Internet name of "Zola." He went from unknown vegetable seller to celebrity as "China's first citizen blogger" in 2007 by posting blogs about a battle between developers and citizens in the southwestern city of Chongqing. The struggle was between developers and one couple who simply refused to move despite compensation offers. Zola's reporting on the Internet about the couple's refusal to leave their "Nailhouse" (a term developers use for stubborn residents) was supported by donations from sympathizers. He gradually turned a local story in a national controversy. Zola spent a few days in jail but the local authorities faced the usual dilemma. His reporting was blocking a major development project, but cracking down harshly would attract more sympathizers. Zola's reporting finally attracted so much national attention that the National People's Congress passed the first law giving private property substantial protection against local authorities who wished to develop it. Zola was also one of those who helped spread the story via blogs and cell phones about the protests in Xiamen, a coastal city known for its beauty, resisting plans to build a chemical plant there. Chinese authorities found it impossible to block these individual blogs and cell phone messages that spread the word about the 2007 demonstration.[34]

Another story that was turned into a national scandal by the new media involved the "Shanxi brick kiln slaves." A television reporter first reported the story about parents being lured by stories of good jobs for their children who were then forced to work in brick kilns in Shanxi province. National attention came only when parents posted photos of their missing children on the Internet. The public was so disturbed that Beijing sent army troops into the area to clean up the problem.

The national government will often stay out of such local controversies and scandals and not interfere with the new media exposing corruption. But there are limits. If the public protests seem to have some political goal or threaten the general public order, the regulators will move quickly to stop them. Isaac Mao, called by many "China's first blogger," spent 3 years from 2002 blogging rather freely about social conditions. A software engineer and a venture capitalist, he encouraged young people to develop as individuals. When he posted an article relating to the Chinese censorship system, his blog was effectively blocked for 80 days. He finally moved his blog and server overseas. He sees a shift of media power to the new media but also a stronger effort by the Chinese government to control them.[35]

The effort by Chinese authorities to control communication may be stronger but some believe that the real new media will make it increasingly difficult. Michael Anti agrees that the mainstream blogs can be monitored but he counts them among the old-media after just a decade of life in China. Blogs are now posted and hosted to the point where they overwhelm individuals with mostly irrelevant information.[36] It is point to point communication that is now the "new media" in China and around the world.[37] "We don't need new media theory to explain blogs in China: blogs are old media," Anti says. "We had no media before 1996 – we had propaganda. In propaganda, the party speaks to you; it's exclusively one-way communication. The Internet introduced the idea of bi-directional media, and created media as we understand it for the first time in 1996."[38]

Anti seems to be talking about cell phones. Sites like Bokee, with thousands of blogs, became a bar to finding the information you want. Anti believes there has to be an exchange of ideas – again bi-directional communication – to keep blogs from disappearing entirely. The new blogs are building an "all to all" communication system that works through social networks rather than blog sites that accumulate them. Some Chinese scholars believe this kind of communication system is even changing the agenda-setting function of traditional media and government.[39] This kind of communication system, like that used by cell phone users in a "one to one" system, is almost impossible to monitor and control.

A New "Public Sphere" in China

According to Chinese communication scholars[40] the "new media," however they are defined, may very well be developing into the "public sphere" that

Habermas[41] says is essential to any democracy. One suggests that the Chinese authorities are simply overwhelmed by the use of the new media by young people and their ability to use it to link with others both in China and elsewhere and to raise questions about the existing regime.[42] The new media are at the frontier of the media changes that are bringing a new "openness," resisted or not by authority, to China.[43]

The Chinese Academy of Social Sciences reported that the Internet is becoming an important political instrument in China. "The Internet has become a prominent forum where the public can make its opinions known to the government," the report said. "It is undeniable that the Internet is building a bridge between the governing and the governed." The Academy predicted that the Internet will become a stronger influence on politics in China as the number of users continues to grow.[44]

Chinese officials realize the dangers that the new media represent. President Hu Jintao sees an uncontrolled Internet as a serious threat. He told party officials in 2007: "Whether or not we can actively use and effectively manage the Internet . . . will affect national cultural information, security and the long-term stability of the state."[45] Chin-Chuan Lee, who has been studying the changing politics of China and its media for decades, agrees. In the government's efforts to keep control of China's media, he says the main battles will be around the Internet and the telecommunications markets.[46]

The most recent battle, however, was not about markets but about a horse. The "Grass-Mud Horse" was an Internet sensation at least partly because its name, "Caonima," can be understood as an unprintable curse word if a different Chinese tone is used. A "grass-mud horse" video on the Internet received more than 1.3 million hits in the first few weeks of the craze. Grass-mud horse toys were soon a hot item on the Internet and were popular on China's university campuses. Countless web users created tales of the grass-mud horse, many of them needling the censors who were trying to get rid of it as part of a clean up of Internet pornography. China's censors finally banned the grass-mud horse from the Internet because "the issue has been elevated to a political level."[47]

Young Chinese, particularly university students, who are the main users of the new media are a potentially restive group if China's surging economy falters. As the twentieth anniversary of the Tiananmen Square student protests approached, Chinese authorities moved to limit and even shut down two of the favorite social messaging sites of these young people: Twitter and Flickr. Fanfou.com, a social networking site in China, carried coded messages created around number series about the 1989 protests in an effort to evade the censors. Some people intentionally used the Chinese character for "blank space" in their messages about the protests, making it more difficult for a computer to read and decipher the message.[48] Government Internet monitors have also shut down message boards on more than 6,000 sites linked to China's colleges and universities. The goal was apparently to halt the spread of discussion among a new generation concerning the 1989 Tiananmen tragedy.[49] The old media were also targeted in the effort to limit discussion. Circulation of Hong Kong's English-language *South Morning China Post*, which had published earlier articles referring to the Tiananmen Square incident, was limited in mainland China. This suggests that China's censors were trying to curb discussion of all contentious political issues. Some readers of the *International Herald Tribune* in Beijing reported that a page with a story on Tibet's Dalai Lama was missing from their copy.[50]

Acknowledgment

The author appreciates the research assistance of Xiao Wenjuan and Siwen Wang.

4

Newspapers

Changing Roles

Historically, Chinese "newspapers" were court messages and memos that were only circulated among imperial family members or elite classes. Modern forms of newspapers were brought into China by Western missionaries in the early twentieth century. Since then, as elsewhere in the world, newspapers have played various roles in Chinese society. In the past three decades, during which China has witnessed unprecedented economic progress and social change, the roles of China's newspapers have also changed in line with the social developments.[1]

Swinging Boundary

As a result of its historical tradition that newspapers only catered for elite political classes, modern newspapers in China have always been at the forefront of political struggles in the nation. This has become more obvious since 1949 when "New China" was founded and later became more ideologically-oriented. Almost all political campaigns since 1949 have been triggered by political editorials in newspapers. This included Mao Zedong's 1966–76 Cultural Revolution, which led China into 10 years of political turmoil, and Deng Xiaoping's 1978 mobilization for reforms and openness, which kindled the nation's economic growth and societal changes that have continued for 30 years. Therefore, newspapers have always been considered a kind of elite media in China, as compared with other media forms such as radio, TV, and the Internet, because they are a necessary and influential editorial platform for all Chinese political sectors to seize in order to influence politics in China.

At present, it is unlikely that China will launch any major political campaigns (like the Cultural Revolution) as, since the early 1990s, the nation has been focused more on its economic development. However, the elite role of Chinese newspapers has continued. Although China has become more diversified in its public opinion sphere, party newspapers are still opinion leaders in China, particularly on political issues, and in fact dominate the newspaper industry at the central, provincial, and local levels across the country.[2]

The reason is clear and simple: despite all the reforms and social changes in the past three decades, media in China (newspapers included) remain, at least politically, within a Communist Concept as defined in the traditional Four Theories of the Press. Newspapers in China, owned and operated by the State, are still regarded as the organs of the Communist Party of China (CPC) and the Government, not the watchdog of the government as is the case in the United States[3] or other western countries. Freedom of press in the Western sense, is still something that is yet to come,[4] although it is now frequently discussed in China and the concept seems to be growing within the Chinese context.

Yet, the amazing two-digit growth of its economy in the past 15 years has led to dramatic changes in the nation's political and social landscape. As part of these changes, media in China are now going beyond the horizons of the Communist concept of the press. While it is true that the Government still exercises control (sometimes rigid) over its media system, a notion to which most westerners would object, control itself does not necessarily mean the stagnation of the nation's media industry. On the contrary, media has become a booming industry in China with its output value amounting to more than 2 percent of the nation's GDP in 2006. Media in China thus fall more coherently into a combination of the authoritarian and development concepts, or state capitalism as is commonly known now.

The newspaper industry in China, of course, can not exempt itself from the fast pace of development in the past three decades. Thus, compared with other media, the Chinese media may experience more ups and downs as newspapers start to wear different hats in the new environment.

While they continue to represent the voice of the Government as an extended practice of its elite role, Chinese newspapers have also assumed more diverse (sometimes contradictory) roles as they made continuous efforts to represent the marketplace and the public. Some efforts by newspapers, such as catering more to segmented readership with specified contents rather than just general propaganda, are aimed at survival in the market resulting from the ending of the government media subsidy in 1993. Other efforts are designed to break political and/or ideological taboos, such as exposure of government scandals and wrong doings, ownership changes, and even IPO endeavors in the stock market, as discussed later in this chapter.

One of the noticeable changes in newspapers in China, particularly in the past decade, is that newspapers are no longer just the epitome of Chinese politics as in the past. Rather, they have started to epitomize the contemporary Chinese society as a whole, which, though still dominated by government, has become more diverse in its power structure. The economic and societal sectors are gaining more influence and gradually shifting the boundary of the dominant government power. See Box 4.1 for a description of the old *Beijing Evening News*.

The changes can be best demonstrated in the famous case of Sun Zigang. He was a 27-year-old university student who was beaten to death on April 20, 2003, in a detention center in Guangzhou in the south of China simply because he did not carry an ID card. The Sun Zigang Case now widely known as a landmark that led to the revision of China's national detention regulations and now even the reforms of political system in China as a whole, was first covered in a news report on April 25, 2003, by the *South News*, a tabloid newspaper of the *Nanfang Daily Group*, one of the largest and most influential newspaper groups in China. This group also owns the *Southern Weekends*, famous for its exposés of wrong-doings and government scandals. The news report attracted nationwide attention immediately and shocked the central government in Beijing. Discussions and criticisms soon went beyond just the death of a university student, but focused more on why and how the killing could have happened. Public opinions in the media not only pushed the police to accelerate the investigation and prosecution of these violent detention center officials, but called for changes in the national detention system. Within 2 months of the first news report, the State Council passed a new regulation designed to deal with beggars and homeless people in cities and also to permanently abandon the word "detention" because of its negative connotation. To some degree, the Sun Zigang Case, together with the SARS epidemics case, which was also widely covered in the West, brought reforms in national policies. These new policies help to protect the weak in the society against powerful government agencies at all levels and are also a leading force in the war against national corruption in all social sectors.

The two cases have also paved the way for newspapers in China to escape government controls in their efforts to expose social evils. A notable

Box 4.1   The Evening News

Beijing had eight daily newspapers but the *Evening News* was emperor. The tabloid usually contained at least 50 pages. Its record size was 208 pages, a tactic that backfired as vendors calculated they could make more selling it as scrap than as news.

The paper cost five mao (US$.07), less than its competitors. With a circulation of 1.2 million, the *Evening News* controlled over half of the local market and had the top advertising revenue of any Chinese daily. Judging by its most ubiquitous ads, its readers were sexually frustrated, but in the market for a cell phone and a car. There was more, much more, and when I handed the paper to the Widow every day, I teased her to read the ads. "The print is too small!" she complained innocently.

The government controlled the *Evening News*, but this was no *Good News Daily* like the other papers in its stable. The front page always ran stories based on announcements ("Register your dog or face a serious fine;" "Junk short-text message senders can be fined 30,000 yuan;" "Welcome the Olympics, stress civic virtue, establish a new wind"), but the inside was filled with crime and citizen misdeeds. Beijing looked very different on the pages of the *Evening News*.

I always flipped to the Police section first, where the headlines included: "Girl lights gasoline on sleeping boyfriend;" "Five-year-old lies next to dead mother for nine hours, thinking she was asleep;'" "Unlicensed sixteen-year-old clubgoer kills migrant with his Mercedes;" "Foreigner smashes taxi window in dispute over fare."

In the *Evening News*, migrants were usually the bad guys, the perpetrators of the most violent crimes, as in the story of a thirty-one-year-old man from Henan province who commandeered a taxi and sped down Wangfujing pedestrian shopping street, killing three people and injuring six. "I wanted to retaliate against society and the rich," he told the judge. "I thought that now, out of ten city residents, nine are black-hearted." He regretted killing the taxi driver.

The saddest part of the paper, and one I studied every day despite knowing better, was the Missing Person ads. The photo of the disappeared was usually an ID headshot, in which the person sat wide-eyed and grim-faced. The description listed what the person was wearing, hairstyle, accent, and mental condition. Many of the vanished elderly, were deaf, neurotic, or "liked to drink alcohol to excess."

It wasn't all blood and bad times in the *Beijing Evening News*. The crime section only took up one or two pages. The rest of the paper presented the contradictions of a city that was both small town and megacity. Peak traffic times filled sixteen hours of every day. A woman got her hand stuck in a latrine hole for an hour. Beijing GDP was at an all-time high. Ten ducks at a central lake fell dead from a virus. Migrant workers crowded public buses when they got off work.

The weather column advised readers what to wear and eat and told how the next day would suit morning exercises, car washing, mountain climbing visiting the beach, and airing out the house. Below the banner on the front page, the day's date was given according to the solar and lunar calendars.

The paper also ran pages of international news, translated from, but not credited to, European and American wire services. It told readers what was in that week's *New Yorker* and other American magazines. A daily page of English lessons explained how a British pub was different from one in Beijing, misconceptions about applying for an American visa, and the meaning of words such as "eggnog" and sayings like "her clock is ticking."

I am addicted to newsprint anyhow, but when locals laughed at me for reading what they considered a rag, they were surprised to learn that American papers didn't have the same windows on foreign culture, no matter how narrow. And in a city whose broadcast media, films, video games, and advertising imitated American forms, the *Evening News* was one of the last products that felt as if it was doing things its unique way, no matter how antiquated.

The Widow showed me another use for the paper. "Run a soapy wet cloth over your windows," she said. "Then dry them with an unfolded page like this." The glass sparkled. "Now, ball up the whole mess and bring it to Recycler Wang. He'll give you a cent or two for it."

From *The Last Days of Old Beijing* by
Michael Meyer (Copyright 2008)
Permission granted by Walker & Company

example was the newspaper exposure of a series of explosions in illegal mines that killed many miners in various regions of China. During the process, newspapers in China, though still owned by the State, tried to represent the public as opposed to government officials. Newspapers are even becoming public domains for diversified opinions to break through local administrative restrictions and even political taboos of the past. Terms such as "democracy" and "freedom," though tailored in the Chinese context or with Chinese characteristics, are openly discussed in the Chinese press although they remain opposed to or different from the Western concepts and contexts.

As a result, opinion and editorial pages in most influential newspapers have, since 2006, become increasingly popular and the number of opinion pages has been continuously rising. Party newspapers like the *Guangzhou Daily* are even leveraging their circulation and advertising on opinion pages that have become popular among local and national readers.

Surprisingly enough (maybe more so to most in the West), these efforts by newspapers to curb the control of government and to expose government scandals are somewhat welcomed and even initiated by the government. This is true despite the fact that Chinese newspapers are pushing beyond the traditional political boundary and even in some ways changing the political and social landscape in China.

Although the restrictive boundaries on newspapers in China are in fact swinging toward more freedom, it does not mean that the government has lost control over the media industry. The government can still exercise different degrees of censorship and control when it wants to. The swinging boundary of media power is more a result of self-motivated reforms from inside the government to improve its own public image and to adapt to an effective "carrot and stick" model. The changes do not signal that the Chinese government is fully relaxing its censorship over the media industry.

On the other hand, it should be admitted that newspapers and other media in China are emerging as a kind of social power, or the fourth estate as it is phrased in the West. Chinese media are exerting more influence via public comments on political and social life and sometimes force the government to pay more attention to discussions in newspapers and on the Internet when they revise public policies. Some of these policies are proposed and executed simply because of a news report as in the Sun Zigang case or the SARS case.

According to a recent survey,[5] most newspaper professionals in China are clearly aware of the contradictory dilemma that newspapers, especially party newspapers, are facing in terms of their public roles. As the openness of a newspaper is often based on the personality of an editor in chief, editors and reporters have learned to balance their political security and business interests by carefully navigating along the invisible swinging boundary, which is subject to changes that may only be understood in a Chinese newspaper newsroom.

Weak Giant

Like China's general economy, the newspaper industry in China has been booming in the past decade, despite competition from TV and the Internet and a shrinking readership. For six consecutive years, newspapers in China have topped the world in terms of newspaper numbers and circulation, leaving behind Japan, India, and the United States. As of December 2006, China had a total of 1,935 newspapers. These included 982 dailies – 12.5 percent of global daily newspapers and 21.7 percent of the average number of newspaper copies published daily in the world. Despite the industry's large size, readership of Chinese newspapers among the nation's population of 1.3 billion is still low compared with other countries. In 2005, readership for daily newspapers only reached 76.84 per thousand population, although this figure has been continuously rising since 2003.[6] The per thousand average readership is 545 for Japan and 198 for the United States as of 2006.[7]

Besides, the overall financial scope of Chinese newspapers is also limited, compared with their counterparts in the United States. Total revenues for China's newspaper industry in 2005 reached over 6 billion yuan[8] (about US$850 million). In the United States, the Gannett Company alone, which owns the *USA Today* and many other newspapers as well as television stations, had total operating revenues of more than US$8 billion in 2006.[9] Newspapers in both China and the United States have suffered declining revenue due to strong competition in recent years from television and the Internet.

One of the reasons for the relatively small financial scope of the newspaper industry in China may be related to the uneven penetration of newspapers in the different regions in China. According to the 2007 Development Report of China's Newspaper Industry, newspaper distribution and access is heavily lopsided towards the big cities along the east coastline of the nation. While the national average readership per thousand is still a bit low,

Figure 4.1   Some readers obtained their election news from wall newspapers, perhaps saving their yuan for morning tea.
Source: Wynne Wang

average readership per thousand for Beijing and Shanghai, two major metropolitan cities in China, has registered 285 and 276 respectively and is increasing each year. The report concludes that the uneven distribution of newspapers reflects the uneven level of information access and economic development in the Chinese society.[10] A national survey has supported this conclusion: readership distribution normally parallels levels of education, income, and profession. Higher readership is often found among white-collar and government employees, people with higher education levels, and those with a greater income.[11] News is also presented on wall newspapers as shown in Figure 4.1.

Dual-Track Systems

Media professionals and government authorities in China have both realized that the newspaper industry is a special industry with dual roles. It can be like an ordinary factory and generate a revenue (mainly through advertising), but it can also be part of the nation's ideological propaganda mechanism. So in the past three decades, newspapers in China have been operating on a dual-track system. They are regarded as enterprises, but they are not placed under the supervision of industry and commerce authorities, like other kinds of enterprises in China. Instead, they are under direct control of propaganda departments, which may issue a lot of dos and don'ts over specific newspaper content and operations simply because newspapers can swing ideological orientations in China.

The dual-track system for the newspaper industry in China, though beyond the understanding of most media professionals in the West, has stimulated the rapid development of the newspaper industry and allowed it to earn its own revenue instead of depending on government subsidies. Meanwhile, the government can still exercise control whenever it wants to. More importantly, this dual-track system has managed to explain and even legalize the current ideological control over the newspaper industry in China from a theoretical perspective. As the dual tracks still lack clear definition and can sometimes lead to a contradictory and conflicting status quo in the newspaper industry in China, the dual-track practice is often referred to as the newspaper industry's "Chinese characteristics." This is another vague but popular term used to explain what is beyond clear definition, at least to date.

Despite the apparent dilemma, media professionals in China have proved themselves creative enough to meet a difficult challenge: they have developed a commercial newspaper industry within an ideological and political framework. This is not only demonstrated in newspaper content, but also in newspaper business operations.

In terms of newspaper content, Chinese newspapers have witnessed a gradual but clear shift from political orientation to non-political content such as entertainment and public services. While it is true that the 438 party newspapers still dominate the nation's political sphere,[12] newspaper content has surely diversified, with popular evening newspapers, metro dailies, service-oriented professional newspapers[13] and tabloids mushrooming in the past two decades. As of 2005, these soft-content newspapers held about 80 percent of the readership market in China, though its total number of papers represents only about two-thirds of the newspaper industry in China.[14]

The dual-track system can also be demonstrated in the internal distribution of the contents of one party newspaper group. While China's central party newspaper, *People's Daily*, is devoted solely to serious and sometimes dull political material, the newspaper group also owns the popular *Global Times*, with a circulation exceeding 1 million. In fact, the kind of serious-soft-content mixture model has characterized all the newspaper groups in China, showcasing the dual systems. Some newspapers, like the Shanghai-based party newspaper *Jiefang Daily* wear the dual-track hats even within the main party newspaper. While its front page (or section) may be devoted to stern political content that follows the party line, the rest of the paper is full of soft and popular content such as society news, real estate news, and advertising.

Diversified newspaper content requires creative skills on the part of Chinese reporters and editors in treating different materials and reforms within newspaper operations. In fact, it demands more political wisdom on the part of newspaper management and, surprisingly, government authorities as well, in order to creatively break through political taboos within an ideological framework.

Newspaper Groups

As all newspapers are owned by the state, management members including the editor-in-chief are all appointed as government officials. Despite their state ownership, Chinese authorities still encourage newspapers in China to enhance their market-driven capacity to grow bigger and stronger and even compete with international media giants. This became especially important after China joined the World Trade Organization in 2001. As early as 1996, however, China started to reshuffle all the newspapers across the nation. One of the major efforts was to pool newspapers in groups.

The first newspaper group, Guangzhou Daily Newspaper Group, was launched in 1996 in the southern city of Guangzhou, which was at the forefront of economic reforms in China as it was close to Hong Kong. The practice soon spread to other parts of the country and since then 40 newspaper groups have been established.

While newspaper groups are expected to sharpen their competitive edge in the market, not all turned out to be successful. As they were organized (or even forced) into newspaper groups via administrative arrangement rather than by market forces, these newspaper groups were sometimes simply a group in name, with no company registration or formal group structure.

Some were only a cluster of similar newspapers squeezed together for no apparent competitive or collaborative reason. Some newspaper groups did initially have what looked like a sensible business structure, but then were forced to accept some less competitive newspapers as well. In Shanghai, China's largest and most cosmopolitan city, two influential papers were the *Wenhui Daily*, which targeted intellectuals, and the more profitable *Xinmin Evening News*, which targeted the general population. After restructuring, both merged into the Wenxin Newspaper Group. The group failed to play on the strengths of both newspapers and lost much of the local readership to the Jiefang Daily Group, the party newspaper group in Shanghai.

Professor Li Liangrong, a renowned journalism professor at Shanghai's Fudan University, cited the current dual-track system in China as a major factor that led to the establishment of successful and not so successful newspapers groups.[15]Although China adopted one uniform national policy for forming newspaper groups, the country is so big and so diverse in its local readership distribution and economic development, the success of any new newspaper group rests largely on how the group's top management interprets and implements the policy. Editors and managers had to balance the local environment and those vague directives to adapt to what reform leader Deng Xiaoping phrased as "Chinese characteristics."

Sometimes a successful newspaper group can even be tied to the personality of a group president. On most occasions, the god of success favors those newspaper presidents who are brave enough to dance with not-to-do policies from authorities and carefully balance between the party line (ideology) and bottom line (market).[16] Sometimes, authorities may even become inclusive enough to summarize successful case studies into a revised policy. However, this does not mean that these authorities have revolutionized the newspaper industry in China. Rather, they are widely regarded as being creative in catering to the local newspaper practices. They are praised for their experimental efforts to create a new model but still with local characteristics as well as the special "Chinese characteristics."

IPO Endeavors

In recent years, these experimental efforts have also been borrowed by confident newspapers groups in China to venture into the capital market. They still operate under the dual-track system but strive to become a real newspaper group in the Western sense. Here again, state ownership does not really mean newspaper stagnation in the stock market, at least for those

Chinese newspaper groups with managers who are clever and creative enough to balance ideology and market.

In fact, five newspapers and newspaper groups[17] were quite successful in their ventures into the Chinese and Hong Kong stock markets with initial public offerings (IPOs) of their stock. This started in 1999 when *Chengdu Commerce Daily* became the largest shareholder of Sichuan Dianqi, a listed company in the inland Sichuan Province, where the Chinese economic architect Deng Xiaoping was born. Although not all five newspapers were successful in the stock markets,[18] their endeavors were seen as a natural result of the competitive newspaper market in China and also as an effort to become more internationally competitive in the future.

It should be noted that the five newspaper groups did not risk IPOs directly in capital markets by themselves. Instead they explored the stock markets via a kind of indirect IPO effort. They either owned a subsidiary company that was listed or invested in listed stocks and restructured a company once they had enough stock to gain control. For instance, in 2007, the Hangzhou-based Zhejiang Daily Group invested 100 million yuan (US$13 million) in two hi-tech companies that had the potential to offer an IPO after selling off real estate projects. The Shanghai-based Jiefang Daily Group purchased more than 32 percent of Xinhua Media, thus becoming the largest shareholder of this 2.2 billion yuan company.[19]

These two ventures by Zhejiang Daily Group and Jiefang Daily Group are listed as the two most important Chinese newspaper developments of the year in the 2007 Development Report of China's Newspaper Industry. These recent IPO endeavors have also been cited by media professionals in China as a signal for upcoming media reform and subsequently political reform in China. They also demonstrate how market-driven business operations of newspaper groups can fit into the dual-track media management system which may be a starting point for transforming the ideological and political framework itself.

Of course, at this stage, the scope of their IPO endeavors is still quite limited and their operations are highly dependent on newspaper advertising revenues. Besides, their business models are also very broad as the mentioned five newspaper groups are really focusing more on non-media or media-related businesses than on media businesses. As a result, their IPO endeavors have identified them as media services enterprises or even department-store enterprises as their investments are entering areas outside the media.

Development Pattern

Due to the different social surroundings in China, the development of its newspaper industry has followed a pattern parallel to the changing social situation. This is characterized in paramount leader Deng Xiaoping's famous motto: "Look for a stone when you cross a river" (Mo Zhe Shi Zi Guo He), meaning you explore and change while you experiment.

As a result, newspaper development in China has seen a continuous swinging pattern while developing and progressing in the past three decades. The swinging pattern traces back to 1978 when China decided to embark on its open and reform course. The nation was then troubled by numerous political campaigns,[20] which appeared to rein in media development in China. However, each campaign seems to have stimulated rather than suppressed the development of China's media, including newspapers. It was not until 1992 that the nation started to become less political and broke from its open ideological tradition. From that time on, the government clearly focused more on economic development as China gradually unfolded itself to the world.

This has been epitomized in China's newspaper development pattern. While its swinging pattern still continues, its swinging scope has come within the dual-track management system as newspapers struggled to balance between the dominating ideology and rising social and market forces.

One basic pattern for newspaper development is the reform pattern from "periphery" to "central" or from "easy" to "difficult." Newspapers, as the traditional organs of the state, used to enjoy a stable monopoly and a hugely influential role in Chinese society. The newspaper industry was regarded as a low-risk professional area in which to earn a stable and even handsome living. However, the economic reforms forced newspapers to suddenly realize that they were not only the reformers but also the reformed as well. On the one hand, newspapers represent the traditional elite classes and their interests; on the other hand, they are also at the forefront of social changes and want to ensure they can also benefit from the ongoing reforms. This dilemma pushed them to engage in reforms in a periphery-to-central or easy-to-difficult pattern, laying a foundation for slow, smooth but continuous development.

For a long time after 1978, the reforms in China's newspaper industry only focused on such areas as advertising and circulation or internal management and financial adjustments. These attempts surely stimulated working efficiency, but did not touch upon the core management system. Fundamental changes did not come until 2003 when the government started to allow external (including foreign) capital into some newspapers. Even though these outside newspaper investments were allowed only under strict governmental scrutiny, they brought a push for more efficient management systems.

The system reform has accelerated changes over newspaper content as well. In the "periphery" and "easy" stage, newspapers in China only reformed their content by expanding weekend editions, especially weekend tabloids that publish more soft content that is popular among readers. Editors have to muster their energy and demonstrate creativity to publish successful soft-content weekend tabloids, which are quite different from traditional party journalism. However, these content changes are relatively easy compared to the challenge of newspaper management reforms.

When private investment moved into newspapers in China, the industry landscape changed. For instance, *Shanghai Daily*, the English daily published by Wenxin Newspaper Group in Shanghai, did not make a profit and was subsidized by the newspaper group before foreign investment moved in. Although it was still confined to the business or non-content aspects of the newspaper, foreign investment did have an impact on content. *Shanghai Daily* soon changed into a tabloid size with more cheerful features and moved away from the unexciting political content found in Beijing's English-language *China Daily*.

In terms of newspaper content, public-journalism or news reports and editorials about scandals have become increasingly influential and popular in newspapers in China. Not only do they attract readers and increase circulation, they also act as a curb on such governmental scandals and expose social wrong doings. More importantly these content changes are creating a fourth estate power for newspapers in the form of public opinion to alter government policies as in the case of Sun Zigang. Although it may sometimes prove to be a more risky dance, by 2007 newspapers added pages for comments and editorials on almost all important public issues. The *Global Times*, a world news daily tabloid published by the central party newspaper *People's Daily*, is devoting at least two full pages to comments and reviews on international relations written by renowned scholars and freelancers and political and military experts from China and overseas. The *Global Times* has gained a reputation among domestic and foreign

Figure 4.2 US President Elect Obama was major news in the *Oriental Morning Post* of Shanghai and others.
Source: Wynne Wang

readers. It has become an important source for news and commentary, especially when China and another nation have strained relations. In 2007 when Germany had diplomatic problems with China, many German companies and organizations inside China turned to reports and comments in the *Global Times* to keep updated about Chinese government views. In 2008 the election of President Obama in the US became major news in over 2,000 newspapers in China (see Figure 4.2).

The second pattern for newspaper development in China is that top-to-down reforms have paralleled down-to-top changes in the past three decades. To some degree, this pattern is also an extension of Deng Xiaoping's motto: "Look for a stone when you cross a river." This time it is true for media professionals as well as government authorities. Since the government ceased their subsidy in 1993 newspapers have been forced to make a profit in the market. Media professionals have been exploring and experimenting with breakthroughs within the national ideological framework. Sometimes, they are lucky enough to solve problems, but most of the time they are confronted with conflicting dilemmas in the newspaper market and also an increasing public demand for transparent governance. Their experimental efforts are sometimes supported by more educated and open officials who are in fact in the same boat as media professionals. These officials also have to swing within the dual-track system to maintain their positions. That is why some newspaper reforms, such as setting up newspaper groups and allowing foreign investment, may be accepted and even initiated by government but some governmental opposition may still appear. This opposition does not mean the end of newspaper reform efforts among media professionals who are used to controls (directives of government dos and not-to-dos). These professionals use their creativity and exercise relevant self-censorship as they push their way through to a policy that government officials can accept. Thus we have this swinging but natural pattern that allows newspapers in China to progress. This development pattern may prove difficult for Western counterparts to understand, even if they think they understand China's culture. The fact is that within this swinging pattern China's newspaper industry has seen unprecedented development in recent decades, paralleling the growth of the nation's economy.

Chinese Perspective

Despite its rapid progress and its increasingly independent role, the newspaper industry in China still faces problems found elsewhere in the world. The 2007 Development Report of China's Newspaper Industry listed at least three major challenges for the newspapers industry. The first challenge comes from the rising new media, which have not only segmented newspaper readership but further reduced newspaper advertising revenue. Advertising growth for China's newspapers in 2007 did not match the nation's overall economic growth while other media advertising did. Also, the newspaper market in China is imbalanced with a stable and expanding market in the East but a shrinking inland market in the West. To make matters worse,

Figure 4.3 Newspaper sales in China remain strong but sales promotions can always help. New subscribers can pick up various gifts at this promotion site outside a grocery.
Source: Wynne Wang

the vast diversity of the newspaper market and the relatively unified and similar newspaper operations in the nation have imposed a limit on overall newspaper revenues in the future. However, newspaper sales remain strong and are promoted through free gifts, other sales gimmicks, and careful positioning of stands (see Figure 4.3).

These challenges, coupled with its dual-track handicap, will surely affect the development of newspapers in China. Again this does not mean an end for newspapers in China and it may not be correct to predict future trends from past practices in China or from Western models.

Most researchers from outside China tend to discuss the newspaper landscape in China from a perspective of press freedom and democracy as a whole. While they surely seem attractive to newspaper professionals in China, these concepts also appear abstract to them. What newspaper professionals care about most is their real development (including survival) in the Chinese surroundings rather than just talking about abstract concepts such as freedom of speech and democracy. They may want to discuss these concepts, but they would like to take on a more pragmatic approach. They care more about what can work and what can not work, particularly in the Chinese environment.

The dual-track system of the newspaper industry is also something that may be beyond the understanding of most Western counterparts. As has been noted, China is a country that needs constant and continuous attention as it is changing fast. What looks contradictory to outsiders may in fact work well in a Chinese society at a certain stage. Therefore, while it is true they are still under the control of the state, newspapers in China are not just a Communist concept any more, but rather a Chinese concept, or to be more exact, an authoritarian concept mixed with a development concept.

This appears to be confusing and contradictory, but it is a true reflection of the current newspaper industry in China. As former US Ambassador Winston Lord concludes, "So often in China, contradictions reflect reality. China is on the move. But the very speed of its pace and rigors of its course will require it to apply the brakes often."[21]

5

Magazines

An Industry in Transition

Compared with other media, the magazine market in China is very much undeveloped. For years, magazine advertising has been the lowest in revenue among the traditional four media, and in 2006 its revenue was even lower than that of the Internet.[1]

China has more than 9,000 magazines. While other media in China do well in the market economy, more than three-fourths of magazines in China are still operating in the planned economy model. These magazines are either Communist Party of China (CPC) magazines published by different CPC organizations or educational and academic journals (See Figure 5.1).

Among the 134 magazines with a circulation of more than 250,000, only 65 have their own subscribers and compete in the marketplace. All the other magazines have a sizeable and stable circulation only because the government requires government offices to subscribe to them. China Comment (Ban Yue Tan), a party magazine summarizing state policy and current affairs gets subscriptions from all branches of the Communist Party in China. Though the magazine ranked among the top 10 in circulation in China for years, no news stand sells it as no one would buy it. Of the 24 magazines with a circulation of one million or more, only seven operate in the market-oriented model.[2]

Since 2006, media in China have been pushed toward a market-oriented system. The state publishing bureau declared in August 2006 that with a few exceptions, such as the major party newspapers and party magazines, all media organizations were to be transformed into state-owned industries and operate in the market economy. Under this policy most magazines

Figure 5.1   Thousands of magazines are published in China, some with English and Chinese content.
Source: Wynne Wang

in China are going to have to fight for survival in an open and very competitive market.

China's magazine market, though very new, has been growing rapidly in recent years. Magazine advertising, though lowest in revenue compared with other media, increased an average of more than 25 percent annually from 1995 to 2002.[3] Magazine advertising's market share has been increasing very fast. In 2004, total newspaper advertising was 11.3 times more than that of magazines, but 3 years later in 2007 the ratio dropped to 9.9.[4]

All media in China are, of course, state-owned, but in day-to-day operations, especially for fashion, sports, technology and even financial magazines, most editors do have the freedom to put whatever they want in the magazine. For some magazines, such as *Elle China* (Shi Jie Shi Zhuang Zhi yuan), a fashion magazine jointly published by Shanghai Translation Publishing House and French Hachette Filipacchi Media, the French side actually operates the magazine independently, appointing and paying all editing staff in China and deciding the content of the magazine. The

Chinese side just checks each issue before it is published to make sure the content does not violate Chinese law.[5]

Chinese magazines, except news magazines, because of their non-political content, are almost the only medium where foreign investors are competing with domestic ones in the market in China. Cui Baoguo, a media professor who compiles media industry reports annually, has very low expectations about the development of local Chinese magazines. He said that the Chinese magazine market has actually been occupied by foreign companies. Almost all profitable magazines in China are owned by joint ventures.[6]

What Professor Cui Baoguo said is quite true in terms of the present situation in China. What is also true is that China's magazine industry is very much in a transitional period. With more magazines entering the market the next few years may see the situation may change. Additionally the digitalization of Chinese magazines will further shape Chinese media markets, especially the magazine market.

This chapter will focus on magazines competing in the Chinese media marketplace for readers and advertising, which, though small in number at present, show the future trend of the magazine industry in China. Four basic categories of magazines will be discussed: general interest magazines; fashion magazines; news and financial magazines; and digital magazines. They either have large circulations, or dominate the advertising market, or they exert political influences, or show the future trend of the industry.

General interest magazines are often quite low in price and enjoy good circulation. These magazines, though state-owned, have editorial policies often adapted to cater to popular taste. Managers change editorial policies and magazine content to suit the market and have taken the lead in the market reform of the magazine publishing system since 1978. Fashion magazines, often published as joint Chinese-foreign ventures and targeting high-income female readers, have the lead in capturing expensive advertising. News and financial magazines, with their political influence and commercial potential, have been an important force in China's magazine market, though they cannot compete in circulation or advertising with general interest or fashion magazines.

Digital magazines, with their easy access both for both readers and magazine publishers, have shown great vitality in China's media environment. Digital magazines have affected the whole magazine industry in China and are shaping its future.

General Interest Magazines: Forerunners in an Emerging Magazine Market

China's media, after a long stagnation in a planned economy, moved into a popular press age in the new market economy that developed after 1978. China's rapid industrialization in its new market-oriented era created a need for a fast flow of information. Urbanization provided large, concentrated audiences for information in China's rapidly growing cities. Hence a popular press grew rapidly, targeting ordinary people, especially millions of new minimally-educated migrant workers who moved to the cities seeking jobs. The metropolitan dailies quickly emerged in cities like Shanghai, Beijing, Tianjin, and Guangzhou. Along with metropolitan dailies came general interest magazines that also targeted these new city residents. With at least 100 cities in China with one million or more residents, these publications had an audience waiting for the right content. Thus, these early magazines quickly gained a large readership and generated good returns from the marketplace.

These magazines, most founded in the 1980s, were at the forefront of overall market-oriented media reform in China. They were the first to try to make a profit in the general market. With their content mostly focusing on stories of love and family, these magazines replaced the serious but dull political magazines that had been the only choice for readers until then. With very few competitors in the market in the late 1980s and early 1990s, this type of magazine soon took over the general interest magazine market in China's cities.

All of these magazines were sold at very low prices since their readers had little cash to spare. They featured short, sensational stories, sometimes true but most of the time all or partially made up by the writers and editors. Still, by 2005, *Stories*, basically a human interest magazine, was one of the top 10 Chinese magazines in circulation and the most profitable magazine in Shanghai, China's largest city. *Stories* is a booklet-size magazine selling at 2.5 yuan ($0.35) a copy, carrying short humorous stories, in simple vernacular Chinese. Though *Stories* does not attract the advertising revenue of a fashion magazine like *Elle China*, in 2005 it generated almost twice more profit.[7]

Two other general interest magazines in the top 10 list in circulation in China in 2005 were *Bosom Friend* (Zhi Yin) and *Family* (Jia Ting). Both contain short, non-fiction articles targeted at women readers. *Bosom Friend* first published in Hubei province in central China in 1985, started with a loan of 30,000 yuan (US$4,000). It now has assets of 500 million yuan (US$70 million). In 2004 alone the magazine generated a profit of about 30 million yuan (US$4.3 million).[8] The magazine is filled with sensational stories of love affairs and crime. Some headlines in the March 2008 issue: "My Love Story with My Scientist Husband;" "Boss and His Secretary: A Game Ends in Blood;" and "Throwing Their Son from a High Building: The Married Life of a Mad Young Couple."

The other magazine, *Family*, based in Guangzhou, has a similar editorial policy. The headlines from the March 2008 issue of *Family* include: "Crazy Father Throws His Two-year-old Son from High Building;" and "A Doctor Uses Love Affairs to Maintain Family." In 2004, *Family* had a circulation of 2.9 million and a profit of 15 million yuan (US$2.2 million).[9] Other magazines of this type, though not as successful as these two, do well in the market by running the same kind of sensational stories, real, or fictional.

These magazines cater to ordinary city residents, especially migrant female workers with little formal education. China now has more than 200 million migrant workers, with low salaries of 500 yuan to 800 yuan (US$70 to US$100) a month. Many are young women working in cities in service industries such as hair salons, massage parlors, and even underground pornography shops. Most of these women have a junior high school education. Popular magazines, being very low priced at two or three yuan (U$0.25–0.40) have great success in attracting these readers. The income of these magazines comes mainly from news stand sales. The only advertising they can attract is for medicines and low end products such as cigarettes and inexpensive clothes and cosmetics.

Although sensational magazines are popular in China's media market, perhaps the most successful general interest Chinese magazine is *Reader*. With a circulation of over 10 million, *Reader* claims it is the most popular magazine in China.[10] Founded in 1981, *Reader* is not popular because of sensational content. On the contrary, *Reader* aims at giving moral lessons by telling uplifting life stories. *Reader* is very similar to the American *Reader's Digest* and, in fact, some stories in the magazine are actually translations from the *Reader's Digest* or other Western magazines. The magazine, though sold for only 3 yuan (US$0.40) attracts better educated and higher income female readers and thus can charge more for advertising targeting this more affluent readership. Since 2004, its advertising revenue has surpassed its circulation revenue. Still, although *Reader* can charge higher advertising rates than the other general interest magazines, it lags far behind fashion magazines in advertising revenue. In China, fashion magazines, often owned jointly by Chinese and foreign companies, continue to lead in magazine advertising revenue.

Fashion Magazines: Leading the Chinese Magazine Advertising Market

In China, magazines with the highest circulation do not usually attract the most advertising. In 2005, none of the 10 Chinese magazines with the highest circulations appeared in the top 10 magazine advertising revenue list. Magazines on the list of top 10 in advertising revenue are usually fashion magazines targeting more affluent white collar females. From 2004 to 2006, the advertising revenue of fashion magazines contributed more than one-third to the total magazine advertising revenue in China. In fact, in the first half of 2006 nine magazines in the top 10 list of advertising revenue were fashion magazines.[11]

Four of the nine fashion magazines belong to Trends Magazines, a group started in 1993 by the China Tourism Association. Since 1998, the group has started joint ventures with several foreign magazines. It bought the copyright of Hearst's *Cosmopolitan* and published *Trends Cosmo* with Hearst Communications. Trends Magazines also cooperated in developing Chinese editions of *Harper's Bazaar, Esquire, Men's Health, National Geographic Traveler* and the British *FHM* (See Figure 5.2).

The most successful fashion magazines targeting high-end readers are these joint ventures. In 2006, all 10 fashion magazines with the highest advertising revenue, besides the four magazines of the Trends group, were joint ventures. *Elle China* and *Marie Claire* are joint ventures of Shanghai Translation Publishing House and French Hachette Filipacchi Media. *Rayli* is a Sino-Japan joint venture, and *Vogue* is a joint venture of China's *People's Pictorial* and Conde Nast Publications.

In the first half of 2006, total magazine advertising revenue in China was about 3.2 billion yuan (US$450 million), while the total advertising revenue of the top nine fashion magazines was about 1 billion yuan ($140 million), almost one-third of the magazine advertising revenue of the whole industry. Beside those fashion magazines in the top 10 list, other joint venture fashion magazines, such as *WITH*, a Sino-Japan production, also attract high-paying advertisers and make good profits in China's media market.

Figure 5.2 Magazines published by Chinese companies in joint ventures dominate the fashion magazine market and take much of the magazine advertising revenue.
Source: Wynne Wang

In the past few years, the increasing revenue of fashion magazines has very much contributed to the overall growth of China's magazine industry. The annual advertising revenue of two fashion magazines, *Trends Cosmo* and *Rayli*, was about 82 million yuan (US$12 million) and 11 million yuan (US$1.6 million) respectively in 2000. By 2006 *Trends Cosmo* was earning 33 million yuan (US$5 million) a month in advertising revenue while *Rayli*'s monthly ad revenue hit 20 million yuan (US$3 million). For *Rayli*, it meant almost 20 times more advertising revenue in just 6 years.[12]

Figure 5.3   Gucci and other Western luxury labels can be found in Chinese.
Source: Wynne Wang

It is no exaggeration to say China's magazine advertising market is dominated by fashion magazines. It is also true to say fashion magazines in China are dominated by joint ventures. Zhang Zeqing, a magazine researcher, observed that in China's fashion magazine market there are no local Chinese fashion magazines. All fashion magazines are related with foreign magazine publishers.[13]

Reviewing the development of China's magazine industry, a Chinese publisher even claimed that all profitable magazines in China are related to foreign investment or foreign publishers. "When will local Chinese magazines be able to compete with those magazines with foreign partners?" he asked. "How long will it take?"[14]

With about 30 years history, the Chinese media market is certainly very much a new market and the Chinese magazine market, as stated previously, is even newer. With little experience in the industry, local Chinese magazine publishers find it hard to compete on their own. World famous fashion magazines entered China's market through cooperation with local publishers and soon dominated the Chinese fashion magazine industry.

Fashion magazines flourished not only because they targeted the right readers, but also because the fashion magazine market was very much undeveloped. Publishing within a planned economy for many years, Chinese fashion magazines didn't have an audience, didn't have fashions to highlight, and didn't have any experienced fashion magazine editors. Foreign fashion magazines, due to their non-political nature, quickly and easily gained access to China's magazine market through joint ventures. With their world famous brand names and experience in magazine publishing, they soon overcame the other Chinese fashion magazines.

On the other hand, the growth in magazine advertising is certainly related to China's fast growing economy. Since 2002, China's GDP has continually maintained two-digit growth. A considerable number of middle class citizens are now a part of the population of any large Chinese city. These people are the target audience of these metropolitan fashion magazines. Figure 5.3 shows the availability of Western labels although Western mannequins are being replaced by those depicting Asian women in order to increase appeal.

News and Financial Magazines: China's New Muckrakers

China has a long tradition of making use of political pamphlets or journals to promote ideas, even to motivate people for a revolution. This tradition continued after 1949 when Communist China was founded. The political journals, being the organizational journals of the Communist Party of China, still play a very important role in the political life of the country.

Official journals such as *China Comment* and *Qiushi Journal* are among the top 10 magazines in national circulation, but these journals are not in the market place. They are Party publications that brief Party members on current affairs and the country's official policies and all Party units must subscribe to them.

In China current news journals appeared in the market in the 1990s. Dozens of news magazines, including *Windows* (Nan Feng Chuang) and *Life Week* (Sanlian Shenghuo Zhou Kai) appeared in news kiosks.[15] Claiming to select news stories based on their news values and to focus on social issues, these magazines tried to make it clear that they were very different from the traditional political magazines.

Like the traditional political journal, these news magazines still target the social elite. However, they are also targeting the emerging new middle class which gradually entered China's economic and political life after the market-oriented economy was officially adopted in 1978. One distinctive feature of these magazines is that they are financially independent and without any government subsidy. They have to survive in the market so attracting readers and advertising and earning a profit have always been major factors influencing the editorial policies of these magazines.

Windows, a news magazine founded by *Guangzhou Daily* in 1985, claims on its website that it is the most influential main stream news magazine and has more subscribers than any other news magazine. In order to cater to the taste of a new middle class in the new market-oriented economy, the magazine has changed its content over time. In the 1990s, the basic story frame of the magazine told of new entrepreneurs starting their businesses with nothing except their ambition and courage – they finally won success and became rich. This was the time when Deng Xiaoping's new policy encouraged Chinese people to develop private enterprises and make their fortunes. In these stories, the success of these legendary figures was justified as part of the process in the development of the whole nation. At that time, *Windows* presented a series of stories under headings such as "Modern Heroes," "The Strategies to Success," and "Views from Entrepreneurs."[16]

As time went by, however, only very few of these business frontier men and women became rich. Most of them became white collar office workers for the few successful bosses or for foreign companies in China or joint ventures. The new middle class suddenly found that they could not really become rich single-handedly. The theme of "original sin" of those successful bosses began to dominate the magazine. From the late 1990s the magazine raised questions about the way these early legendary figures had made their fortunes. In the meantime, intellectuals started to turn their eyes toward the lower social classes who had become victims in this economic reform process. At this point some of the stories began to question the entire social system. Since 2003, *Windows* has had the slogan, "FOR THE PUBLIC GOOD" on its cover and after 2006, it even started to list people of the year who made great efforts working for public good. Together with a few other news and financial magazines in China, in recent years, *Windows* seems to have contributed to a new trend of muckraking in China.

Caijing Magazine, a magazine founded in 1998 in Beijing, is the only news magazine in the top 10 in magazine advertising revenue in 2006.[17] It first made its name in 2001 by exposing an illegal deal in China's stock market. In 2003, the magazine further distinguished itself in covering the

SARS epidemic and was awarded an international investigative reporting prize. In 2006 it was the first publication to report on Shanghai's social security fraud, the biggest corruption case in China. The investigation finally led to the fall of Chen Liangyu, the Communist Party Secretary in Shanghai.[18]

Both *Windows* and *Caijing Magazine* focus on major problems of a Chinese society in transition, from constitutional debates, public affairs, and civil rights to the rights of reporters themselves. What distinguishes these magazines from others, especially other general interest magazine and fashion magazines, is their sharp exposure of all kinds of corruption. In a time when the Chinese government is trying to curb corruption and is still looking for a Chinese model of modernization and democracy, these magazines find themselves in a political environment that seems likely to ensure their own survival.

The successes of *Windows* and *Caijing Magazine* set a model of muckraking in China's magazine market. Other news magazines, though less successful in the market, are following the model. Muckraking is not only a good marketing strategy for news magazines, but also a very important social responsibility which China's media need to adopt in a transitional society.

Going Digital: A Technology that May Shape China's Future Magazine Market

China's digital magazines, or e-magazines, started to develop very recently. Until 2005, there were only 20 e-magazines in China, but since 2006, the number of e-magazines has increased dramatically. By 2008 there were about 700 e-magazines in China, almost 35 times more than 3 years earlier.[19] The sudden booming of e-magazines is largely related to investments by several big venture capitalists in e-magazine servers. Big e-magazine servers in China, like POCO, Xplus and ZCOM, each obtained more than 10 million yuan (US$1.4 million) from venture capitalists. Total venture capital in the area amounted to about 60 million yuan (US$9 million) in 2005 and 2006.[20] Advertising revenue of e-magazines in China more than doubled in 2007, from 90 million yuan (US$13 million) in 2006 to 200 million yuan (US$30 million) in 2007.[21]

Most readers of these e-magazines are well-educated. A 2006 report released by iResearch group shows that about 44 percent of e-magazine readers have college degrees and another 27 percent have associate degrees.[22] Most e-magazine readers are between 18 and 35 years old, the majority of them are female and their income is between 2,000 and 6,000 yuan (US$300–$600) monthly, putting them squarely in China's growing middle class. This may explain why the most popular e-magazines are fashion magazines, which account for 74 percent of magazines read online.[23] This coincides with research carried out with traditional magazine readers in 2003, which showed that a typical magazine reader was a female about 34 or 35 years old with an associate college degree.[24] That means most e-magazine readers are very likely traditional magazine readers. Another study of fashion magazine readers shows that half of the e-magazine readers will not buy the printed version.[25] That shows printed magazines are actually losing their readers to e-magazines.

With most magazines turning to e-versions and the development of some online only e-magazines, the trend is likely to continue. This trend seems to bring more opportunities to China's magazine industry which has a very small market share with their printed versions compared to other media.

This easy access to the market via e-magazines opens the door to new players in the magazine industry. Magazine servers, newspapers, even radio stations and celebrities have started e-magazines. POCO, an e-magazine server, has four e-magazines each with more than six million readers. *Lan*, an e-magazine founded by TV anchor Yang Lan, claimed that the magazine was downloaded more than one million times in the first 3 months after it was founded.[26]

Moreover, some traditional magazines, such as literature magazines, which are not very competitive in the market because of the high cost of production and poor circulation, found new readers through their e-versions. Eight literature magazines which have very low circulation for their printed versions are in the top 20 list of 2006 e-magazine readers of Longyuan Periodical, an e-magazine server with 1600 full-text periodicals (http://cn.qikan.com). Among them, two literature magazines, *Dangdai Bimonthly* and *Harvest*, rank second and third on the list, and *National Geographic*, an elite magazine with limited circulation, is also in the top 20.

In this sense, e-magazines are reshaping China's magazine industry not only in exploring more market space for magazines as compared with other media, but in the inner structure of the whole industry as well. If we take the readers of the new e-magazines, who are mostly younger than traditional magazine readers into consideration, we can optimistically estimate that, with time, the new e-magazines will gain more and more readers. With the growing popularity of e-magazines, it is likely that the whole magazine industry might be restructured in the future.

Being a new market, the magazine market in China is very much unregulated. Magazine circulation is often confirmed by the magazine itself and some figures are not credible. Even the amount of advertising cannot be calculated accurately as most magazines give big discounts to advertisers while listing much higher prices for advertising space. Although, according to the law, no magazine can be published without a license there are lots of magazines without licenses on the market.[27]

In terms of magazine market advertising share, it seems that there is still much space to develop. In 2007, China's magazine advertising accounted for only 5 percent in total media advertising share. In 2005 French magazines had a 20 percent advertising share, American magazines had a 15 percent and Japanese magazines 12 percent. It may take years for China's magazines to compete with other media and to become a real industry but the trend can clearly be seen.

6

Radio Broadcasting

Deregulation and Development

In 1976, when Mao Zedong passed away, people in China sat under loud speakers attached to the walls of public places to listen to the news. At that time, radio was still a luxury for most people. They listened to loud speakers broadcasting at least once a day starting with *Internationale*, a song about fighting against social injustice and building a new world.

Like other media in China, radio carried no advertisements at the time. Radio stations received full financial support from the government. In the late 1980s, as people's incomes rose, more people could afford TV sets. Television gradually grew and the influence of radio declined dramatically.

In recent years, however, with more people commuting to work, radio, as a medium that people can access in cars or buses, has revived in the big cities. At present, radio in China is an industry with great profit margins. International companies have invested in Chinese radio and a great variety of programming has developed. This has already changed the scene of media in China. One of the basic reasons for these changes is the deregulation of China's radio industry.

China's Radio Between 1949 and 1978

Without appreciating the media situation in China between 1949 and 1978, it is almost impossible to understand the present situation of China's media. Between 1949 and 1978, radio was the Chinese people's main source of news, as all newspapers were distributed through mandatory subscription and only a few elite could access them. The "news," mainly government announcements, came via cable and then often through loudspeakers. There were millions of these loudspeakers in China, set up and maintained by all units of government. Farmers and workers started their day when loudspeaker announcements began each morning.

Radio stations were set up in line with the country's administrative system. Stations were operated by central government, provincial governments, municipal governments, and county and town governments. As government organizations, radio stations were mainly responsible to each level of government. Their main tasks were to publicize government policy and educate people. A limited number of entertainment programs were broadcast.

The Emergence and Boom of China's Radio Industry

In 1978, China's leader, Deng Xiaoping, started to reform the economic system of the country. All media organizations, especially those receiving full financial support from the government, were told to start generating their own revenues.

The first commercial advertisement in China was posted in *Tianjin Daily*, a local newspaper, on January 4, 1979. The first commercial radio advertisement, a commercial for shampoo, was broadcast on March 15 of the same year by Shanghai People's Radio.[1]

As government organizations, radio stations were only required to pay a 5 percent income tax on their revenues. In the meantime, all the equipment and operating costs were covered by the government.

The "extra" money generated from selling advertisements and other sources soon enabled radio stations to accumulate a considerable amount of capital. These radio stations were soon expanding their programming and services. The number of radio stations increased dramatically. In 1981, there were only 114 radio stations in China. By 1999 the number had grown to 1,363, more than 10 times the number in 1981.[2] Competition among radio stations contributed to the industry boom. Station managers who generated more revenue were promoted to more important posts, while part of the profits went to staff members as bonuses.

The Decline of China's Radio in the 1990s

The golden times ended in the late 1980s. Benefitting from the economic reforms, many people in China were able to afford color TV sets. With its obvious advantages, TV soon dominated the advertising market.

Radio, on the other hand, having been the only sound medium that provided the Chinese audience with news for almost four decades without a strong competitor, was not producing appealing programs. Attracted by the new TV medium, talented reporters and anchors also left radio stations to seek jobs at TV stations. Some of the most popular anchors on China's Central television (CCTV), like Cui Yongyuan and Bai Yansong, originally worked for China National People's Radio, the central Beijing station that broadcast programs to the whole of China for many years. Radio declined quickly and soon became a so-called "weak medium" compared to newspapers and television.[3]

Deregulation and the Revival of China's Radio Industry

At the beginning of the new century, China's radio industry showed signs of revival. By October 2004 some 1,489 radio stations in China were broadcasting 1,686 programs for a total of 24,503 hours a day. China's National People's radio had 62.3 million listeners, accounting for 52 percent of the population over 4 years old.[4] Listeners were also listening for longer. Daily listening time increased from 70 minutes per person in 2005 to 97 minutes in 2006. In 2007 listening time per person dipped to 89 minutes.[5]

Radio station revenue increased 20 percent yearly between 2000 and 2004 while the National People's Radio revenue rose 40 percent annually.[6] Among the traditional media, radio advertising increased the fastest. From 2000 to 2006, the average annual increase in radio advertising was 35 percent. Total market share for radio advertising also increased, from 2.3 percent in 1997 to 3.6 percent in 2006.[7]

For most countries in the West, the revival of radio is closely related to new technology, especially digital technology. In China, technology only partially explains the revival of the industry. The main force was the new media environment brought about by the booming economy of the country, changing lifestyles and most importantly, the deregulation of the media.

China's booming economy has created a strong need for advertising. Radio is very competitive in attracting advertising. Radio ads are much cheaper than television or newspaper ads, while some popular radio programs have large audiences. New radio formats, such as interactive programs, have attracted many new listeners owing to the popularity of mobile phone

Figure 6.1 A TV advertisement for a music show in Chinese and English.
Source: Wynne Wang

short messages. Radio advertisers can target the audiences they want to reach because different groups tend to listen at different times. People with college degrees tend to listen to radio in the morning, while people above the age of 55 tend to listen to the radio any time of the day. From 2005 to 2007, more than 20 percent of morning radio listeners were white collar workers.[8]

A widespread English-language learning fever has also contributed to the popularity of radio among young listeners. Students, especially college students, use radio to learn English. Advertisements for radio programs appear bilingually (see Figure 6.1).

More newly affluent people have adopted new lifestyles that bring more radio listening. With the growth of China's cities, more people are spending more time traveling to and from work. Private cars are also becoming more affordable. In Shanghai, for example, the municipal government has been trying to discourage people from buying cars by charging up to 30,000 yuan (US$4,300) to register one. However, the number of cars still increased rapidly. The car market in China grew more than 20 percent in

2003. In Beijing, the increase was 36 percent, and the number of auto-mobiles reached 1.8 million in 2004, with half of them private cars.[9]

In just 10 years the revenues of a service program, *Beijing Traffic*, grew from 3 million to 150 million yuan (US$20 million), an increase of 50 times. This was much more than the entire annual advertising revenue for Beijing People's Radio, the sponsoring station just a few years earlier.[10]

The changing of China's media policies, especially those regarding management and investments from private and foreign sources, greatly stimulated the development of the radio industry. The loosening of government controls on radio management allowed stations to develop numerous new programs, especially entertainment programs. Satellite stations of big national or provincial stations were granted more freedom to produce and broadcast their own programs. More importantly, they could sell advertisements by themselves. Therefore, these local stations gained more financial and managerial independence from their mother stations.

In January 2003, at the National Conference of Radio, Television and Film, Xu Guangchun, head of China's Radio and Television Bureau, declared the year 2003 as "The Year of Radio Development."[11] To counter audience segmentation and answer new listener demands, all major radio stations could develop their own programs in news, music and sports and sell their own advertising. The experiment with this kind of management model was started in 1992 when Beijing People's Radio took the initiative to let its seven divisions manage their own advertising and retain the profits. The model was gradually copied by other stations. By 2003, the Government considered it the model for radio stations across the nation.

The deregulation regarding private and foreign investment also had an almost immediate impact on China's radio industry. In September 2004, Beijing People's Radio joined with Phoenix Satellite TV and established their own advertising company. Phoenix, based in Hong Kong, is largely owned by Rupert Murdoch's News Corporation. In 2005, Beijing Global Qifu advertising company invested 20 million yuan (US$3 million) in the music programs of China National People's Radio, while Bori Communications and a Shanghai communication company jointly invested 6 million yuan (US$850,000) in another program of National People's Radio, *The Voice of the Metropolitan*.[12] Although foreign investment is limited to 49 percent of total capital, deregulation opened the door for foreign investment in China's media industry.

Deregulation changed the sources of income for almost all radio stations in China, which now operate mainly on the revenue generated from sell-ing advertisements. As early as 1992 in Shanghai, China's largest city and its economic capital, TV and radio station revenue passed 200 million yuan (U$30 million), 10 times more than the subsidy from the government.[13]

Most importantly, media policy in China always lagged behind media practice. Almost all the officially approved deregulation policies had been in effect, at least on an experimental basis, somewhere in the Chinese media long before the policy was formally implemented. In fact, the deregulation boundary has always been pushed by China's media.

Problems to be Solved by Future Deregulation

With a long history as a government organization, radio in China faces many problems in its development as an industry. Deregulation is the only way to solve these problems. In the view of the radio industry, one development needed is the formation of commercial radio networks. In 2003, just 454 radio programs developed by one station were shared with other stations. The total volume of this "network" trading was only 1,015,000 yuan (US$145,000).[14] For news, individual stations rely on their own local staff or on Xinhua, the official government news agency. A survey completed in 2000 showed nearly 70 percent of news came from the local station reporters while the rest was mostly from Xinhua. At some local stations, 90 percent of their news program content is from Xinhua.

A big problem is that news program reporters and editors lack sufficient freedom to choose what to report. Since local radio stations are still run by the local government, station staff have to spend much of their time covering numerous meetings attended by local government officials.

The old system of management has been an obstacle for further development. Radio stations operate with the same personnel policies that apply to local government offices. On the one hand, radio stations directors cannot fire people who are unable or unwilling to do well. On the other hand, those who do well soon get promoted to administrative jobs so the station director loses a good program emplooyee. In some radio stations, one-third of the staff members do all the work.[15]

The Future of Radio Development in China

Formerly considered a weak medium compared to newspapers and television, China's radio industry is now developing fast. There is still room for greater development and much greater profit. China has the second largest radio market in the world, but its potential market could surpass the United States, the current leader. By the end of 2002, China had only 1,882 radio stations, less than one-sixth the total in the United States.[16] The market share ratio of radio compared to TV in China is 1 : 10.5, while in some developed countries like the United States or Britain the ratio is 1 : 4.[17]

The rapid increase in revenues in recent years also shows radio's great potential. In 2000, the average revenue of a radio station was 20 million yuan (US$3 million), while in 2004 the revenues of 12 radio stations in the country each surpassed 100 million yuan (US$12.5 million). One popular program on Beijing People's Radio Station, generated 150 million yuan (nearly US$20 million) in 2003.[18] In 2006, radio advertising increased 47.2 percent, much faster than the 18.2 percent average increase for China's media industry. In 2008, the revenues of seven radio station passed 200 million yuan,[19] while Beijing People's Radio, the most pro-fitable radio station in the country, claimed revenue of 560 million yuan (US$80 million).

Most radio stations target city listeners. While there are still great profit margins for stations in the cities, even greater profit margins may exist in the vast countryside that is currently largely ignored. As a convenient and cheap medium, radio has more advantages in its ability to cover distant rural areas where TV signals can hardly reach. In a 2001 survey, 62.8 percent of villagers owned radios and there were 467 million listeners in the rural areas. However, the first radio station targeting these areas was set up only in 2003 in Shanxi Province.[20]

The need for a bigger market will push China's media companies into different areas to break down the regional administrative fences. With China's central government media as the exception, media are often restricted to their home administrative regions. To gain profit from economies of scale, local media in China have been seeking cooperation with other regions. However, this kind of the cooperation has been quite limited. The main obstacles come from local government officials, who consider the local media their own channel to the people. These officials fear that media that cross regional boundaries cannot be controlled by them and could carry news that criticizes the local government. Even though there will be obstacles, in a market economy driven by profit margins, cooperation between media of different regions will continue.

The need for better programs and more capital is an important motivation for China's media to cooperate with foreign media. Media in

China are still learning to adapt to the new media environment brought about by the market economy. Most radio stations in China are eager to cooperate with foreign media to gain new ideas to produce programs that cater for local listeners. Foreign companies, especially big companies, on the other hand, would like to expand their markets in this most populous country in the world with its now booming economy. Economically, the cooperation would bring benefits to both sides.

It is hard for China to break out of its old inefficient management system, but new management systems will be formed within the framework of the old system. The cooperation of radio stations with advertising companies, even companies from other industries, will introduce new management systems into this industry. Some programs on China's Central People's Radio have developed this way. The new form of ownership has already brought about a new management system within the framework of the old system. We can expect these changes soon to spread to the whole of China's radio industry.

Like radio in other countries, the digitalization and convergence of radio with other media will characterize the development of radio over the next few years. This means almost a revolution in radio station ownership and program production in China.

On November 15, 1996, the Zhujiang Economic Program in Guangdong was first broadcast online. By the end of 2003, eight radio stations in China had started broadcasting online. China Radio International is broadcasting online in 39 languages, claiming to be the website using the most languages.[21] Afterwards, online broadcasting developed very quickly.

At present, in terms of ownership, there are three kinds of online radio stations in China: government radio; commercial online radio; and private amateur online radio stations. Government online radio, such as popular online radio Yinhe Radio (radio.cn) was set up and run by two state media: China People's Radio and China Broadcast Website. Commercial online radio stations often developed from former commercial websites. These stations were originally part of commercial websites and then developed into independent online radio stations. Radio stations like QQ Radio (http://fm.qq.com) and Mop Radio (http://radio.mop.com) were part of two commercial websites before they became independent online radio stations. Amateur online radio stations are run by individuals and groups with an interest in radio. These stations, such as Firefly Radio (52yhc.com), are more like a platform for radio amateurs to share programs they like, mainly music and entertainment.

With the merging of traditional media and new media, online radio will exert strong influences on traditional radio in program production and management. Since 2007 several online radio networks have been established. These online radio networks make it possible for radio stations in different places to broadcast online. For example, new online network broadcasting has brought different radio stations together. Radio Sina (radiosina.com), a commercial online radio station, has cooperated with 10 city radio stations, including Shenzhen news radio and Hunan Satellite Radio, to broadcast online.

The founding of online radio stations, to some extent, has brought about the biggest deregulation in China since 1978. For the first time, individuals can broadcast to the general public through the Internet, which could hardly been imagined for traditional media. Furthermore, commercial and amateur online radio stations are private. In this sense, online radio is the first privately-owned and managed medium in China. It is not an exaggeration to say online radio is a revolution in ownership and program production.

7

Television

Entertainment

Television plays a quintessential role in the lives of virtually every Chinese. Not only does television physically reach 96.23 percent of the country's 1.3 billion people, but broadcasting has great symbolic importance as well. In Shanghai, the Oriental Pearl Broadcast and TV Tower in the Pudong "new area," with its distinctive double-onion silhouette shown in Figure 7.1,

Figure 7.1   The Oriental Pearl TV and radio tower is 468 meters (1,536 feet) high. It is the third highest broadcasting tower in the world. It has shops, restaurants, and even a museum in its upper areas.
Source: Wynne Wang

Figure 7.2 The new Beijing headquarters of Central China Television (CCTV). The spectacular building was completed after the 2008 Olympics.
Source: Xiaopeng Wang

serves as the symbol of the modern city. In Beijing, the US$800 million leaning double towers of Central China TV (CCTV)'s gargantuan new headquarters shown in Figure 7.2 send a clear message: "irreverent, a can-do spirit and extremely confident."[1] The CCTV tower, which was damaged by a fire in February 2009, ranks as the second largest office building in the world, after the Pentagon.

That structure, as well as about 10,000 other new buildings that were constructed in time for the 2008 Olympics, gave Beijing a more modern, profile. Some old-time residents did not support the modernization enthusiastically as they saw old neighborhoods disappear. During the

17 days of competition, August 8–24, some 2,500 hours of programming aired – 1,000 more hours than for the 2004 Athens Games. The Beijing Games had an estimated record-breaking audience of more than four billion TV viewers worldwide.

During non-Olympic days, the average person's daily viewing time amounted to nearly 3 hours in 2006. During the past two decades of rapid growth, TV broadcasters adjusted to changes in audience viewing patterns with better market-oriented strategies, although they still must conform to the government's ideological guidelines. China's mass media are ranked as "not free" by the Freedom House organization.

China's TV audience was merely 80 million in 1978, but now numbers as many as one billion people, the largest TV market on the planet. In 1990, China ranked second to the United States in number of receivers, but it has since catapulted to first place, with about 400 million TV sets; ownership of color TVs per 100 urban households zoomed from 59.04 in 1990 to 137.43 in 2006.[2] Today, in addition to CCTV's national network, provinces and cities also have their own TV stations. Internationally, two of CCTV's channels, the Chinese-language CCTV-4 and the English-language CCTV-9, are broadcast around-the-clock to global audiences in more than 120 countries. All this development has occurred in just 50 years.

History

Although the People's Republic of China was founded in 1949, Chinese television did not begin until May Day in 1958 when Beijing Television (BTV) went on the air. Only about 30 TV sets existed in the capital city to receive BTV's abbreviated contents. The twice-a-week programming lasted 2 or 3 hours each day, including the first TV drama, "A Mouthful of Vegetable Pancakes," aimed at encouraging frugal food habits during a period of adversity. Later in 1958, a channel was established in Shanghai, similarly carrying only minimal content.

Within the following years, many other provinces, municipalities directly under the central government, and autonomous regions began to set up local TV stations. By 1961, 26 TV stations were already established throughout China, although the political turmoil and economic adversity caused by the later Cultural Revolution (1966–76) largely hindered the industry's further growth for the next 15 years. Nevertheless, some progress occurred, such as a pilot run of color programming broadcast in 1973 by BTV in Beijing.

In July 1976, BTV began a trial airing of national TV news on more than 10 regional TV stations across the nation; that program turned into "*Xinwen Lianbo*" (News Broadcast) in 1978, arguably the most authoritative and influential program on television. Mao Zedong, who died in September 1976, did not see or make use of the medium's potential.

In 1978, after Mao's death and the end of the Cultural Revolution, BTV was renamed China Central Television (CCTV). CCTV now reaches every corner of China and encompasses 16 channels. English-language CCTV-9, launched in fall 2000, broadcasts to both Chinese and overseas viewers.

Alongside China's economic reform and opening up, the 1980s and early 1990s witnessed the TV broadcasting sector's growth in leaps and bounds. In the early 1980s, a complete national TV network emerged, which linked provincial stations to transmitting, channel-switching, and relay stations. TV stations at both national and local levels were able to carry color broadcasts on the Phase Alternation Line (PAL) system. Starting from 1983, authorities began to loosen up the centralized TV broadcast system by allowing regional municipalities and counties to set up their own TV stations to join national- and provincial-level counterparts to form a four-level broadcast mechanism. As a result, the number of TV stations in China surged from 52 in 1983 to 202 in 1985. The official statistics indicate that, as of 2005, China had 302 national and provincial TV stations and 1,932 municipal and county-level broadcast stations, with a total of nearly 12.6 million broadcast hours of TV programming yearly.

Today these provincial satellite TV stations, with national coverage and their various niche markets, have developed distinct personalities. Often gathered into groups for better management and financial support, they creatively use limited resources to launch entertainment-oriented programs. Provincials' endeavors have paid off as, in 2006, their combined market share rose from the previous year's 16.9 to 19.1 percent. While provincial satellite TV broadcasters have gradually strengthened their market positions, those provincial non-satellite TV stations and lower municipality- and county-level stations have felt increasing pressure from competition and faced a dropping market share.

Revenues and Ratings

The dominant player in China's multi-level TV broadcast system is still CCTV, with its vast resources, personnel, coverage base, and government support.

In 2006, CCTV garnered approximately a 35.2 percent of the market share, which ensured its number 1 market position.

Despite stiff competition in the marketplace, the TV industry's robust growth has resulted in financial rewards. In 1982, China's TV and radio broadcast industry reported revenues of merely 8.8 billion yuan (US$122 million), but in 2006, the figure soared to 109 billion yuan (US$15.1 billion), or an average annual growth rate of 22.3 percent. Among the major contributors was revenue from TV advertising, whose value reached 45.3 billion yuan (US$6.29 billion) with an 11 percent annual growth. Also, earnings from cable TV subscription amounted to 25.2 billion yuan (US$3.5 billion), accounting for 23 percent of the broadcast industry's total revenue.

Advertising requires accurate audience measurement to set acceptable rates for purchase of TV time. Compared to other countries, China's TV viewership measurement started rather late. In 1986 CCTV conducted China's first large-scale, nationwide poll that sampled TV audiences in 28 domestic cities. In 1987 a larger study by CCTV and major provincial TV stations covered, for the first time, audiences in both urban and rural areas. With the breakneck development of the TV industry in the 1990s, a fast-track need arose for companies such as AGB Nielsen Media Research that could handle more professional and more accurate audience measurement.

By far the main player, with an 85 percent market share, is CSM Media Research – a joint venture between China's CTR Market Research and the giant Taylor Nelson Sofres (TNS) Group. As the world's largest broadcast audience measurement firm, it surveys the Chinese people as well as Hong Kong's 6.4 million audience members. This operation covers some 54,000 homes with 178,800 panelists, who measure in excess of 1,000 main channels and nearly 400 radio frequencies every day.

AGB-Nielsen Media Research, by contrast, has about a 10 percent market share that encompasses major metropolitan areas and provinces (as of October 2007, greater Shanghai, greater Beijing, and the provinces of Guangdong, Zhejiang, Jiangsu, Shandong, Fujian, Sichuan, Liaoning, Chongqing, and Tianjin). It has installed its proprietary system in more than 11,000 households, representing some 471 million Chinese TV viewers.

Broadcast Regulation

Broadcasters have adapted to changes in markets and audiences' viewing patterns, although they still must conform to general ideological guidelines set by authorities. Given its important role in China's cultural industry in government's eyes, the country's TV broadcasting sector has been under rather strict supervision, primarily by the State Administration of Radio, Film, and Television (SARFT). This government agency lies directly under the State Council (similar to the US president's cabinet), which has the role of making media policies, issuing operation licenses and directives, and determining programming themes. Such supervision is in strict accordance with the fundamental ideological guidelines by the Propaganda (or Publicity) Department of the Communist Party of China (CPC) Central Committee. For example, regulations promulgated in 1997, 1999, and 2000 applied specifically to TV dramas.

Apart from such state-level supervision, local provincial, municipal, and county-level governance also oversees broadcasters.

Despite the existence of multi-layered supervision, TV broadcasting in China has seen a major shift from a stern-faced political propaganda machine running in a monopolistically structured and highly hierarchic system for decades to become more market-oriented and audience-friendly. This new approach can be shown by the emergence of specialized stations in the early 1990s that focused on the economy, entertainment, education, women, urban matters, children, and other areas. With relatively more autonomy, such stations signaled a trend towards decentralization and specialization that helped to counterbalance television's original political and propagandist role.

Entertainment programs, especially those launched by regional broadcasters (sometimes created specifically to compete with CCTV's offerings), have been under scrutiny by authorities. SARFT has, in recent years, unveiled a series of orders and punished quite a number of TV stations in order to uphold high moral standards in entertainment fare shown on domestic TV screens. Crackdowns are exemplified by the ban of Chongqing TV's "The First Heartthrob" in 2007 for its "vulgar content" and "bad taste."

Rules also govern other specific content. Since in China crime must not pay, one Chinese-Hong Kong co-production had two endings, one for Hong Kong and one for mainland viewers. Furthermore, depictions of and talk about sex are forbidden. In a 2004 adaptation of "Sex and the City" titled "Falling in Love" the four characters' stylish fashions reveal less and look softer than those of Carrie Bradshaw and her friends in the US series. In this female-targeted drama the four independent professional Chinese friends retain a traditional femininity even while they buy, buy, buy. Other clones include "Home with Kids" (based on "Growing Pains") and "My Siblings" (based on "Friends").

Rules on co-productions went into effect in 1994. Other regulations impose quotas on foreign TV imports.

Imports

The fast growth of China's TV market since the early 1980s brought about an ever-increasing demand for TV programs. In 1979, CCTV aired the first foreign TV drama series, "Povratak Otpisanih," which was produced in the former Yugoslavia. Translated and dubbed, it depicted resistance activities in Nazi-occupied Belgrade during World War II.

Later, as the central authorities gradually lifted the ban on importation by granting large regional and city TV stations the authority to buy foreign TV programs, more fare from abroad began to flow in. Among the earliest widely popular entries were "The Man from Atlantis" – the first US imported drama after the 1979 establishment of China-US diplomatic relations. Other early imports included the US shows "Garrison's Gorillas" and "Dallas." Japan provided "Doubtful Blood Type" and "Astro Boy" – the first imported foreign cartoon – and from Hong Kong came "Huo Yuanjia."

The popularity of imported foreign TV programs continued throughout the early stage of China's opening up and economic reforms until the mid 1990s, when the authorities began to curb imports with a string of rules that restricted the broadcast of foreign content during the prime viewing time. Currently every province and provincial city level TV station has to abide by an annual quota system. In 2005, China imported a total of 72,640 hours of TV programs worth some 401 million yuan (US$54 million), including 202,370 episodes of foreign dramas that accounted for about 4.5 percent of the total broadcast dramatic programs that year.

Gradually imported programming lost its position as priority choice for Chinese viewers. Programming from Taiwan, Hong Kong, and Korea dominated the imported TV drama market, while fare from Europe and the Americas became far less welcome. For instance, the Chinese market reaction to imported US TV series like "Desperate Housewives," "ER," "Band of Brothers," and "Everybody Loves Raymond" was rather lukewarm. By contrast, CCTV-1 ran a popular prime-time, 50-episode series on Hong Kong martial arts star Bruce Lee that a mainland crew filmed on the mainland, Hong Kong, and Macau, as well as foreign locations. In 2000 14.3 percent of dramas were imports.

Content

Despite quotas that keep imports low, outside influences affect TV content indirectly but significantly. Evoking criticism for copycatting practices, the amateur shows "Dream of China," "My Show," "My Hero," "Super Girl," and "Happy Boy" strongly resemble "American Idol," itself a copy of Britain's "Pop Idol." Moreover, CCTV's "Happy Dictionary" and "Win in China" are modeled on "Who Wants to Be a Millionaire" and "The Apprentice." In fall 2008, "Ugly Wudi," based on "Ugly Betty," debuted on Hunan Satellite Television, with plans for 400 episodes rather than the usual 20 to 40. Despite some viewer's complaints that the actress' old-fashion braids and sweaters looked ridiculous in the current era, ratings were high. Notably, all these cloned shows are non-violent.

A combination of regulations and cultural norms keeps violence at extremely low levels. Both sex and violence "run counter to traditional family values and the spiritual civilization" of China.[3] On seven CCTV channels in 2000 in Beijing, one study found that only 16.3 percent of prime-time shows contained violence, compared to 67 percent of shows on US prime time.[4]

As noted above, the average Chinese person watches television for about 3 hours (176 minutes) a day, mostly entertainment (non-news) content. Despite some highly popular talent shows like "Super Girl" and the fall 2008 karaoke hit from Hunan TV "Beat the Mic," TV dramas have remained the preferred TV genre. According to SARFT, among the total 12.59 million TV hours aired in 2005, TV dramas contributed nearly 44.5 percent (followed by about 11.8 percent for advertising, 11.7 percent for news programs, 10.7 percent for special service programs, and 9.3 percent for general entertainment).

Dramas

More than 4.4 million episodes of domestic TV dramas as well as 202,370 episodes of imported TV dramas were aired in 2005. Also in that year, more than 193,000 hours (20,000+ episodes) of 945 TV dramas were produced, involving a combined investment of 3.07 billion yuan (US$415 million).

A CSM Media Research study revealed that the Chinese viewers watched an average of 56 minutes of TV dramas per day in 2004. Advertising revenue from TV dramas amounted to 9.3 billion yuan (US$1.26 billion) for the broadcasters.

Episodes run daily until (like Latin American telenovelas) the story reaches its end. In general, audiences in the north prefer historical fare, while modern love drama attracts more viewers in the east and south. Also, time cycles characterize the types of dramas aired.

One popular subgenre of domestic TV drama is historical subject matter. In the 1990s, historians, novelists, and then TV scriptwriters delved into the Qing Dynasty (1644–1911); "almost every single Manchu emperor who worked for a strong state has been made the hero of a serial drama."[5] For example, the reign of the emperor Yongzheng (1722–36) was made into a 44 episode, 100+ character drama based on a contemporary novel.

Next, dynasty dramas ceded their place to contemporary anti-corruption dramas as the new primetime audience favorites in the early 2000s. Supported by the central authorities, crime dramas overcame all other genres, both as novels and as TV dramas. Then in 2004, SARFT restricted showings of all crime dramas, due to heavy doses of sex, violence and raw power struggles, until after 11 p.m. Thereafter, dynasty dramas such as "Genghis Khan" returned to the TV screens.

In 2003, another revisionist trend reevaluated the short Republic era (1911–31). In "Marching toward the Republic," Dr. Sun Yat-sen's appearances are "always associated with uplifting and at times sentimental music."[6] Not all critics approved of the drama, however. The government banned reruns on CCTV or provincial stations. Since the show emphasized democracy, apparently it threatened the current Chinese system.

In 2005, "The Great Emperor Hanwu" depicted, in 58 episodes, the reign (156–87 BC) of this long-ago leader at a then record-breaking budget of US$6.02 million. With 1,700 characters, it featured a Taiwanese actress as the emperor's grandmother, increasing its popularity in Taiwan. Why a switch from the recent Qing to the prosperous Han empire, which reached to central Asia? There is a parallel to China's current growing influence and pride as its people gain wealth and its preparation for the Olympics.

Foreign Influences and Dramas

The 1980s saw huge popularity of imported family-life melodramas; for example, 450 million Chinese saw the 1976 Brazilian telenovela "The

Slave-girl Isaura." Home-grown family-life productions soon followed. In China, as in Latin America (but differing from the United States), well-known movie stars appear in prime-time TV soap operas. The lead character of "Yearnings," aired in 1990, was a beautiful woman of traditional virtue who appealed to the family values of the largely middle-aged and elderly regular TV viewership. Its rousing success spawned a wave of copycat family sagas into the 2000s. One example, Nobel nominee Lin Yutang's "Moment in Time," adapted from the 1938 English-language novel set in the Republic era, omitted the novel's complexities and concentrated on love triangles.

The "trendy" genre originated in Japan in the late 1990s as a conscious effort to attract young, unmarried women with disposable income. It featured fashionable clothes, pop music, and trendy locales. The genre came to China via Korea when the trendy drama "What Is Love all About?" debuted on CCTV in 1998, starting a wave of imports. Korea has now overtaken Japan as the prime drama exporter to Asia. China and Taiwan, both accounting for about 20 percent of Korean exports, were the top consumers of Korean TV programs in 2001–3. Korea's trendy dramas, unlike Japan's, have "a rare synthesis of modern lifestyles with Confucian moral and ethical codes . . . Cultivating or practicing such concern for others involves effacing oneself."[7]

Love-themed "idol" dramas appeal to college and high school youth, while "pink" dramas cater to working females in their 30s. Chinese copycats of both soon followed the Japanese-inspired Korean imports, beginning in 1994 with "Love to the End" and followed by titles such as "Love in Shanghai," "Real Love," and "Love Letter." By 2005, idol dramas set in the present time ranked as the most popular TV genre, followed closely by urban (including pink) dramas and then crime (including anti-corruption) and historical (mostly costume) dramas.

Animation

Animation currently produced in China, such as the adventure story "The Question of Naughty Blue Cat 3000," is designed for children aged 3 to 10. They often have didactic intentions, such as teaching children to study hard and be obedient – for example the series "Black Sergeant." Although parents may approve of such fare, adolescents and older teens find them bereft of dramatic artistry, "monotonous and boring." Moreover, the same audience finds parent-approved cartoons related to history, such as "Journey to the West," lack a sense of modernity, while "Japan's animation products enjoy a variety of topics covering modern trends."[8]

This author found college students in China adept at downloading Japanese animation, such as the naughty-boy series "Crayon Shinchan." The director of the School of Animation at the Chinese Communication University confirmed too, in early 2009, that within as few as 3 hours or so of an episode appearing on Japanese TV, it would have been subtitled in Chinese. Older episodes of the Japanese series "Famous Detective Conan" were legally available on various stations in China, but because of a government ban intended to encourage local animation recent series such as "Death Note" have been banned.

Reality Shows

James Fallows says that "the curse of Chinese TV, apart from its being state-controlled and de facto censored, is the proliferation of stupid low-budget 'reality' shows."[9]

Although cruel in its "PK" (Player Kill) segment, nevertheless CCTV's "Win in China!" has many redeeming qualities. In this adaptation of "The Apprentice," contestants are "killed" as determined by audience vote or a panel of judges. In the final, live episode (December 2007), one grand champion was chosen from five remaining contestants of the show, which had started with thousands of initial candidates.

Instead of a high-salary job as in "The Apprentice," creator Wang Lifen offered seed money for new entrepreneurial ventures with a top prize of US$1.3 million. After 33 episodes, advertising agency manager Zhou Jin, one of two women among the final 12, won, even though she took a short maternity leave during the competition. She had strong backing in the blogosphere because of the way she handled her pregnancy.[10] "There is no religion in China, so it is very important to promote the right kind of values," creator Wang said. "Today for our society, the entrepreneur can be our hero."

Game shows

Like "Win in China!" many game shows are based on overseas formats but not legally licensed. For example, China's participation in the worldwide

"Millionaire" phenomenon includes both a shoestring budget version and a CCTV clone with high production values. ("Who Wants to be a Millionaire?" was created in the United Kingdom in 1998 and was exported to the United States in 1999.) By 2000, producers in Anhui Province had created "Super Great Winner," a low-tech version where the "poll the audience" lifeline amounted to a show of hands, while to "phone a friend," the player chose someone in the audience; the Anhui show also added a musical chairs segment that Regis Philbin would never have recognized. Despite its dissimilar title, CCTV's "Happy Dictionary," which also debuted in 2000, stays closer to the Western "Millionaire."

The low-budget "Super Great Winner" is an example of one of four basic game show types: the *mixed-format* program.[11] "Happy Dictionary," especially at the big-money stage, is a *knowledge* quiz. The venerable "Lucky 52," which premiered on CCTV-2 in 1998, was China's first *interactive* game show; in other words, viewers at home can play along in most of the segments. For example, if stylish host Liyong asks, "What anniversary is symbolized by gold?" viewers at home find themselves yelling "50! 50!" at the screen. Two contemporary game shows exemplify the *spectator* format: a strong-man contest between teams of midgets; and a CCTV "Family Feud"-type show involving physical stunts by a father, a mother, and their elementary-school child. The dating/matchmaking shows popular on provincial channels also fall into the spectator category.

The genre is so malleable that shows can emphasize luck or strategy, require bookish or common knowledge, involve time pressure or proceed leisurely and feature civilians, celebrities, or both. Hunan TV's "Happy Camp," which debuted in 1997, has celebrities participate in game segments interlaced with performances. Even a casual channel surfer will notice the preponderance of young male-female host duos, rather than the Regis Philbin model.

New Year's Programming

Hundreds of millions of Chinese families gather in front of their TV screens on the lunar New Year's eve (in January or February), watching the annual variety performance gala broadcast live on CCTV networks. Debuted on CCTV-1 in 1983, the event has become a modern ritual observed by a majority of Chinese households. Beginning at 8.00 p.m. on New Year's Eve and lasting for nearly 5 hours, the gala usually comprises entertainment programs like traditional Chinese folk arts, popular dancing and singing, short comedy sketches, Chinese cross-talks, scenes from Chinese opera, magic tricks, and acrobatics.

According to a survey by Nielsen Media Research, 214 million Chinese in more than 100 million families, or 70 percent of the national total, tuned in to the 2008 CCTV gala. While the event has turned into a viewing habit for Chinese families, thus becoming an advertising cash cow for CCTV, it has in recent years received increasing criticism for showcasing timeworn routines and too-familiar entertainers. Also, its audience has demonstrated much disparity as, for example, the same Nielsen study showed that only 4.59 percent of the TV audience in the booming southern Guangdong Province watched the 2008 gala, while 25 percent or 24 million out of 93.67 million watched the show in the populous eastern Shandong Province. Meanwhile, the CCTV flagship show has been challenged by influential regional TV broadcasters like Shanghai's Dragon TV and Hunan TV that present their own variety shows to vie for a bigger market share.

"Super Girl" and Variety Shows

Like the New Year's show, everyday variety shows can feature celebrities' performances, such as CCTV's "Super Variety Show" launched in 1990. A different experience, the amateur talent contest, has also caught the public's attention, highlighting public participation, low entry standards, and high interaction with participants.

Among these amateur talent shows, Hunan TV's "Mongolian Cow Sour Yogurt Super Girl" was easily the most successful. Modeled on "American Idol," but featuring only young female singers, it went on air in 2003, receiving a fairly healthy market share. Realizing the huge market potential, Hunan TV revamped the program the next year. Backed up by carefully designed marketing, promotion, and production strategies, the show quickly caught the public eye and became, via cable, a national viewing sensation. The audience remained under the spell of "Super Girl" in 2005, when success was even more miraculous. The show attracted over 150,000 participants, and an estimated 30 percent of the country's TV sets, or 210 million viewers, tuned in to the event's episodes, demonstrating that province-based ratings could match those of the CCTV annual New Year's extravaganza.

More significant is the participation of the Chinese people in a nation-wide "election." The top three finalists received more than eight million votes by paid cell phone text messages, involving an estimated 540,000

zealous fans. Panned by the official media "for vulgarity and manipulation" of fans, the show was praised as "a victory of the grass-roots over the
elite culture" and (in the West) for promoting democracy and freedom.[12]
The nationwide mania continued in 2006. SARFT thereafter banned gossip,
screaming fans, and outlandish hair and clothing.

The success of "Super Girl" spurred Hunan TV to launch "Happy Boys'
Voice" in 2007 – not "Super Boy," since SARFT would not approve another
talent show titled "super." In fact, authorities had been concerned about the
popularity and "worldliness" of "Super Girl," and critics from the state-run
CCTV once panned the show for being "vulgar, boorish, and lacking in
social responsibility."[13] Although "Happy Boy" met with great success in
2007, SARFT later banned such talent shows from prime-time television
(7:30–10:30 p.m.) and thus basically put an end to this extraordinary TV
phenomenon.

Changes and Challenges

New forms of television, such as Internet protocol TV (IPTV), handset TV,
and mobile TV (used on public transport facilities), are posing an increasingly serious threat to the traditional television industry. At the end of
June 2008, China for the first time had the largest number of Internet users
in the world, 253 million people, surpassing the United States. Moreover,
China has 550 million cell phone users. Content production resources will
no longer be monopolized by traditional TV stations, deepening audience
segmentation and reshuffling revenue sources. Another development is the
increase of cable TV subscribers, which totaled approximately 140 million
households by the end of the first half of 2006. Among them were about
12.6 million cable digital TV users.

As well as film, piracy affects television programming. Broadband
access and streaming sites represent a "troubling development for entertainment executives and copyright lawyers" for countries "with lackluster
piracy enforcement efforts, like China."[14]

According to SARFT's plan, China's radio, TV, and film production,
as well as broadcast, cable network, and satellite transmission, will all go
digital by the year 2010. By 2015, China's content production, broadcasting, and transmission systems will all be digitized.

Analog TV systems and networks will be shut down eventually. These
and other transformations will deeply change the public's TV consumption

patterns; new modes for entertainment, education, business transactions, and daily communication, such as pay TV, will also bring huge business opportunities.

The lackluster export market presents another challenge. In 2004, earnings from exports of Chinese TV dramas amounted to merely US$6.5 million, accounting for nearly 80 percent of the total export value of TV programs. SARFT statistics also indicate that, in contrast to more than 72,640 hours of imported TV programs in 2005, China exported only an egregiously disproportionate 6,680 hours of programs.

Generally speaking, most of China's TV drama exports are targeted at the overseas Chinese communities, especially in Asian regions, and drama series like those adapted from classical Chinese literary works or those with historical settings, as well as some costume dramas, have been the most popular, especially in Taiwan. However, competition pressure from rivals like Korean TV's dramas has been increasingly keen in recent years for Chinese TV program exporters, while cultural, linguistic, and even political barriers are still in place to prevent China's TV programming from fully tapping the international market.

The central authorities of China aim to open the TV industry to private companies and telecommunication firms, both domestic and overseas. However, there has been considerable criticism of the sternness, uncertainty, and micro-managing of government-directed administrative interferences. For instance, the strict limits on prime time TV drama content will lower profitability.

The lack of political parody comes in for criticism, given the popularity of "The Daily Show" and similar programs in the United States. A *China Daily* columnist bemoans the fact that "making parodies of mainstream culture is still sadly not acceptable to many people and institutions in our society."[15] Video Web content is similarly controlled, such that it blocks YouTube and has punished or shut down video sites deemed pornographic, violent, or violating vague national security laws. A later edition of this book would surely include scenarios not even imagined today.

The latest challenge to China's entertainment industry came in 2009 when the World Trade Organization (WTO) ruled:

> that China must start allowing more foreign imports. This should mean more U.S. films, music, and books will enter the Chinese market. The trade dispute has been going on for years, however; trade experts warn against expecting any big changes in the near future.[16]

8

Television

News

After the 2008 Olympics the biggest story in Beijing was no doubt the spectacular February 9, 2009 fire that put CCTV's magnificent new head-quarters out of commission just before it was to open. The public throughout China and the world could, via the Internet, see the flames devouring an adjacent hotel and searing off the special alloy skin of the CCTV building, the largest in the world after the Pentagon. However, they could not see any of this on CCTV whose staff could have covered the fire by looking out the windows of their nearby offices. Several reports stated that the fire was started by firecrackers set off by CCTV employees to celebrate the Chinese Lantern festival. They could have provided some dramatic reports from the scene.[1] But the government quickly ordered that the story be kept off CCTV and told all other news outlets to wait for the official report. The Internet joke that quickly circulated was that CCTV had created the biggest story of the year and then failed to cover it.[2]

Han Han, one of China's leading writers whose blog was ranked the second most popular in the country, immediately posted a report of the fire. The blog was quickly censored but by then it was being reposted all over China by other bloggers. CCTV's refusal to report what nearly every citizen in Beijing had witnessed and bloggers throughout China knew about once more damaged the credibility of a news operation already under severe attack.[3]

Less than 2 years earlier Chinese officials had tried to bolster CCTV's credibility after an embarrassing fake story got onto the national network. A freelance journalist at a Beijing TV station reported that a city bakery was mixing cardboard with the dough in its buns. He later admitted he had staged the story, which put the public into a panic over their fears of contaminated food. The story added to the damage done to China's reputation by reports that it was exporting contaminated food and drugs.

Infuriated Chinese officials cleaned out a reported 3,000 or more CCTV employees, many of them freelance contract workers. Many remaining employees had their salaries cut as Chinese officials reportedly decided that the entire CCTV operation had become overstaffed and needed closer control.[4]

In January 2009 a group of Chinese intellectuals published a letter accusing CCTV of being full of "propaganda aimed at brainwashing the audience." The letter said the news programs were a large part of this. Wang Jianhong, a CCTV deputy director, defended the news broadcasts, saying that CCTV had covered the 2008 Sichuan earthquake, the Tibetan riots and the tainted milk scandal with "timely and sufficient reports."[5] Just a week later CCTV cut off the Chinese interpreter of the inaugural speech of US President Barrack Obama after he mentioned the word "communism" in the same sentence with "fascism." The *Washington Times* commented: "What had begun as a promising exercise in openness degenerated into a familiar display of paranoia from the country's publicity department." The *Times* noted that Obama's full speech showed up the following morning on the state-run, but English-language, *China Daily* and also on some Chinese language Internet sites.[6]

News and Politics at CCTV

CCTV, as a government-owned operation, faces numerous problems in trying to report the news. First of all, CCTV clearly cannot directly criticize the government or established government policies. For example, its news editors must be alert to block any story that would suggest that Taiwan is a separate country and not part of China. More problematic situations arise with a news event that demands immediate coverage and there is no clear policy on what to report or how to report it. When the biggest disaster of the new century – the 9/11 attacks on New York and Washington occurred in 2001 – Phoenix TV in Hong Kong was on the air quickly with a bulletin that could reach 150 million Chinese via its satellite. However, CCTV was essentially paralyzed by policy questions that had to be cleared through government ministers. Chinese leaders require advance notice of any news with worldwide impact about to be broadcast by CCTV. In 1986 CCTV had quickly broadcast a report on the explosion of the

Challenger space craft before alerting China's leaders. It was considered CCTV's "boldest moment" by Dean Lei Yuejie of the Department of TV and News at the Communication University of China but CCTV's action did not impress the country's political leaders. "It was the first and last time in history that central government leaders got no advance report," said Dean Lei. "I thought that *Xiawen Lianbo* (the main evening news broadcast) would thereafter arrange the news according to newsworthiness. However, this wasn't approved by the executive department. Even the 9/11 terrorist attacks didn't make the news headlines."[7] Meanwhile, the Internet, CNN, BBC and Hong Kong's Phoenix TV were fully reporting the 9/11 tragedy. Everyone in China who could get access to these channels did so almost immediately.

In a study of coverage of the 9/11 attacks by China's major media, Prof. Li Yinbo of Huazhong University faulted CCTV for its dull and superficial coverage. CCTV was not far behind in its initial reports but treated the 9/11 attacks as just another routine story in its foreign news summary. Phoenix was the first television channel in China to report the 9/11 attacks just 25 minutes after the first jet hit New York's World Trade Center, although it was still 15 minutes behind Sina.com's first Internet report. CCTV was only 10 minutes behind Phoenix TV with a short item on its *Broadcasting Now* program, making it the last story in its usual end-of program international news summary. CCTV then continued to provide short reports on the tragedy as part of its regular news programs.[8]

In contrast, Phoenix TV, which had started its InfoNews channel only 8 months earlier, was on the air with a special program, "The US Under Terrorist Attack," less than an hour after the first plane hit the World Trade Center. There then followed 35 hours of news reports, reactions from around the world, and background information. Its audience soared to 60 percent of Chinese viewers. Its coverage was so thorough that many television stations simply relayed its programs. University students in Shanghai and other cities banded together to rent rooms in tourist hotels where they could receive Phoenix and other international TV news reports. CCTV meanwhile continued with its "monotonous and superficial coverage" that brought angry letters from its audience protesting the poor reporting. CCTV, true to its mandate to be a channel to provide government information to the people of China, kept pushing the 9/11 story aside for official announcements and reports. During much of the 9/11 coverage period, half of CCTV's evening *Xiawen Lianbo* news program focused on a policy address by President Jiang Zemin.[9]

Summarizing CCTV's coverage Professor Li wrote in *Television & New Media* in 2002: "CCTV did nothing but make the old media system look very dull and conservative, whereas Phoenix TV reanimated the old media and made it shine in this age of the Internet." Rather than paying attention to its audience, CCTV relies on the official Xinhua News Agency for news and lets the government's journalistic guidelines confine its coverage, he said. Li called on CCTV to make "profound reformations in its management and operation in order to become a high-quality source of information and to be more competitive in future competition." [10]

The Challenge of Phoenix TV

Phoenix TV has a substantial advantage over CCTV because of the different level of censorship in Hong Kong. This represents a direct challenge to CCTV because Phoenix TV is "eroding their legitimacy and audience size."[11] It also has been able to avoid the "protocol news" about the comings and goings of China's Communist Party leaders that fill up so much of CCTV's news programs and bore so many of its viewers. Phoenix has also been careful in its commentary to adopt what one researcher called a "bystander" position, carefully presenting all sides of an issue and not suggesting one position is more authoritative than another. Its commentary programs tend to be direct even when dealing with sensitive mainland issues such as the arrest of journalists. Phoenix is so successful at finding the line between acceptable and forbidden news and commentary that it also distributes a weekly news magazine to a relatively small audience of less than 100,000 on the mainland.[12] Phoenix TV is clearly after a large mainland audience with lots of news from China in its broadcasts. Two Phoenix programs aimed directly at that audience are *Mainland Q&A* and *Jing Xing on Changan Street* (the most famous old street in Beijing). Still, Phoenix was careful not to intrude too obviously on CCTV. Phoenix calls its news program *Zixun* (Infonews) rather than *Xinwen* (News), the name of CCTV's main news program. However, Phoenix clearly wants to compete with CCTV for the mainland audience. Wu Xiaoli, a Phoenix TV news anchor said: "Someone says that the Phoenix InfoNews channel wants to be China's CNN. I say we are more ambitious. We want to be both China's CNN and CNBC."[13] Phoenix TV's ambitions are just part of what some in China see as a wholesale assault on China's culture. In 1993 a Beijing journalist said he sometimes felt that Hong Kong was "starting to buy up mainland culture wholesale."[14]

Chinese journalists working at CCTV have been trying to escape oppressive government controls for years. Hu Yong, a journalism professor at Beijing's Peking University, said the most depressing time during his 10-year career as a journalist was his few years at CCTV. "Restrictions and limitations on reporting were present everywhere. Sometimes we had to race to make the news before the order came down to censor the news." Hu said he and his colleagues admire the "desperados" in the mainstream media brave enough to try to act like professional journalists. He added that some of these "desperados" at CCTV did their best to report on the school collapses that killed so many children in the 2008 Sichuan earthquake.[15]

Even with CCTV support, its reporters face some risks when they try to act like professional journalists. The experience of a CCTV reporter identified only as "Ms. Li" suggests the continuing tensions even when the official national media try to report on local government problems. In November 2008 Li went to Shanxi province to investigate a land dispute. When she returned to Beijing, four Shanxi police officers arrested her at her apartment and charged her with accepting a bribe from one of the parties in the dispute. Earlier, CCTV employee Wang Huai was arrested in Shanghai by police from Henan Province who returned him to Henan where he was jailed. Wang had criticized officials there on his personal blog.[16]

Despite resistance, especially at the level of local government, Chinese officials in Beijing often cite the media as being important in the fight against corruption. Wu Guanzheng of the Communist Party's Political Bureau told a CCTV audience that "media publicity was vital" in the national campaign to prevent corruption. He said that authorities "should listen to the voice of media to improve their work." Wu added that the media should stick to the "right orientation" in trying to guide public opinion.[17]

CCTV's news coverage has often been dreary by Western standards. *Xinwen Lianbo*'s lead stories had to focus on what the Communist Party and its leaders were doing that day. New government policies had to be explained to its viewers before reporting the day's news events no matter how dramatic they were. One study found that 50 percent of the program time was taken up by political stories. The Chinese audience did, however, always pay close attention to the final five minutes of CCTV's 7 p.m. *Xinwen Lianbo* ("Simultaneous Newscast") program. For years the program regularly provided a short summary of foreign news from Western sources.[18] The format of *Xinwen Lianbo* has hardly changed since its start in 1978. The activities of the Communist Party and its leaders always lead the news program followed by about 20 minutes of domestic news and five minutes of foreign news. There are two presenters, usually a man and a woman, who always take a serious tone and speak in formal Mandarin. The program is repeated later in the evening and dubbed versions are available in at least some minority languages.[19] An early presenter said the style was always "clear and rich in tone," "majestic," and "precise." From 1989 to 2006 the same main newsreaders were used. There is no "happy talk" that is common between news anchors on Western television news programs. The style of the program was so rigid that when the news presenter asked to change his hair style his request was rejected by CCTV executives. The program's signature music did not change in more than 25 years. Composer Meng Weidong became known throughout China as "the man whose music you hear every day."[20]

The content of China's news has also been rigidly controlled, especially in the early years of Communist control. In 1958 when the harvest failed it was officially announced that China's wheat output that year had overtaken that of the United States, wrote Jung Chang, who lived through the period. In her book, *Wild Swans*, she wrote that the official explanation for the starvation deaths of 30 million people during the 1959–62 famine was that Russia had forced payment of a huge Korean War debt and the country had been the victim of natural calamities.[21]

According to a 2007 CCTV survey, *Xinwen Lianbo* remains its top program, attracting 500 million viewers. The program is even uploaded on to YouTube by Dowei, a Chinese news network. CCTV can claim an audience this large by counting all the viewers on the major provincial and city channels who are more or less forced to watch the 7 p.m. program since it pre-empts all others. Local news programs could have a larger total audience if they were all counted together. Also, whatever *Xinwen Lianbo* claims as its audience size it has clearly been losing viewers to Phoenix TV and Shanghai's Dragon TV in recent years. Shanghai's Oriental Satellite TV used to have its own 7 p.m. news broadcast but as of July 2007 it switched to CCTV, reportedly because CCTV did not want that competing with *Xinwen Lianbo*.[22]

Despite the strictures placed on it by government policies, CCTV has had some impressive and even venturesome news programs. On September 25, 2008, TV viewers in China could watch on CCTV the launch of the Shenzhou VII spacecraft, carrying three Chinese astronauts into earth orbit – followed by coverage of a space walk and their successful return to earth. These live broadcasts, despite the risk of a possible failed launch, space walk, or reentry, symbolized a metamorphosis for China's government-controlled news media.

However, the refreshing transparency of the space mission coverage does not translate into other arenas. CCTV news is still "censored and packaged largely to show the country's happy, harmonious moments."[23] As the only national network, CCTV's audience is "vastly larger than every major television network in the United States and Europe combined."[24] For example, while NBC felt proud to draw 29 million Olympics viewers in prime time, the Olympics opening ceremony in China drew an average audience of nearly 500 million. Cities and provinces have their own local programs. For example, Beijing TV 1 airs *Beijing Xinwen* ("Beijing News") at 6:30 p.m., but like almost all other stations it then carries the national CCTV "*Xinwen Lianbo*" at 7 p.m.

Xinwen Lianbo: Still on Top with the News

Among all mass media in China, *Xinwen Lianbo* has stood without rival "in view of geographical coverage, audience size and visual imperatives," ranking as China's "dominant and most authoritative source of news, information and ideas."[25] No commercials may air during the newscast, but many, and at premium prices due to the vast audience, bracket the program. This domestic Mandarin-language national newscast is potentially the most-watched news program in the world. The program is scheduled for 30 minutes but can be extended. To cover the death of China's leader Deng Xiaoping in 1997, for example, for more than a week *Xinwen Lianbo* was longer than 30 minutes.

In addition to the nightly news, CCTV runs an all-news channel, which draws on a growing number of foreign bureaus. However, the contents (and omissions) of the 30-minute *Xinwen Lianbo* give viewers most succinctly "the Chinese viewpoint of . . . the world . . . and how it was to be seen."[26]

Although *Xinwen Lianbo* is clearly the leading CCTV program, other news and public interest programs are very popular. *News from Taiwan* ranks number 11 in CCTV's top 20 programs. Second in terms of audience is *Focus Interviews*. This discussion program sometimes investigates corruption and inefficiencies, especially in provincial and local governments. Critics claim that the program too often spends little time on the problem but focuses for the most part on what the government is doing to fix it. Topics it chooses to address are already on the government's reform agenda, they claim. Another very popular program is *Law Today*, which sometimes takes up cases of ordinary citizens who have legal problems, often those cases which have attracted public attention. One program discussed the case of CCTV employee and blogger Wang Shuai who was arrested by Hennan Province police and jailed for criticizing local officials. CCTV's commentator discussed a citizen's right to criticize government policies but focused on how the government could prevent future incidents.[27]

Some have reported that officials have used the popularity of these programs to trap critics. Feng Bingxian received a message from an individual claiming to be a reporter with a CCTV discussion program. Feng was in dispute with some local government officials over some property. He was in hiding because the local government officials had ordered his arrest. According to a friend when Feng went to meet the CCTV reporter, he disappeared. A businessman from Hainan Island and a drug company official on their way to CCTV interviews were reportedly arrested when they went to Beijing.[28]

The 7 o'clock News in the 1990s

T.K. Chang , in a massive project, analyzed 840 stories airing on *Xinwen Lianbo* in 1992 (when media reform began), 754, in 1996, and 582, in 1998 (when CCTV celebrated its fortieth anniversary). The central question he addresses is: How did China see (construct) the world? The *putonghua* (Beijing dialect Mandarin, CCTV's standard language) newscast's worldwide coverage is limited and highly selective and includes about 28 per cent of all stories received by the editors. The program clearly emphasizes Chinese news for the Chinese people.

Chang found that CCTV covered 88 total nations with the following 10 entities the most prominent: United States (in 11.7 percent of stories); Russia (9.9 percent); the United Nations (8.2 percent); Yugoslavia (5.0 percent); Japan (4.8 percent); Israel (4.4 percent); the Palestine Liberation Organization (4.1 percent); the United Kingdom (3.7 percent); France (2.5 percent); and Germany (2.3 percent).

By far, North America outstripped all other regions – even East Asia. Although little pre-1990s research exists to enable comparisons, Chang notes that in 1985, the United States likewise occupied first place on CCTV news. In the 1990s, on *Xinwen Lianbo*, two US images appeared: "the positive display of US technological and scientific accomplishments was counterbalanced by a negative depiction of US society." The CCTV gatekeepers, who are government employees, "thus created a symbolic social reality about the United States that was based on facts, yet regimented according to the Chinese political purpose."[29]

Chang also found much more violence (terrorism, disasters, accidents, wars and destruction) in international than in domestic news, such that the newscast portrays China as "a peaceful, safe country as opposed to other countries out there.[30]

The 7 o'clock News: Recent Trends

Cooper-Chen examined the same news show in fall 2005 (170 stories aired October 31 to November 6).[31] Comparisons with Chang's study of the 1990s revealed the United States as still the most prominent country in 2005 and Asia as the most-covered region. As earlier studies had found, the United States and a nation's own region tend to dominate news coverage. As in the 1990s, China's selection of world news clearly emphasized violence, making China seem much more peaceful than the outside world.

In 2008, 3 years later, Cooper-Chen analyzed 60 stories during 1 week of *Xinwen Lianbo* (September 21–27). In both 2005 and 2008, gender equality was conveyed by the choice of anchors (even though males accounted for the bulk of actual newsmakers) – always a serious, unsmiling male and female duo from a stable of regular presenters. Regular features, such as "Comrade Pioneers" (2005) or "30 Years of Progress" (2008) took up many minutes of time during the newscasts. The segments did not resemble US network news features such as ABC's "A Closer Look" or "Person of the Week." They did not deal in depth with current news, but appeared to have been planned and produced far in advance.

By 2008 the program's dominance was somewhat fading, given the plethora of viewing options at 7 p.m. Other than Channel 1 and the news channel, no other CCTV outlets carry *Xinwen Lianbo*. There are also numerous other non-news local channels (nine choices for Beijing TV alone) that do not air it. However, its reach remains vast in that all provincial flagship stations still must carry the program. In 2008, Japan and the United States were the most covered nations in the abbreviated international roundup that typically ended each newscast. As in the past a typical beginning of the newscast involved a national figure greeting guests at some sort of ceremonial function.

When the TV audience sees a newsmaker alight from an airplane, shake hands, smile, propose a toast, speak to an assembly, cut a ribbon, lay a wreath, wave, smile and ascend into a plane, they are watching protocol news. Such news can vacillate between one pole – "harmless but of little interest . . . lacking credibility . . . [being] very boring and almost never exportable" – to the opposite pole, in that the "ceremonial comings and goings of national leaders paled in the face of the real problems of development."[32]

Protocol news dominated both the 2005 and 2008 CCTV broadcasts. To cover these "grip and grin" TV portrayals of top government leaders looking official, cameras typically pan over orderly rows of listeners or guests as the official speaks, followed by a long stretch of hand shaking. These scripted events contain no analysis or criticism.

The media no longer ignore unscripted events, but they give them a protocol rather than critical spin. In earlier times, the 1976 Tangshan earthquake, which killed an estimated 800,000 people, merited only a brief mention in the *People's Daily* the following day. The short story was followed by extensive coverage of party leaders' expressions of concern and their praise for the heroic rescuers' efforts. Reports gave no casualty figures or damage estimates. Not until 1988 did the media reveal the complete story of the earthquake.[33]

Concern about public panic and China's image are used to override Chinese authorities' responsible disclosure of negative news and events.[34] Now the events such as the 2008 Sichuan earthquake are covered, but CCTV emphasized images of officials "consoling victims and reporting tales of rescue efforts. Images of death and anger over shoddy school construction were censored."[35] In sum, the media in China tend to create an illusion of normalcy.[36]

TV News to Overseas Audiences

To audiences beyond China (but also available in China), CCTV International broadcasts four 24-hour news channels: in Mandarin (CCTV-4); English (CCTV-9); French (CCTV-F); and Spanish (CCTV-E).

CCTV-4 is aimed at a worldwide Chinese-speaking audience but it starts off every day with a program focused on Taiwan. "Across the Strait," another 15-minute program, comes up again during the day suggesting how important it is for mainland China to reach the Taiwanese audience. Ties between China and Taiwan have increasing in strength for decades, especially in business and cultural ties. Direct China-Taiwan flights that avoid a long detour via Hong Kong started in 2005. The CCTV-4 schedule is then filled with news programs, cartoons, and shows about cooking, sports, science, film, health, and business plus advertising segments. Some history and travelogues ("Light of Chinese Civilization") and dramas ("Snowing Homeland" and "The Policemen and Their Lovers") are also scheduled. Programs are mostly in Mandarin, but there are some in news reports and business programs in English. CCTV-4 devotes a good deal of time to covering Chinese sports stars such as Yao Ming in the US National Basketball Association. The star's activities, families, and personalities are the focus of the programs rather than the actual NBA games. Chinese-Americans who have been successful in their new country (a mayor, a police chief, a beauty queen) also get featured. Much of the information apparently comes from overseas Chinese-language newspapers. Medical programs apparently attract an audience since they are frequently shown. Examples are a program on autism and another that showed a mother in China donating part of her intestine to save her son's life. Viewers have noticed that CCTV-4 is slow on covering breaking news, perhaps reflecting the usual hesitancy with any news story that may have policy implications. Such stories are sometimes left to CNN and the BBC for the first 24 hours.

On October 1, 2007 CCTV-E and CCTV-F became separate channels. Earlier these channels aimed at Spanish and French speakers were together on a single channel. Most programs, including Chinese soap operas, are subtitled. News broadcasts are in Spanish on CCTV-E and in French on CCTV-F. Schedules do not show any programs particularly aimed at Spain and Latin America or France and the large French-speaking audiences in Africa and elsewhere. Many programs on the French and Spanish channels are reconfigured from the English-language international channel.

CCTV-9, the English channel launched in 2000, claims an audience of 45 million via six satellites. Like CNN International, it carries commercials and more accurately could be called a news-and-features channel. Long before CCTV-9 began broadcasting, CCTV aired English-language news bulletins in 1986. China's new efforts to reach English speakers via CCTV-9 is clearly to present a different face of China with a moderate and neutral news programs and many feature programs on Chinese culture and its people. Jirik, who worked for CCTV, found CCTV-1 the main source of Channel 9's Chinese news, while wire services such at Reuters and the Associated Press provided the foreign news.[37] The following programs were being aired in late 2008: "World Wide Watch" (7 p.m. Beijing time);

"News Hour" (noon Beijing time); "New Frontiers;" "World Insight;" "Up Close;" "Travel in China;" "Travelogue;" "Sports Scene;" "Rediscovering China;" "Nature & Science;" "Documentary;" "Dialogue;" "Culture Express;" "Chinese Civilization;" "China Today;" "Center Stage;" "Biz China;" "Asia Today;" "Around China;" and "Learning Chinese."

"World Wide Watch," airs between 7.00 and 7:30 p.m. in China, the same time as *Xinwen Lianbo*, the main CCTV newscast to China. "World Wide Watch is," as would be expected, more consciously world-oriented than *Xinwen Lianbo*.

In one analysis, 165 stories from "World Wide Watch" (October 18–30, 2005) were coded based on their content.[38] Reflecting the newscast's title, only a few stories were purely domestic. Crime stories in domestic news only appeared twice, but were much more prevalent in international news. As Chang found regarding the English news in the 1990s, the CCTV worldview of China as more peaceful than the world out there continued into the 2000s. Also confirming other CCTV studies, the United States stood out as the most prominent country in the world news.

An analysis of 7 days in fall 2008 further confirmed the United States as by far the most-covered country and Asia as the most-covered region in "World Wide Watch." Japan, Germany and the United Kingdom ranked equally as distant second-place countries; neighboring Russia and South Korea ranked third. Latin America and Africa were virtually ignored.

An April 2009 "World Wide Watch" report, with Annie Fu presenting the news in formal but meticulous English, was, as would be expected, more consciously world oriented than *Xinwen Lianbo*. It included the following items in its 30-minute format: 1) Violence in Thailand; 2) UN condemning North Korea's rocket launch; 3) Signs of an easing of US–Cuba relations; 4) China's navy involved with pirates off Somalia; 5) Sri Lanka war; 6) Lebanon violence; 7) Anti-Russian protests in Georgia; 8) China's human rights plan announced; 9) China's tax revenues fall; and 10) Need to export Chinese culture to foreign markets. A world weather report was presented at the end by a Westerner along with a scroll showing weather conditions in cities around the world exactly as seen on CNN. There were two advertising segments in the program including one for beer complete with dancing Chinese models.

The list of stories shows CCTV-9 is including more foreign items that focus on violence and criminal activity. This suggests that TV news editors in China increasingly accept that international audiences want these types of stories. And, of course, these stories of violence and crime in foreign places also reinforce the theme that China is a more peaceful and harmonious society. In a study of news broadcasts aimed at the Chinese audience such as *Xinwen Lianbo*, Dong and Chang found this was an increasingly strong theme in foreign news aimed at the Chinese mainland audience.[39] They looked at the broadcasts between 1992 and 2004 and said there was a "shocking" increase in reports of foreign crime and violence, especially from smaller countries. There was a continuing news focus on all activities of China's main rivals, the United States and Russia, but coverage of the rest of the world focused on the "hot spots" (Iraq, Sudan) while the rest of the "Third World" made the Chinese news only when disaster struck.

Channel 9's reach for an English-speaking audience has changed substantially in a decade. A 2001 study by Scotton comparing news broadcasts by CCTV-9, CNN and BBC showed substantial differences.[40] For example, CCTV-9 started its 2001 program with a report of a Communist Party conference on the role of the media in Chinese society. The program consisted largely of officials meeting formally with the announcer's voice-over explaining what was happening. Next, a segment about the opening of the Party Congress in Beijing, which mostly showed long rows of Party members sitting at a meeting. The third news item was on an international topic, the UN considering Iraq issues. The order of the news items was different but except for the two China-focused lead items on CCTV-9 all three news programs had similar content. All three included film of a plane crash in Luxemburg and a train fire in Germany, indicating that all three programs used the same news agencies for international video. This suggests that television news editors in Atlanta, Beijing or London will select many of the same news stories for broadcast if they are not under some government or political constraints. A TV producer confirmed that with visuals available, such non-political segments are always useful to fill out a newscast. Thus, these broadcasts reflect that the emerging global media are blurring the lines between politics, language, and nationality.

Two items that appeared on both CNN and BBC were not shown on CCTV-9: the shoplifting arrest of a Hollywood actress; and the tell-all book by a former butler to Britain's Princess Diana. When asked about this omission, a Chinese broadcasting official replied: "CCTV does not deal in gossip."[41]

Like Mandarin Channel 4, the English-language channel had numerous travelogues and cultural programs – film tours of the Grand Canal, the Silk Road and Buddhist temples plus a program on Chinese Opera and the

Shanghai Tea Festival. Channel 9's sports program highlighted the careers of the NBA's Chinese basketball stars, no doubt with much of the same material shown on Channel 4. "Biz China," a 15-minute report, was shown several times during a 24-hour news cycle. Figures in China's yuan were translated into the equivalent in dollars for foreign viewers.

A Changing US Image

Combining all the content studies of English-language news, the image of the United States has undergone a change. Chang had found a "counter-balanced" US portrayal – lionized for technical achievements, but denigrated for social ills.[42] However, in 2005 and 2008, it could be argued that almost all of the stories were negative – clearly in the case of the financial crisis stories of 2008. The admiration for US technical achievements seems to have disappeared, overshadowed by China's launch of three astronauts as noted above.

The CCTV worldwide newscasts, which have an audience of millions, are "not journalism as we understand it in the West," according to China expert Orville Schell. He also noted, that the "ponderous forms of censorship . . . are just more obvious in China" than in certain other countries.[43]

Further, viewers may not realize that the CCTV "reporters" are actually narrating outsourced video with CCTV-approved scripts. Only rarely do original stand-up stories appear. Chinese TV news producers face the same problems as their colleagues elsewhere. They need visuals to fill their news hour. However, the officially approved script must be used to explain to the audience what it is viewing.

Six anchors revolve in the daily English newscast, including New Zealander Ed Maher, Canadian James Aitken, and a stable of Chinese broadcasters. In additional to Maher and Aitken, about three dozen foreigners work at CCTV-9, performing roles such as editing scripts, checking grammar, and narrating stories. There is a Belgian woman who presents the news on the French-language channel. Maher, however, stands out as the pioneer. In 2003, CCTV hired him as its first Western news anchor "to shake its image as a stodgy government mouthpiece."[44]

Maher, who has tried gallantly to learn *putonghua*, worked for China Radio International for 6 months before he accepted his job at CCTV. He was the first non-Chinese news anchor at CCTV-9, starting in 2003 as the channel began to revamp its English-language programs. His rather solemn presentation is not far removed from the standard set by CCTV's Chinese anchors. A native of New Zealand, he worked in Australia as an unconventional weatherman, sometimes using carrots or ice cream cones as map pointers. He ceased this career in 1999 to care for his wife, moving to China in 2001 after her death.

Not bothered by criticism of himself as a sellout, Maher points to the progress that Chinese news reporting has made in the 30 years since the repression of the Cultural Revolution. It was after that revolution (1966–76) that television became a mass medium, spurred by the show trial of Mao Zedong's widow and the "gang of four" during 1980–81.

Maher and the other non-Chinese presenters represent an effort to make CCTV-9 an international channel reaching out to an international audience. CNN does the same with the stable of foreign anchors seen on its international programs. The difference, according to Maher's critics, is that CNN attempts to present a complete and balanced news report while CCTV presents only the officially approved version of the news. Maher maintains that since he joined CCTV the station has become less rigid, reporters more relaxed and there has been a move, however slight, toward balanced news. Whether the news is balanced or not, everyone at CCTV must keep in mind the requirement to follow government policy. More bluntly, a CCTV official put it this way: "If you like working here, obey the rules. If you don't like the rules, get out."[45] That sentiment could, of course, apply to all news workers in China who are essentially government employees.

An Ambitious Plan for CCTV's Future

China will have to attract more foreign television professionals to CCTV if its ambitious plans to launch a 24-hour international TV news channel in English continues to move forward. China wants to create a channel modeled on Al Jazeera, the 24-hour Arabic-language news network that has captured much of the Arabic-speaking audience with its strong cover-age of the Middle East. Al Jazeera has also launched an English-language channel which is attracting some viewers. China has two problems to overcome before it can have a successful international television channel, says Prof. Li Xiguang of Beijing's Tsinghua University. Those are "a great shortage of good journalists" and the urge to control.[46] No doubt China can train more Chinese journalists and attract more foreign journalists to

CCTV but China is not likely to give up control of the media. "Control of the media is absolutely paramount for the Communist Party," says David Bandurski, head of Hong Kong University's China Media Project. "They are not going to dispense with the notion that media control is central to their power in one fell swoop." In fact, argue some critics of the plan, China will have to undergo political reform before it is going to reform CCTV and its other media.[47]

China is apparently very serious about having a news channel to compete with CNN and BBC. It is reportedly willing to invest billions and even set up the station outside China, possibly in Singapore or Thailand, to gain credibility. China's propaganda director, Liu Yunshan, stated that such a channel is essential to the future of China. "It has become an urgent strategic task for us to make our communication capability match our international status," he said. "In this modern era, who gains the advanced communication skills, the powerful communication capability and whose culture is more widely spread is able to more effectively influence the world."[48] However, journalism professor Yu Guoming of Beijing's People's University said if the new TV channel is to reach an international audience, one that has been relying on CNN and the BBC for years, China is going to have to change its approach to the news. CCTV's English, French and Spanish channels are not successful "because they ignore the Western audience's requirement of balance," said Yu. If the China's international TV news channel is to be successful, it cannot be used as a propaganda outlet. Gong Wenxuiang, journalism professor at Peking University added, "If the medium lacks credibility, it is unthinkable that it will improve the country's image."[49]

China does have image problems abroad. In a 2008 survey of 23 countries the Pew Research Center found that in only seven did a majority have a favorable view of China. It is doubtful whether a government-operated TV will help. The United States government set up an Arabic-language news channel, Al-Hurra ("The Free One"), in 2004 to improve its image in the Middle East. The Arabic-speaking audience showed little interest in it.[50]

Anthony Fung, who interviewed many CCTV and Phoenix TV staff members, does not see how CCTV can compete with CNN and BBC. Phoenix TV is so far ahead in both international and even mainland news that Chinese government officials consider it an important information source. CCTV is burdened by its necessary caution and delay whenever there is a political element to a news report. In China's current political setting, at least, says Fung, CCTV "cannot be reincarnated in the form of modern media like CNN or BBC."[51]

Acknowledgments

The authors would like to thank Dr Charles Chen for his assistance with translation of *Xinwen Lianbo* stories, Maria Waltner for her analysis of "World Wide Watch" and Siwen Wang for the analysis of Phoenix TV programs.

9

Xinhua

The Voice of the Party

Xinhua is by some measures the world's largest international news agency. Its free or low cost reports from Beijing in six languages – Chinese, English, Russian, Arabic, French and Spanish – to more than 130 countries makes it a major institution in the field of international news. It is subsidized and controlled by the Chinese government and Xinhua's content reflects government policy and avoids issues that China considers politically "sensitive." The Associated Press (AP), whose members and clients must pay hefty fees for its news service, sends its reports from New York and other cities in four languages to 121 countries. As a commercial operation serving clients in many countries, AP tries to be neutral or balanced in its reports although it is regularly accused of being biased or at least reflecting the Western and capitalist values.[1]

Which news agency is actually the world's largest depends on how you count agency assets. Xinhua, which is much more than just a news agency, has more than 7,000 employees, perhaps as many as 10,000 by some estimates. Some 1,900 of them are journalists, according to one report.[2] AP lists 4,100 staff members and reports 3,000 are journalists. Xinhua has five regional offices and says it has news bureaus in more than 100 countries; AP claims 243 bureaus in about 100 countries. Xinhua has an office in all of China's 31 provinces, in 50 additional cities, plus one office that deals with military matters. AP has about 150 offices in the United States.[3]

Xinhua tries to control the news coming into China and the news flowing from China to the rest of the world. For China's media – 2,119 newspapers, 369 TV stations, 306 radio stations, and 9038 periodicals by one count[4] – Xinhua is the only source allowed for news from outside China. Foreign reporters who want to send Chinese news out of the country

must first get press credentials from Xinhua or one of two other government agencies: the General Agency of the Press (GAPP); or the State
Administration for Radio, Film and Television (SARFT).[5] Xinhua tries to
enforce a unified propaganda line throughout the Chinese media. For
certain official events and announcements all Chinese media must carry
only the Xinhua reports.[6] These reports are particularly recognizable on
the news programs of Central China Television (CCTV) as they always
come at the start of the program, have no video and focus on government,
military or diplomatic matters.[7] Since Xinhua is a conduit for Party and
government political statements,[8] those who want to keep up with the
various political currents in Beijing have to pay close attention to Xinhua.[9]
Overall Xinhua reports have a much greater impact on its people than the
Western agencies have on their people.[10]

Xinhuanet is Xinhua's website and claims to be just behind CNN and
BBC in numbers of visitors. Its task, as reported on its English-language
website, "China View," is to "publicize China and report the world."
One of its most popular web programs is "VIP Studio." Various people
including government officials appear, sometimes in online discussions
with viewers in China and overseas. Topics and guests are carefully chosen
to avoid "sensitive issues."[11] Xinhuanet clearly enjoys a preferred place
among news gatherers, at least in Beijing. Its website boasted that it was
present in the Great Hall of the People for the 2002 press conference
of the Chinese and US presidents, while "the White House press corps
remained outside and filed stories based on what they saw and heard on
television."[12] The content of Xinhuanet, as a web version of Xinhua, is
controlled by the Chinese government. Through Xinhua the government
tries to control the news content of all web portals in China. Sina.com,
China's largest news portal, with 95 million registered users and 450 million
daily hits, does not have its own reporters. Legally, Sina.com and other web
portals can get their news only from Xinhua or the Party's main newspaper, the *People's Daily*.[13]

Xinhuanet uses the same six languages as Xinhua. Both are developing
a Portuguese-language service. In 2009 both had numerous stories focusing on Portugal and activities in Macau, the former Portuguese colony that
became part of China again in December 1999, but the stories were in English.
Xinhuanet was also advertising for native Portuguese speakers to work
as editors.[14]

Xinhua is one of 11 agencies reporting directly to the State Council, which
is one level below the Politburo, China's top governing body. The State

Council has always used Xinhua to enforce its monopoly over most media content throughout China. Some news could be generated by local media, but all political or "sensitive" information could only come from Xinhua.

As an agency clearly controlled by the Chinese government and the Communist Party of China, some call Xinhua "the world's biggest propaganda agency."[15] However, Xinhua's leaders have historically seen no conflict in serving the Party and being conscientious journalists. On its fiftieth anniversary in 1981, Xinhua Director Zeng Tao congratulated the agency for its "fine tradition of observing the Party line, adhering to the Party's leadership, maintaining close ties with the people, seeking truth from facts, being scrupulous and conscientious in every aspect of news work, and serving the people wholeheartedly." Party General Secretary Hu Yaobang added that journalists should use the news to focus on the good when reporting about life in China. Hu said Chinese journalists should not try to emulate the West when writing about the capitalist world and "definitely should not paint too rosy a picture or publish so-called objective reports" about that world.[16] There is an alternative news service in China, China News Service, founded in 1952. At the start, China News Service represented itself as independent of government but it was actually operated by the Chinese government. China News Service is much smaller than Xinhua and has developed to serve mainly overseas Chinese plus Hong Kong, Macau and Taiwan.[17]

Xinhua's Early Years

The Communist Party of China's first news service, Red China News Agency, was set up in 1931 in Jiangxi Province. The agency was mostly concerned with producing the Party newspaper, *Red China*, to promote the Party's political ideas. It also printed *Reference News*, a compilation of foreign news and commentary about China, for Party leaders. In 1937, after the Communists had made their famous "Long March" to escape annihilation by the opposing Nationalist armies, the news agency was renamed Xinhua (New China). During this period Xinhua was considered the "throat and tongue" of the Party, developing sources of information for Party leaders and faithfully presenting the Party's views to the public in China through its newspaper *Red China* and broadcasting to the world.[18] After the communists took over China in 1949, Xinhua became the national news agency and the major, and for most the only, source of information for the Chinese public. Xinhua was important to Mao Zedong as he pushed various national efforts such as the Great Leap Forward of 1957–9 to make Communist China into a more economically stable and independent nation. Mao rarely used the fledgling Chinese television network but utilized Xinhua regularly to reach out directly to China's masses.[19] To distribute the leaders' messages to the Chinese people and also to fulfill its roles as collector of information for the Chinese leadership and presenter of China to the world through five foreign languages, Xinhua needed a large staff. By the 1980s Xinhua already had an estimated 5,000 or more employees.[20]

Illustrating Xinhua's role as a government agency is the fact that Xinhua journalists who get sent overseas hold diplomatic passports. This enables Xinhua correspondents to be in countries such as North Korea and Myanmar that bar most foreign journalists. Some of Xinhua's foreign correspondents have operated as both diplomats and reporters. This was clear in Hong Kong before the British left when China earned a large portion of its foreign exchange via trade through that port.[21] Xinhua's office in Hong Kong provided news and was also a diplomatic channel, even hosting diplomatic receptions.[22] A Xinhua correspondent in West Germany was the chief negotiator in establishing diplomatic relations between the two countries and in 1972 became China's first ambassador there.[23]

Xinhua positioned itself as a "Third World Agency," establishing many bureaus in Africa in the 1980s when Western news agencies had only a few.[24] Xinhua's charter spells this out. It says Xinhua is to "fully reflect in particular the aspirations, demands of the third world."[25] Xinhua was a supporter of the New World Information Order (NWIO) in UNESCO that Third World countries tried to establish in the 1970s to counter what they saw as bias toward and poor coverage of their countries by Western news agencies.[26]

Searching for Non-government Revenue

Xinhua like all Chinese media was heavily dependent on government subsidies before China's reform movement began in 1978. Subsidies were then gradually withdrawn from the Chinese media as China moved its economic system toward "market socialism" or "capitalism with Chinese characteristics."[27] Xinhua, the *People's Daily* and other major Party organs kept some of their subsidies but, noting the trend, Xinhua moved to develop other sources of revenue. It had a monopoly until 2003 on distribution and sale of school textbooks and also started advertising, public relations, and photography businesses. It also published hundreds of books per year and, until they were split off into a separate Chinese firm, ran a large chain of bookshops.[28]

Xinhua clearly saw that its days of living on generous subsidies were over even though it was able to persuade the government to keep providing some support because of its central role in China's media system. Its many non-media businesses included a farm and a real estate firm in the 1980s. As a result of objections from other media as well as a number of corruption scandals, in 2002 Xinhua news divisions were prohibited from engaging in profit-driven enterprises. Nevertheless, Xinhua continued to have more than 500 "economic units" under its control though most of them seemed to lose money. As loses mounted Xinhua regularly lobbied government officials to increase its subsidy. The Chinese government kept providing subsidies to Xinhua and has even increased them substantially since 2000 as the agency is vital to its control of information flow within China.[29]

Xinhua has always produced publications that provided some revenue. A former Xinhua editor identified 40 publications that the agency published in the 1990s although, again, some were probably money losers.[30] Some of the leading media enterprises that Xinhua was involved in by 2009 were:[31]

Xinhuanet, its online portal;
Xinhua PR Newswire, a press release service for Asian companies;
Xinhua Daily Telegraph, a daily newspaper full of Xinhua wire reports;
Reference News, a daily digest of the international press;
International Herald Leader, a report on global affairs;
Economic Information Daily, a financial newspaper;
Modern Express, a metro daily in Jiangsu;
Globe Magazine, a biweekly news magazine;
Outlook, a weekly news magazine;
Oriental Outlook, a weekly news magazine;
China Comment, published every 2 weeks, focusing on politics, social issues;
Chinese Journalist, a monthly journal about the media;
China Securities Journal, a daily newspaper published in Beijing focusing on financial news; and
Shanghai Securities News, a daily with a focus on financial news.

Xinhua sells material from its audio-visual department to television stations, but has been consistently blocked when it has tried to move into television itself.[32] Xinhua officials realized that even with its vast size and reach inside China, Xinhua did not have the impact on the Chinese audience that CCTV's 7 p.m. *Xinwen Lianbo* news had on its many millions of viewers.[33]

China and the WTO

As the December 2002 date for China to join the World Trade Organization (WTO) approached, it set up an ambitious plan to re-organize its media. Party leaders wanted to create conglomerates that could compete on a world level in the WTO era. By December the State Agency for Radio, Film and Television (SARFT) announced it would combine China Central Television, China National Radio, China Radio International, the China Film Group plus Internet production operations. More central control of China's media, especially of China Central Television (CCTV), could work to Xinhua's advantage. The news agency had continued to lobby the state agency that controls television (SARFT) to operate a national television channel but had made no progress. When the chief of SARFT moved to become head of Xinhua, the agency believed its fortunes would change. The new Xinhua head petitioned SARFT to approve a Xinhua television channel. The new SARFT director, however, simply cited the former chief's memo denying Xinhua's request a few years earlier.[34]

The Xinhua rivalry with Central China Television (CCTV) was typical of the situation throughout China's media industries and was the primary reason why the conglomeration plan did not work out. There were just too many entrenched bureaucrats in the individual media entities who would not cooperate. Local officials, for example, did accept some newspaper consolidation but resisted strenuously any effort to take away their control of provincial and city television stations. These stations provided them with substantial revenue as well as political platforms. The conglomeration plan looked to them like a move by Beijing to take both political power and revenue from local authorities.[35]

While not usually generating as much revenue as local television stations, the growing Chinese metropolitan dailies were also considered important assets and political platforms by local officials. These newspapers had their own journalists to report on crime, violence, and local corruption, and to provide lots of human interest articles for their growing number of readers.

Their editors also set up their own exchange systems to collect news from other areas. Overall, they became less dependent on Xinhua for news.

The editors of these metropolitan dailies had two problems with Xinhua. First was Xinhua's notoriously slow pace in editing and sending out news. Xinhua was by tradition not interested in "timeliness" since it was a Western concept that did not fit with the government's political concerns.[36] Xinhua's slow pace did not particularly concern China's leaders until 1994 when 24 Taiwanese tourists died in a boating accident. Several days after the accident, despite resistance by local government officials, Xinhua released a short article with few details. Relatives of the victims assailed the Chinese government, accusing it of hiding the facts. A few months later China's State Council ordered Xinhua and other Chinese media to improve the "immediacy and accuracy" of reporting unexpected events. However, the order only applied when reporting for overseas audiences.[37]

The second problem for the metro editors was Xinhua's traditional focus on "good news" to show China as the harmonious society depicted by its leaders.[38] Chinese leaders and thus Xinhua believed this was the news the agency should provide for both foreign and Chinese readers. A 2005 study of Xinhua's French pages on the Internet found 80 percent gave a positive view of China. The percentage (70–80 percent) that Elliott[39] reports is the accepted Xinhua formula for balancing good and bad news. Bad news does appear on Xinhua – crime, traffic accidents, mining disasters, earthquakes, even corruption – but the emphasis as in the disastrous Sichuan earthquake is always on government efforts to help the victims or correct the problems. Criticism of China and some of its policies, albeit cautiously handled, is also clear on Xinhuanet forums.[40]

The metro editors wanted more stories about crime, violence, and tragedy that they believed their readers wanted and Xinhua was not supplying. They increasingly used their own exchange networks to obtain this news from around the country.[41] Competitive pressures also persuaded these editors to take up popular local causes such as environmentalism and consumer rights independent of central guidance from Xinhua.[42] One reason that Xinhua was not responsive to the needs of these large-circulation city newspapers was its close relationship to Beijing's *People's Daily* and other major Party papers. To gain government subsidies, it was vital that Xinhua please the editors and the influential readers of these publications. These were the people who ultimately controlled Xinhua's financial well-being and gave the agency its important political status. Even the journalists who worked for Xinhua believed they were successful only if they were published in the

People's Daily and other major party publications. Thus, Xinhua for years paid little attention to distant provincial and city newspapers.[43]

Decline of the Party Newspapers

Unfortunately for Xinhua, two developments weakened its relationship with these Party newspapers. First, as government financial subsidies declined and strict control over content eased in the late 1980s, the Party papers began to develop their own staff to produce more stories. This meant less room for Xinhua articles in the limited number of pages, sometimes as few as four, that these papers could print daily. Also, these Party newspapers began to lose readers and advertising to the metropolitan dailies that were attracting readers with plenty of local news and less Xinhua material. The number of Xinhua stories on Central China Television (CCTV) news programs also steadily declined in the 1990s.[44]

The city newspapers and the evening provincial dailies that local governments were encouraging as new revenue sources were growing fast. In 1979 there were only 69 newspapers in China but by 2002 there were more than 2,100.[45] Advertising revenue flowed to the city newspapers as their circulations grew and in 1995 Xinhua tried to tap into it by starting to charge a fee to its subscribers. Unfortunately for Xinhua, of course, the subscribing newspapers with the most income to pay for its services were the metropolitan dailies that were less interested in the Xinhua content and less dependent on the agency for news. Also, free news and information on the Internet forced Xinhua to sell its service at discount prices. It had to rely more and more on its own publications, including newspapers that competed with some of its clients, to generate the revenue it needed to replace the diminishing government subsidies. Xinhua's directors recognized that the metropolitan newspapers were gaining political as well as economic power as their readership and advertising grew while the Party newspapers gradually lost their power. Xinhua was, therefore, forced to adopt a market-oriented view of the news for its long-term survival.[46]

"News" at Xinhua

A basic problem that Xinhua had from its beginning is that its journalists had little interest in information as "news." An American who worked as a Xinhua editor in the 1990s reports that he was in "a newsroom in which it is difficult to detect the slightest interest in news."[47] He found it could take days for Xinhua to edit and transmit a story from overseas. Almost every story about China was copied from newspapers and the top priority was not the quality or importance of a story but the number of stories a journalist produced. This continued as a priority into the 1990s since the number of stories published in various Xinhua outlets became linked to the journalist's bonus.[48] These priorities may have been a consequence of new cautions that arose among Xinhua staff members after the 1989 Tiananmen Square protests and the military intervention. An Asian editor had found Xinhua's news service much stronger in the 1980s but believed the agency's journalists lost their initiative after those who showed signs of supporting the 1989 protesters were disciplined.[49]

Xinhua does recruit talented people to be its journalists. Top university students who are considered completely loyal to the Communist Party are sought out. Xinhua will even take on promising high school students as "amateur correspondents" and send them to a Party school. When they return to Xinhua as full-time journalists, they are considered more "politically reliable" than some university graduates who may have been exposed to dangerous ideas.[50] Graduates of the agency's program report that the training that the new Xinhua journalists get at the agency emphasizes the political role of Xinhua. Critics complain that Xinhua reporters, even those who are sent abroad, do very little reporting and spend their time copying material from various publications.[51] If Xinhua journalists do cover an important event, they receive advance "guidance" on how to cover it from the Propaganda Department of the Party's Central Committee.[52] The Xinhua stories sent to its subscribers, whether from reporter or editor caution, disinterest, or lack of journalism skills too often end up as barely useable by the newspaper editors. A top editor of *Beijing Youth*, one of China's best known papers, complained that Xinhua's reports on breaking news events sometimes lacked basic details and rarely provided needed background.[53]

Early in the 2000s a researcher found Xinhua journalists were conflicted about the definition of "news." Many were frustrated by dealing every day with dozens of local Xinhua bureau reports that were outside their definition of "news." As one Xinhua journalist said, most of the reports are "none-news" about routine works of local governments. "But," he said, "I had to deal with them."[54] Xinhua, on the other hand, will ignore or give very few words to important events that relate to political problems. In 2005 Xinhua ignored the death of a former propaganda director who had relaxed media controls during the 1989 Tiananmen Square protests. It gave just 60 words to the 2005 obituary of Zhao Ziyang, former prime minister and former secretary general of the Communist Party of China. Zhao had been banished in 1989 and spent 15 years under house arrest for sympathizing publicly with the student protesters.[55]

Xinhua Tries Investigative Journalism

In an effort to get more news into the thriving metropolitan newspapers, Xinhua in 2000 set up a department for investigative journalism. There are still "sensitive topics," but Xinhua journalists have learned that fast action can keep them relatively safe. "We must respond very promptly and take action very quickly," one Xinhua journalist said. In order to avoid censorship, he added, "We must act quicker than the Central Propaganda Department."[56] Xinhua also had the same problems editors at other news services have with lengthy investigative reports: newspapers lacked enough space to print them. Most of these reports were, however, posted on Xinhuanet. There are still sensitive areas that may result in a story being "killed" without explanation. Local Xinhua bureaus are also sensitive to investigations which might interfere with their relations with local governments.[57]

Xinhua has also had management problems. Xin, who has studied the agency extensively over the past decade, described its operations as "chaotic" in both journalistic practices and business operations.[58] Another study portrayed senior Xinhua managers as very cautious editors who make sure no controversial material gets publicly distributed and each day set the political guidelines for their subordinates. To some of their subordinates these top editors are known as "pandas," since they are perceived as sleeping through most of the day.[59] The caution at Xinhua is understandable. In 2003 Xinhua's editor-in-chief was severely reprimanded and a staff member was fired after they released to the public what they thought was a routine government report about the SARS epidemic.[60] A large number of Xinhua journalists also received a salary reduction, an action widely seen as a collective punishment for the error.

Reaching Out to Foreign Readers

Elliott sampled Xinhua's English-language stories from 1950 through the 1980s studying 4,674 releases. The Xinhua releases, in effect, reflected what the Chinese government believed at the time to be the news, or at least the news it wished to present. Most of Xinhua's news releases were out of date by the time they were distributed, normally coming 2 days after the event and sometimes even 8 days later. Asia was the focus of the largest group of stories. Africa and Latin America got much more attention than in the Western news agencies. Europe and North America went up and down but became more important in the 1980s, particularly in the latter part of that decade when China's "opening" began to take effect. Economics stories increased substantially in the late 1980s with Xinhua gathering more of the international news and becoming less dependent on other news agencies.[61]

In 2009 Xinhua's English-language stories, available on the Internet on "China View," were as up to date as those of any other news service. For example, Xinhua, CNN International and the BBC carried the same story about the Iranian President's hopes for better relations with the United States and President Obama within minutes of each other on May 25. Stories are changed so rapidly on these Internet sites that comparisons are difficult. Noticeable, however, was the emphasis on news about China on "China View," suggesting that it was not competing with CNN or BBC for viewers seeking international news. Six of the top 10 items on a "China View" snapshot at midnight (Beijing time) on May 25 were stories about events in China or involved Chinese officials. Checks of "China View" did find periods when none of its top 10 stories directly involved China (e.g., May 27 at midnight Beijing time), but there were usually some Chinese items among the other stories listed. CNN on May 25 had no US items among its top 10 stories and the BBC had no stories about the United Kingdom in its top 10, suggesting they were looking for an international audience. One top story on Xinhua reported a "suspected new flu case" in China. Within a few minutes this had been dropped to "Other top stories" and replaced by a report on "Confirmed, probable flu cases in US rise to 6,764." China's other news agency, China News Service, is clearly serving a Chinese audience either at home or overseas. For example, at midnight (Beijing time) on May 27 nine of its top 10 stories related to China (the other reported North Korea's nuclear plans).

A team of viewers checked and translated Xinhua's six websites (Chinese, English, Russian, Arabic, French, Spanish) posted on May 27 at midnight Beijing time to determine to what extent Xinhua tries to construct its news reports to serve different audiences. On the Chinese-language website nine of the top 10 stories were about China or the activities of Chinese leaders. On the English website, "China View," none of the top 10 stories focused on China. On the other four websites about half of the top 10 stories were about China. It was difficult to find any special focus to attract Xinhua's presumed target audience to its Russian, Arabic, French or Spanish websites. Each had one top 10 story about something happening in the general language or cultural area – one story on Russia, Pakistan, France, and Latin America. Different formats of some web pages (English, French) allow sections devoted to activities in that language area. The French web page had two stories concerning French-speaking Africa.

Conclusion

The metropolitan newspapers' success shows the "practical deregulation" of China's media to allow more market influence. Xinhua will survive if it can successfully change from a political to a market relationship with these major clients. It needs, as Xin pointed out, "a mixture of Party logic and market logic."[62] One test for Xinhua will come if China goes forward with its plan to spend billions to expand the reach and improve the credibility of its international media. The emphasis seems to be on television with plans for more foreign anchors and even a broadcasting site outside China in Singapore or Thailand to present a balanced media face to the world. Xinhua, always competing with Central China Television (CCTV) for influence and money, will insist that its established international news service and the prominence of Xinhuanet makes it eligible to participate in this effort. In fact, Xinhua reportedly has plans to launch its own 24-hour television news channel.[63] Yu Guoming, vice dean of the journalism school at Renmin University in Beijing and a consultant to the government on the plan, confirmed that Xinhua plans to create a 24-hour international news channel that would broadcast in English. Yu said the goal was for China to improve its image abroad and to create an international news organization.[64]

One problem for Xinhua is that the plan to create an international news channel seems to have conflicting goals: to reach an international audience and to improve China's image through, we expect, a considerable amount of news about China. Xinhua is capable of providing an international news service. At times its website has an array of international stories. At other times, however, it is too heavily focused on news about China to attract and keep an international audience that has access to CNN and the BBC. These news sources consistently put international news first. News from the "home country" (CNN – United States; BBC – Great Britain) gets into their reports only when there is true international import.

A more difficult problem for Xinhua to overcome if it is going to attract an international audience will be its credibility. Yan Lieshan, a Chinese author and columnist for *Southern Weekend*, said any perception that Xinhua cannot report freely will doom the "great external propaganda" campaign. Westerners, as another columnist pointed out, mistrust even their own media. International viewers are not going to abandon CNN and watch a TV channel run by Xinhua unless it can establish credibility.[65] Allowing Xinhua to report free of government control would represent a major change in Chinese policy. The policy has been followed by Xinhua for decades and is articulated in its own publications. A 2001 editorial in *Chinese Journalist*, a Xinhua affiliate and an authoritative source of information and guidance for Chinese journalists, stated: "Whatever the changes, the (media's) nature as party and people's mouthpieces must not be changed; the party's control of the media must not be changed; the party's control of the cadre must not be changed; and the correct opinion guidance must not be changed."[66] That statement does not seem to suggest that a new Xinhua free of government and Party control is in the near future for China.

10

Advertising

Wings for the Media

Although the mass media in China are still like caged birds, over the past 30 years they have grown strong wings strengthened and powered by advertising.

A Glimpse of Chinese Advertising in 30 Years

Since advertising became legal again in China in 1979, shortly after the country began an economic reform and reopened to the outside world in 1978,[1] it has experienced phenomenal growth. From humble beginnings the industry has grown to become one of the largest advertising industries in the world today.[2] In 1979, advertising revenue accounted for 0.002 percent of China's gross domestic product (GDP) and in 2003 0.92 percent the highest so far in terms of advertising's share of China's GDP.[3] In 1979, advertising revenue in China was approximately 10 million yuan (US$1.43 million), and fewer than 1,000 people were employed in the industry; by 2007, advertising had grown into a 174.1 billion yuan (US$25 billion) industry with more than 1.1 million employees.[4] Over the past 30 years, advertising in China has grown at an average annual rate of 35 percent average annual rate, one of the fastest growth rates among all industries in the country.[5]

Research has identified a strong, positive association between China's economic development and advertising growth. For example, 1985 and 1993 were two high points in China's economic growth, at 25 percent and 13.4 percent, respectively. Those years also witnessed the fastest growth rates in advertising business volume in the country, at 65.75 percent and

97.57 percent.[6] While China's annual advertising industry growth rates between 1981 and 1994 were found to be highly correlated with the nation's annual economic development rates in the same period, the correlation between the annual increase rates in retail sales of consumer products and the annual advertising industry growth rates in China during those years showed that each grew at almost the same rate.[7]

It is not therefore surprising that advertisements are ubiquitous in China today – in airports, on taxis and buses, on billboards, in subways, in shopping malls, in sports venues, on radio, television, the Internet and mobile phones and above all, in magazines and newspapers (see Figures 10.1 and 10.2).

Figure 10.1   Chinese advertisements can be big and dramatic as this Samsung advertisement in Beijing demonstrates.
Source: Hong Cheng

Figure 10.2   A Reebok advertisement on a Beijing street attracts attention. No translation is needed in the world of international consumers.
Source: Hong Cheng

Hosting the Olympic games boosted China's advertising market by 22 percent to US$35 billion in 2008.[8] Olympic-related advertising receipts alone reached a record high of more than US$5 billion.[9] A continuing increase of 19.5 percent to US$42 billion in the following year was forecast by GroupM, a US-based marketing communication company.[10] In fact, two-digit growth has been the "norm" for the advertising industry in China.[11]

The rapid and sustained growth of advertising in China has been fueled by two major forces. The first comes from China's robust economic development. Since the initiation of economic reforms in 1978, China has become one of the world's fastest-growing economies. From 1979 to 2007, its real gross domestic product (GDP) grew at an average annual rate of 9.8 percent. Real GDP grew 11.4 percent in 2007, the fastest annual growth since 1994.[12] With 200 million Chinese regarded, in the eyes of global marketers, as "serious consumers" growth is expected to increase dramatically in the near future.[13] The large middle class, estimated at 197 million in 2008,[14] has turned China into a "king-maker" market that neither foreign nor local marketers can afford to ignore.[15]

The second force shaping China's advertising industry comes from the intense interfirm competition that has been occurring as the country continues to deregulate its markets, especially since 2001 when China became an official member of the World Trade Organization (WTO).[16] Amid intense interfirm competition, advertising has become an indispensable tool, not only for multinational companies (MNCs), but also for local firms that challenge the MNCs' competitive positions.[17]

To local Chinese advertising shops, the most intense competition comes from transnational advertising agencies (TNAAs). Since China reopened its doors to the outside world, TNAAs have rapidly entered this booming market. By 2006, there were 38 TNAAs joint-ventured with Chinese local agencies and 497 foreign-invested advertising shops in the country, generating a total of 13.24 billion yuan (US$1.89 billion) in revenue. Although TNAAs only represent 0.4 percent of the advertising agencies in China, they garnered 21 percent of the business volume in the country that year.[18]

However, the picture is not all rosy. Although by 2007 advertising revenue in China totaled 174.1 billion yuan (US$25 billion), a 10.7 percent increase on the previous year, it was the first time since 1979 that advertising growth was behind the GDP growth of the country – the GDP grew by 11.4 percent. In fact, Chinese advertising growth has been slowing down since 2004, with increases of 14.8 percent, 14.4 percent, 11.1 percent, and 10.7 percent in 2004, 2005, 2006, and 2007, respectively.[19] This recent slow-down in growth rate is attributed to the stagnation of government regulation. The advertising industry in China, like its counterparts in other countries, has experienced numerous changes and challenges in the past 10 years, such as the rapid growth of new media and drastic media segmentation.

Government regulation in China, however, is far behind the changes and unable to meet these new challenges.[20] For example the *Advertising Law of the People's Republic of China* became effective on February 1, 1995 when online or mobile advertising did not exist, yet no update has ever been made to this first but simplistic law on advertising.

A Close Look at Chinese Advertising Media

In the 1980s, newspapers were the largest advertising medium in China. In 1991 and 1992, television surpassed newspapers in advertising revenue for the first time, and became the largest advertising medium in the country.[21] In 1993 and 1994, TV returned the honor to newspapers; since 1995, however, television has regained and maintained its dominance as the largest advertising medium in this fast-growing market.[22] Currently, advertising provides more than 80 percent of revenue for the four traditional media that offer advertising (newspapers, magazines, radio, and television). Some media experts in China believe that the traditional media rely too much on advertising, which is directly affected by various economic sectors and government policies. On the contrary, some new media outlets, such as Sohu and Sina, two leaders in China's online advertising, receive less than 40–50 percent their revenue from advertising.[23]

Owing to the challenges from digital technology-based media, (e.g., online advertising, mobile advertising, LCD and plasma screens in office buildings, grocery stories, convenience stores, supermarkets, and other commercial spaces) traditional mass media advertising (mainly carried by newspapers, magazines, radio, and television) has for the first time since 1981 had only a single-digit increase and newspaper advertising, for the first time since the early 1980s, did not increase at all.[24]

Newspaper Advertising

Since the late 1970s China's newspaper industry has developed rapidly. In 2004, the number of newspaper titles reached 2,137, about 11 times more than that in 1978 when the economic reform began. The newspapers are owned by 1,200 publishers and press groups across the country. As the dominant position of government subscriptions have been taken over by individual subscriptions, competition among newspaper publishers has become more intense as they seek to attract readers. In 2003, newspaper advertising revenue reached 24.3 billion yuan (US$3.5 billion), accounting for 22 percent of the total advertising revenue in the country.

In 2002 newspaper advertising revenue in China increased 19.5 percent and in 2003 the increase was 30 percent, compared to an increase of 9 percent in 2004 and 8 percent in 2005, growing much more slowly than advertising in other media.[25] This slow-down in the growth of newspaper advertising revenue is due to multiple reasons. First, five of the 10 largest product categories for newspaper advertising (including telecommunication, automobile, real estate, pharmaceuticals, and office equipment) reduced their advertising in newspapers.[26] The second reason was stricter government regulations on pharmaceutical advertising due to a large number of illegal advertisements in this area. The third reason was the challenge from the fast-growing new media, which significantly reduced people's newspaper reading time. Between 2001 and 2005, adult individuals' average newspaper reading time declined from 45 minutes to 40 minutes per day. Among those in the 18–50 age range, daily newspaper reading time dropped by about 13 minutes on average; even the average reading time of 51–60 age group, who tend to read more, went down by 9 minutes a day over the 5-year span.[27]

Magazine Advertising

Although the revenue of magazine advertising in China is still increasing every year, there too the rate of increase began to slow down between 2001 and 2005. In 2005 for example, magazine advertising revenue increased by 18 percent, the smallest increase in 3 years. This trend is consistent with the entire advertising industry in the country, which has entered a period of slow increase. A major reason for the slow-down in magazine advertising revenue is the decline in magazine readership.[28]

However, the picture of magazine advertising in China is not all that gloomy when looked at more closely. Even though magazine readership is declining overall, the decline has been slowing down. For example, magazine readership declined by 7 percent between 2004 and 2005, but it only declined by 4.9 percent between 2004 and 2005.[29] At the same time, the percentage of those loyal and regular "core readers" of magazines has increased even though overall magazine readership has decreased. Specifically, the percentage of white-collar readers aged 25 to 44 with a college education and relatively high personal income has increased.[30] This change in the readership demographics may account for the continuing growth in magazine advertising revenue despite the decline in overall magazine readership – the growing core readership is attracting more marketers.

Among all magazine categories, fashion magazines are the most profitable. In 2005, their advertising revenues reached 2.3 billion yuan

(US$333 million), taking 40 percent of the advertising revenue of all magazines. Fashion magazines were also the only magazine category in China that had an advertising revenue above 1 billion yuan (US$143 million) that year.[31]

A noticeable trend in the Chinese magazine market is the increasing number of international titles, approximately 40 in 2005. *Elle* is among the most successful.[32] Its circulation grew from 300,000 in 2001, when China had just entered the World Trade Organization (WTO), to 400,000 in 2005. Although this circulation was less than half that of *Shanghai Style* (the most popular local fashion magazine with a circulation of about 900,000) *Elle* (with 90 percent of its readers high-income and well-educated females) attracts 20 percent of all advertising spending on fashion magazines in China.[33] Foreign advertisers are often reluctant to purchase advertising space in local magazines because of "the absence of independent and reliable consumer measurement mechanisms" in the country.[34] While upmarket-franchised magazines like *Elle* tend to pitch their advertising space at a higher rate, their brand reputation delivers high-profile clients.

Chinese fashion magazine readership is mostly female. A study of 38 fashion magazines in China found that 82 percent of the readers were female, with only 18 percent male.[35]

TV Advertising

Advertising has become the major source of revenue for television in China, accounting for more than 90 percent of its total income,[36] the highest percentage among all media categories in the country. Due to competition from new media like online TV, cell phone TV, office building and shopping center TV and mobile TV, the growth of advertising revenue for all traditional media has begun to slow down. Some factors accounting for this slow-down are similar to that for newspapers and include the decrease in real estate and pharmaceutical advertising caused by increasingly strict government regulation in those areas.[37]

At the same time, TV advertising revenue is becoming more concentrated on the most competitive TV stations. For years China Central Television (CCTV), China's sole national TV network and its "window on the world"[38] has been taking the lion's share of China's TV advertising revenue. In 2007 CCTV's advertising revenue reached 10 billion yuan (US$1.4 billion), accounting for about one-third of the entire TV advertising revenue in the country. It took CCTV less than 30 years after broadcasting its first commercial in 1979 to reach this revenue mark. In 1992 CCTV's advertising revenue was 100 million yuan, only a tenth of its advertising revenue just 15 years later.[39]

One of the biggest current media events is CCTV's annual auction for selling its primetime advertising resources for the next year – this started in 1994.[40] The primetime resources include dozens of spots before and after the nationwide news and weather reports, as well as special programs like the annual Chinese New Year's Eve Gala,[41] – the most-watched show on Chinese television.[42] In the 2009 auction title sponsorships were also offered, a new "weapon" on CCTV-2's economics program.[43]

The 2009 CCTV advertising auction garnered 9.26 billion yuan (US$1.34 billion), a jump of 15.29 percent from the sales of the previous year and a record high in the 15-year-history of CCTV auctions.[44] This gigantic annual media event is often labeled as "an important barometer for China's TV market,"[45] "a barometer of the media business' health" in the country,[46] and "a bellwether for China's broader economy."[47] Additionally, these "typical" labels, the record advertising sales of 2009 were seen as "a confidence indicator"[48] for the growth potential of the Chinese economy, in a period of global economic turbulence.

While the CCTV annual advertising auction is cheered for its success and innovation by the government, news media, and advertisers, its critics call it "a monopoly game."[49] The criticism is based on the rationale that CCTV is "both the government's mouthpiece and a powerful conglomerate,"[50] and one "can't find a second media [outlet] like CCTV in China, so it does not represent the overall ad market."[51]

To offset CCTV's monopoly, many local TV stations have extended coverage, via satellite, from their home provinces to multiple provinces or even the entire country, giving some competition to CCTV. In this regard, Hunan Satellite TV is a shining star, having become the third most profitable satellite TV station in the country, following CCTV-1 and CCTV-5. In 2008, it launched its hit soap "Ugly Betty," a format bought and localized from Televisa, the Mexican TV conglomerate, achieving strong ratings by attracting 242 million viewers.[52]

Tailing behind Hunan Satellite TV are Anhui Satellite TV and Beijing Satellite TV. The top 10 provincial TV stations take more than 65 percent of advertising revenue generated from all provincial TV stations. Whereas, the advertising revenues of those less competitive local TV stations continue to decline.[53]

Radio Advertising

Although radio as an advertising medium has been challenged by television and the Internet, the past a few years have witnessed a rapid growth of radio advertising. Its revenue increased from 1.5 billion yuan (US$220 million) in 2000[54] to just under 5 billion yuan (US$710 million) in 2005, with an average annual increase of 40 percent.[55] In 2005, 13 local radio stations made the 100-million-yuan mark (US$14.3 million) in advertising revenues. The three radio stations with the highest advertising revenues were Beijing Radio (450 million yuan, US$64 million), Guangdong Radio (249 million yuan, US$36 million), and Shanghai Radio (223 million yuan, US$32 million).[56]

One of the major reasons for the sharp increase in radio advertising revenue was the significant increase in the number of private cars. In Shanghai, for example, there were more than two million motor vehicles in early 2006, which gave rise to a 10-million "mobile population" on any given day, accounting for 56.3 percent of the population in the metropolis. To reach this large "mobile population," advertisers bought more than 300 million yuan (US$43 million) in radio time from the Shanghai Media Group (SMG). This group of media resulted from a merger of the People's Radio Station of Shanghai, East Radio Shanghai, Shanghai Television Station, and Oriental Television Station.[57]

Internet Advertising

In 2005, online advertising revenue in China reached 313 million yuan (US$45 million), a 42.1 percent increase on the previous year, surpassing the advertising revenue of magazines and nearing that of radio advertising.[58] Thanks to the Beijing Olympics, online advertising revenue surged 65 percent in 2008 from the 7 billion yuan (US$1 billion) of 2007 and was expected to grow another 40 percent in 2009.[59] Sina, Netease, QQ, and Sohu are the four largest Internet portals in China.[60] Between 2001 and 2005, the advertising revenues of Sina, Sohu, and QQ increased from 170 million yuan (US$24 million), 80 million yuan (US$11 million) and 10 million yuan (US$1.4 million) in 2001 to 680 million yuan (US$97 million), 470 million yuan (US$67 million) and 250 million yuan (US$36 million) in 2005 respectively.[61] In the month around the Beijing Olympics, CCTV earned 600 million yuan (US$85 million) from its online advertising, far above any single media outlet in China.[62] CCTV's online advertising revenue for all of 2008 was estimated at 2 billion yuan ($300 million).[63]

With a rapid adoption rate, increasing broadband penetration, and a young, well-educated population, the Internet is quickly becoming the medium of choice for the youth in China, which provides strong incentives for marketers to advertise online. The US-based eMarketer, a research company on Internet marketing, forecasts that by 2012 China's online advertising revenue will reach 29.2 billion yuan (US$4.2 billion).[64] Another more optimistic estimate from the Chinese media was that in 2008 Internet advertising revenue in the country had already reached 17 billion yuan (U$2.4 billion).[65] It was projected to be more than 50 billion yuan (US$7 billion) by 2011, surpassing that of newspapers and becoming the second largest advertising medium in China.[66] No matter which estimate was most accurate, one thing is for sure – the Internet is by far the fastest growing advertising medium. A 2008 report of CTR Market Research, "the leading market information and insight provider in China,"[67] predicted that Internet commercials will be among those who suffer least from the global financial crisis.[68]

With 250 million Internet users, Internet advertising market is not only appealing to marketers but also to media research companies. In late 2008, Nielsen Online formed a joint venture with the parent of ChinaRank, a Beijing-based publisher of website rankings, to track Internet use in China. Called CR-Nielsen, the venture is "the first company authorized to compile and publish standard Internet data, such as traffic and ad-spending figures, on the Chinese market."[69]

Mobile Advertising

Meanwhile, with an increase of 82 percent in 2008 (again, thanks to the Beijing Olympics) and 47 percent in 2009, mobile and LCD advertising spending in China was expected to surpass that of Internet spending in the near future.[70] The emerging field of digital media has begun to eclipse the market share of traditional media, especially newspapers and television.

Out-of-home Advertising

Out-of-home advertising is also growing fast in China. It includes advertising in airports (see Figure 10.3), subways, taxis, public buses, and other

Figure 10.3 Don't forget that gift! Check-in desk at Shanghai airport.
Source: Hong Cheng

vehicles (see Figure 10.4). LCD and plasma screen advertising in office build-ings (see Figure 10.5), grocery stories, convenience stores, supermarkets, and other commercial spaces is growing especially fast. Airport advertis-ing alone occupies tens of thousands of square meters, seeing a growth rate of 50 percent annually. The 2008 advertising revenue of the terminal building of Capital Airport in Beijing, for example, reached 760 million yuan (US$108 million), up 81 percent from the 420 million yuan (US$60 million) in 2007.[71]

As noted earlier, advertising provides at least 80 percent of the revenue for the mass media in China today. This high percentage has given strong wings to the mass media. This reduces the media's dependence on government funding and promises more opportunities for creativity and variety in media products.

However, like the media industry itself, the advertising industry has to adjust quickly to meet the challenges of audience and media segmentation, as well as the rapid development of technology. While the competition between the traditional media and the online and mobile media continues

Figure 10.4 Advertisements in Chinese metro stations are ubiquitous and very big.
Source: Hong Cheng

Figure 10.5 The advertisement giant by some standards, is typical of those found on building walls in Chinese cities.
Source: Hong Cheng

to grow, more and more marketers will pay increasing attention to their clients' needs and the interactions between brands and consumers, rather than merely resorting to the traditional one-way marketing. Only by adjusting to these changes can the advertising industry maintain its high-speed growth. Some advertising experts in China predict that "in the near future, the marketing strategy will see a fundamental change, in which a company will put its web site at the center of its marketing package, integrating a variety of channels."[72]

11

Public Relations

In the late 1980s, there was a popular 24-episode TV drama in China called *Gong Gua Xiao Jie* (Miss Public Relations). The story was about the life and career of a beautiful and ambitious female public relations manager from Hong Kong, who came to Guangzhou and worked in the hotel communication management business. It was perhaps the first time the term public relations ever received attention of a Chinese audience. The TV program paralleled the birth and early adolescent years of public relations as a profession in China.

A report from the 2007 annual survey by CIPRA (China International Public Relations Association)[1] showed the continuous rapid growth of the PR industry: Within 1 year, earnings from PR services grew from 8 billion yuan (about US $1.17 billion) to 10 billion yuan (about US $1.47 billion), increasing by 25 percent. The corporate communication and marketing communication service for automobiles, electronics, IT, daily staples, health insurance, and financial industries have the top six portions in the PR market, while PR services in sports, government, non-profit organizations and real estate companies are also making steady progress. The largest PR firms and agencies, most located in Beijing, Shanghai, Guangzhou, and Chengdu are, as expected, taking the biggest share of this growing public relations spending. This growth has gradually led to increased demands on a profession that aims to help organizations achieve their goals.

Brief History

China's new openness policy in the early 1980s increased attention on public relations as organizations looked to them to help achieve their goals.

In 1980, Shen Zhen She Kou Hua Sheng, a construction design and consulting company, established the first local professional public relations firm in China. In November 1984, Guangzhou Bai Yun Shan Pharmaceutical Factory set up the first public relations department in any of the state-owned enterprises in mainland China. It allocated 1 percent of profits for public relations and soon after sales and profits of the factory improved rapidly.[2] This historic event was reported in a news article published by the Chinese financial newspaper, *Economic Daily*, that said "the work of public relations in Guangzhou Bai Yun Shan Pharmaceutical Factory is like a tiger that has grown wings." An editorial in the same edition was headlined: "Study socialist public relations seriously." Two years later, *People's Daily*, the biggest newspaper in China, also published the news article and editorial.[3]

In 1981 Black saw the debut of Western style modern public relations practice in China in the joint ventures with foreign firms in the Shenzhen Special Economic Zone.[4] Public relations also employ Western characters such as Mickey Mouse in their public relation campaigns (see Figure 11.1). Many other companies throughout China soon developed their own public relations departments, emphasizing the Western model of public relations in building healthy media relations. By the early 1990s, there were 100,000 people employed in the public relations industry in China. The majority of them worked as part-time personnel in the in-house PR departments of various organizations in the private and public sectors, while others worked as full-time practitioners in local agencies and forged links with international PR firms. Major international public relations firms were soon appearing in China. As early as 1985 Hill & Knowlton and Burson-Marsteller set up subsidiaries in China. By 1991, there were more than 30 other PR firms nationwide providing advice and services in marketing, customer relations, and communication for businesses that did not have their own PR departments. Toward the end of the 1990s, there were 1,200 PR firms with a combined workforce of 30,000 to 40,000 people, 5,000 to 6,000 of them professionals.[5] In these early years of the development of public relations in China, only a few state-operated enterprises had PR departments, although almost all Sino-foreign joint ventures had such departments to "further the objectives of the enterprise; organize large-scale propaganda activity; subsidize social public good causes; assist in marketing the business."[6]

A 2006 Chinese government report suggested the extent of growth in the public relations industry. "The public relations industry in China," the report stated, "'has maintained an annual growth rate of more than

Figure 11.1   Mickey Mouse is a useful figure in any advertising or public
relations campaign in China or anywhere else in the world.
Source: Wynne Wang

30 percent over the past two years thanks to China's rapid economic
growth and growing exchanges with foreign countries,' a senior Chinese
PR professional said in Beijing on June 23."[7] Li Daoyu, head of the China
International Public Relations Association (CIPRA), said at the 2006
China International Public Relations Congress: "As part of the modern
administration concept that China is beginning to embrace, PR is playing
an increasingly important role in China today."[8] A survey of the association revealed that the annual volume of China's PR business reached
6 billion yuan (about US $850 million) in 2005, up 33.3 percent on the
previous year.

Strenski and Yue credited the PR profession as playing a pivotal role in China's national economy. Public relations' scope and goals range from developing positive images for businesses and generating new product publicity to planning large scale promotion campaigns for marketing and social welfare activities. Other PR activities include providing business information and consulting services, coordinating programs and services for government and government agencies as well as the businesses that work with them, and also providing crisis management expertise.[9]

Background

The burgeoning of China's modern public relations industry has several fundamental roots. These include the changes in the economic system resulting from Deng Xiaoping's open door policy and his promotion of a market economy. Also important were changes in the government's political ideology, which has gradually shifted toward open dialogues with the West and has embraced long-term gradual political reform led by the Communist Party. Wu highlighted the typical Chinese-style flexibility by quoting Deng Xiaoping's famous remark in 1992: "It doesn't matter if the cat is black or white; so long as it catches the mouse, it is a good cat."[10] During his tour of Southern China in 1992, Deng called on all Chinese people, regardless of their social status or political beliefs, to put aside the ideological argument, and place making-money as the first priority. Since then, China's central government has adopted a "less-ideological, more practical policy to integrate its economy into the global competitive system".[11] To do this, Deng said, China needed "Four Modernizations," in agriculture, industry, national defense, and science and technology, in order to build a strong nation of unique Chinese Socialism. Many saw the public relations role as transmitting the messages of modernization to the Chinese public.

During the 2005 National People's Congress, the Chinese Government under the President Hu–Prime Minister Wen Administration proposed the ideology of constructing "*He Xie She Hui*" (a Harmonious Society). Since then, it has become the new dominant social and economic vision and goal of the new Chinese central government leadership, which has been projected at almost all walks of life in Chinese society and visualized in all kinds of media messages. Thus, it is crucial for public relations practitioners in China to effectively manage conflict and competition internally and externally in all kinds of situations in order to achieve the construction of this Harmonious Society.

Cultural Trends

China's fast economic development and churning consumerism have motivated many Chinese people to pursue profits and financial status, but they also created confusion in terms of priorities in life. In the new era of "market capitalism" how is the balance materialism and spiritualism achieved? While Western philosophy infiltrated the Chinese intellectual elite in the 1980s and 1990s, its lack of fundamental connection to the agriculture-based utilitarian Chinese cultural soil prevented its widespread adoption within the large Chinese population. Western culture has shed light on individual development and democratic principles, but it did not provide practical solutions to questions raised by the general Chinese public. Since the 1990s the Chinese people have started to look back to ancient Chinese philosophy as an oasis in a modern material world full of conflicts and confusion.

In 2007 Professor Yu Dan of Beijing Normal University conducted a seven-part daily series on the well known program "Lecture Room" (*Baijia Jiangtan*) broadcast on Channel 10 of Central China Television. This educational show on the *Analects of Confucius*, a collection of Confucius' brief aphoristic fragments, was an unexpected success with the Chinese audience. The Professor became a popular celebrity and the *Analects of Confucius* have become popular among the general public in China again. The success of this cultural program in some ways reflects the dynamic fusion of different ideologies and cultural traditions in China in the past 30 years. In addition to the Communist ideology, that continues to dominate the mainstream media and a public advocacy for an egalitarian selfless, classless society as an ideal,[12] the classics of ancient Chinese philosophers have re-nurtured the contemporary Chinese society as it undergoes rapid changes. It can provide some guideposts as this new Chinese society tries to balance materialism and spiritualism

For example, to balance individual pursuits and societal needs, Confucius laid out a hierarchy on the role and duty of a person in society. This hierarchy consists of "*Xiu Shen*" (cultivating oneself), "*Qi Jia*" (regulating the family), "*Zhi Guo*" (making the state peaceful), and "*Ping Tian Xia*" (having universal peace under heaven). Achieving a balance in life depends on the ability and resources the person has, with each level building upon the achievement of the other. This casts light on the collective trend for individuals in China to pursue personal happiness as their life priority, but at the same time fulfilling duty to the family, the community, and the nation.

The Confucian emphasis on personal relationships, honesty, high moral standards, and loyalty to one's group affects every aspect of individual and organizational life, and tends to mix personal and public relations.[13] This fundamental belief to some extent explains the preferred communication style among public relations practitioners in China. According to Chen, due to the Confucian emphasis on group loyalty, Chinese find it difficult to accept "purely business transactions" and the "calculated, impersonal, strictly contractual approach of most Western business deals." Chen further pointed out that "while a relationship may exist for purely business reasons, Chinese prefer transactions to be carried out on a more personal, warm, human level."[14] At the organizational level, Chinese are intensely tied to their own companies and institutions, and work and negotiate for the total institution, not merely for personal enrichment. Confucian values also support the principles of applying a human face or expecting human characteristics in a business situation; as a result, "trust, respect and acceptance in a business deal hinge on the degree to which the parties involved trust, respect and accept each other as people."[15]

Another related cultural phenomenon that can be easily detected is the rising patriotism in times of conflicts with external publics. The Confucian stresses loyalty to groups at all levels – the family, the work group, and the nation as a whole – and has some distrust of outsiders. Traditionally one prefers group members over non-members. Especially "at the national level, the Chinese have long been somewhat xenophobic, showing loyalty to the nation and culture to the exclusion of outside influences."[16] This loyalty also demands strong central government leadership and its quick reaction in external crises. As Chen and Culbertson noted, one special challenge faced by Chinese PR practitioners is that Chinese tend to blame leaders more quickly when things go wrong.[17] Thus, there is a particular need for Chinese leaders, especially government officials, to act quickly and decisively in dealing with a crisis and to communicate their decisiveness. For example, the 1999 bombing of the Chinese embassy in Belgrade created widespread protests in China against the United States and NATO, protests initiated by Chinese college students and joined by the general public in China's major cities. There were banners and loud threats to boycott US imports. Chinese government officials reacted quickly because they knew the Chinese public expected them to do so. The collective memory of the Chinese people includes the two humiliating nineteenth century Opium Wars and the devastating twentieth century Japanese invasion. The collective pride and vision of being an "awakening sleeping lion" has constantly united the Chinese people, regardless of internal conflicts and disagreement on domestic issues, when confronted by external threats to the unity and stability of China as a nation. It is crucial that public relations practitioners who become involved in such national issues remember this.

Defining Public Relations in China

It is not easy to define the practice we call "public relations" in the Chinese context. As Yu pointed out, "various factions within China argue about the role and value of PR." Some people defined PR as just "the work of etiquette and reception done by Miss PR and Mr. PR" while some others simply see PR as another type of advertising, or no better than "just a means of propaganda."[18] The official definition of public relations as stated on CIPRA's website is: "Public relations is a kind of service business that provides professional service to satisfy clients' public relations needs (i.e., information communication, relationship reconciliation, and image management) so as to make business profits by using research, program planning, implementation, evaluation, and consultancy."[19]

In Chinese public relations is called *Gonggong Guanxi*. In Black's view China has adopted the same definitions and functions of public relations as currently accepted in the United States and Europe.[20] Still, many Chinese PR practitioners and scholars advocate the uniqueness of the concept in the Chinese context and call for an awareness and understanding of the subtlety of practicing public relations in China. To do so, one must understand the linguistic roots of *Gonggong Guanxi*, the Chinese translation of public relations.

Gonggong means public. From a historical and cultural perspective, China has had an elite-authoritarian-governing political and social system for thousands of years, which fostered political apathy. This resulted in the two dominant social characteristics: a low-level of average privacy awareness among Chinese people, and a net-veined social construct structure. Wu explained that, in China, every person can be treated as a knot in a well-woven net: "If you touch one of them, all other knots connecting with it, sometimes even the whole net, will respond."[21] In English, the same word "public" is used as both an adjective (as in "public relations") and noun (as in "general public"). In Chinese, however, we need two different words: the adjective *Gonggong* (as in "*Gonggong Guanxi*" or public relations) and the noun *Gongzhong*, which means a group of people involved in an issue in society.

Wu argued that there is no "public" in China and that "in reality, it is nearly impossible to require Chinese people to differentiate clearly the 'public' part and the 'private' part of their societal behavior."[22] However, the clearer definition and valid identification of Chinese publics might be contingent upon many situational factors in different perspectives. For example, PR practitioners working for cosmetics companies are able to segment and identify different publics among female consumers, such as high-end consumers, household buyers, etc. Generations are now becoming one important item at the matrix of strategic public identification in China. The terms "70 *Hou*" (born after 1970), "80 *Hou*" (born after 1980), and "90 *Hou*" (born after 1990) might function similarly to the terms "baby boomer" or "X generation" in the United States. These Chinese terms are frequently used in public forums with topics ranging from fashion and entertainment to education, job markets, and social issues.

Guanxi means relations, relationship, connections, social networks, or special interpersonal relationships. If the publics can be visualized as knots, then relations become the net linking the individual clusters of knots. *Guanxi* can carry different connotations depending on the context. Defined as "a strategically constructed network of personal relationships" it is identified as one of the most challenging barriers confronting American public relations firms,[23] *Guanxi* can carry the meaning of power, social status, and resource transmission. Wu noted that it is vital for people living in China: A well-established "*Guanxi* net" can guarantee the success of the person who sits in the center of the web, and maximize one's profit while minimizing one's risk at the same time.[24] At the organization level, a good *Guanxi* can help an organization obtain positive media coverage, acquire a favorable policy from bureaucratic officials, and sometimes prevent a crisis from occurring or at least eliminate negative consequences. Therefore, *Guanxi* is a long-term identification, maintenance, and improvement process. The exchange of reciprocal benefits between two sides marks the beginning of a higher-level relationship, rather than an end of a temporary business contract, which is in contrast with most Western style business partnerships or networking. It is crucial for any one practicing PR in China to build up and nurture a long-term and mutually beneficial "*Guanxi* net".

Related to *Guanxi* is another important concept in Chinese culture: *Mian Zi* (Face) – *Mian Zi* literally means face, though it actually refers to "image" and "reputation" in terms of how one is perceived and valued in the eyes of others. To save someone's face and to give face to someone is critical in interpersonal communication among Chinese people. If two people or two organizations are in a good *Guanxi*, they must take care of each other's *Mian Zi*. There might be disagreements between these two parties, but both should consider preserving and repairing, if necessary, the *Mian Zi* of the other party. Chen highlighted that, China's "collectivism and long-term emphasis on virtue contribute to a major idiosyncrasy of Confucian societies – preserving face."[25] PR practitioners need to plan their activities carefully so that they do not create a situation in which an individual or an organization might encounter loss of face or damage to their public image. As Drobis said, "In China, protecting one's 'face' is regarded as a very serious matter and the use of humor to communicate a message – especially at the expense of another person – can upset or offend an audience."[26] Therefore, *Guanxi* (emphasizing personal relationships) plus *Mian Zi* (emphasizing the drive to save face) require the Chinese PR professional to cultivate public relations as a people-based process driven by interpersonal relationships, mutual respect, and benefit-focused communication management between organizations and publics to help achieve the clients' goals and objectives.

The goals of China's PR profession cover a wide range of areas and include the promotion of positive images for businesses and new products, providing consulting services and business information, and crisis management expertise.[27] Public relations in China is moving in the direction of more strategic communication management, especially in multinational PR firms, in many corporations, and even local PR firms. The majority of PR services, however, are still limited to event planning, press conference hosting, and basic media relations.

Wu provided a checklist for PR practitioners on how to achieve an effective public relations performance in China:[28]

- strengthen cooperation and communication ties with government departments at all levels;

- employ regional strategic communication strategies and take into consideration China's diverse ownership patterns, management levels, and geographic diversity while mapping out PR strategy;
- balance using traditional state-owned propaganda media and the modern commercial media driven by advertising and marketing revenue; and
- build long-term mutually beneficial personal and organizational *Guanxi* networks prior to executing any PR campaigns.

Public Relations Practice in China

The PR practice areas in China include government, corporate communications, travel, sports and entertainment, nonprofits and NGOs (nongovernment organizations), trade associations, financial and investor relations, and health communications. Public relations has played important roles in building and polishing national and organizational images and identities, nurturing media relations and providing media training, cultivating employee relations, handling crisis communication at all levels, and implementing reputation management. However, different sectors of the industry clearly demonstrate different attitudes toward public relations.[29] For example, small corporations tend to regard PR practitioners as technicians focusing on image and publicity. Medium size corporations tend to see the PR professional as the key communication facilitator in relations with employees, clients, and other external publics. Large firms tend to involve PR people in strategic planning and corporate culture building. By 2007, among the Fortune 100 Chinese Corporations, only about 30 had specifically designated departments dealing with public relations and corporate communications, according to their official websites. The names vary from public relations, human resources, external relations, strategic development, to communications, public affairs, and sales management.

These different names reflect the varied assignments a PR professional in China may have to adopt. Kate Wang, Director of Corporate Communications for Caterpillar, who has worked in Beijing for 9 years, suggested the breadth of a PR assignment during an interview with the author (September 2008). She said that corporate communication for Chinese companies must "further the company's reputation, support its mission, and create goodwill." In addition, she added, the PR professional must "actively seek positive news coverage and respond to inquiries with answers that are prompt, courteous, and as informative as possible."

Foreign PR firms, especially American firms, have brought their own views of public relations to China. There were five American public relations firms in Beijing by 1997: B&B International Ltd.; Burson-Marsteller Beijing; Edelman Public Relations; Fleishman Hillard Link, Ltd.; and Hill and Knowlton.[30] Several more opened offices in the next few years. Local Chinese PR firms started to bloom in the late 1990s. By 2006, there were more than 2,000 domestic public relations firms in mainland China, almost five times the number of multinational PR firms in the nation.[31]

Some top multinational PR firms in China are: Ogilvy & Mather Worldwide (entered China in 1995, main Clients include KFC, Audi, IBM, eBay, LG); Edelman Global Public Relations (main clients include New York Life, TCL); Burson-Marsteller (entered China in 1985); Hill&Knowlton (entered China in 1984, main clients include Motorola, KFC, Coke Cola, HP, Nestle); Ruder Finn (entered China in 1996, main clients include Audi, Johnson & Johnson, CE, Citi Bank, O'real); Weber Shandwick (entered China in 1993, main clients include Microsoft, Amazon.com, Bahamas, Boeing, Coca Cola); Ketchum-Newscan; and APCO Worldwide Inc. Examples of top Chinese public relations firms are: Blue Focus (main clients include QQ, LG, Lenovo, Canon); Marketing Resource Group (main clients include Hui Yuan Juice); China Global Public Relations Company (main clients include Apple, IBM, Compaq, Motorola, Ericsson); Broadcom Consulting (main clients include China Mobile); Highteam PR Consulting Ltd.; eVision; EBA Communications; D&S Consulting (main clients include HP, OKI, NEC, Intel, SAMSUNG, NOKIA, SAS, KFC, San Yuan Group, Jin Long Yu, Yili, and JAC); and Science PR.

According to Scott Kronick, managing director of Ogilvy & Mather Public Relations in Beijing, the difference between public relations in the United States and in China is how it is practiced. "China is a market of fundamentals. You must get the fundamentals of PR right first, before getting too creative and technical. My understanding of the United States is that PR is becoming much more specialized. We are following that path in Asia, but it will be some time before it develops to the level of the West. First, get the fundamentals right. Then, extend from there."[32] He cited the need for public relations practitioners who speak English and Chinese and who know Western-style public relations. Kronick described four public relations needs he saw in China:

- awareness and education campaigns since understanding of companies, their brands and products is much lower than in Western markets;

- government access since the government permeates every sector of the Chinese economy;
- information and understanding via market research to help clients understand the complexities of different situations; and
- client support and event management to help clients figure out how to execute PR strategies locally in China.

During a conversation in 2008 Public Relations executive Kate Wang pointed out that local firms with their understanding and integration of local Chinese culture in their communication activities have a clear advantage. She feels, however, they also "lack in the proper training and development of talent" and "are running at much lower profit margins and therefore do not invest as much in employee retention." According to Wang, local firms are considered the low-end service providers, as they do more event management than providing strategic consulting. In her interview, Wang said that, given China's great needs for PR consulting in both the public and private sectors, "local firms are going international and the international firms are localizing, with the general trend of becoming more professional at all levels."

Government PR

China's official policy on reform and freedom as well its ongoing political and economic reforms have made Chinese officials more aware of the value of public relations activities. There has been a pervasive spread of Western-style public relations among governmental entities as part of their political strategies. Reforms in public administration since the mid-1980s have moved the government towards efficiency, transparency, accountability, public participation, and fairness. Public relations need to communicate these changes via the government's public messages.

In a survey conducted among Chinese government officials, Chen found that the Chinese government at both central and local levels is "slowly but surely beginning to abandon its old propaganda schemes, and adopting government PR measures to promote itself."[33] The new Hu–Wen administration in China especially emphasized listening to the domestic public's voice, tailoring policies to public need, and strategically utilizing public relations to make an impact on China's economic development and international diplomacy.

The overall goals of China's public relations programs are to obtain public support and to advance political and commercial interests at home and abroad. They may focus on specific issues and concerns but will also concentrate on building or repairing China's national image, as it did in its 2008 Olympic campaigns. During and after the SARS crisis in 2003, China set public health as one of its top priorities and has been highly aware of the need for health information and more innovative approaches when delivering health messages to the public. China's Ministry of Health (MoH) and its technical arm, China's Centers for Disease Control and Prevention (C-CDC) have recognized the need for more effective social marketing and health PR for more effective health communication. They are looking to the US Center for Disease Control (US-CDC) for a collaborative project to help address this need. China's CDC and the US CDC have built a long and trusting relationship on which China's CDC has created distinctive plans "tailored to the nation's needs, audiences, resources, and infrastructure."[34]

Consumer Relations

The Chinese government has a strong commitment to continuing the economic development that has so dramatically changed the country over the past 25 years. The increasing purchasing power of millions of Chinese consumers has attracted the attention of Western companies and created intense competition among domestic and multinational manufacturers. Chinese consumers are becoming more sophisticated and product-quality driven. This is a change from the late 1980s and 1900s when foreign goods were perceived to offer intrinsically higher quality. Effective public relations can help both domestic and international clients develop identifying brand messages to Chinese consumers. Public relations can help establish favorable brand and product attitude and help Chinese consumers make choices.

To respond to the government's advocacy and the consumers' calling for more socially responsible companies, it is critical for companies to reach out to communities by forming strategic partnerships, organizing special events, and disseminating effective messages. For companies promoting products of innovation, they need to use public relations to educate consumers about the uses and benefits. Corporate Social Responsibility (CSR) has become one of the hottest topics among Chinese PR practitioners.

They have started to work with clients on public affairs and social issues such as education, poverty, health and the environment. Zhao noted that, "while CSR initiatives can focus on a number of issues from labor standards to fair trade practices, China's CSR situation is dominated by environmental regulations encouraged by the State. PR campaigns are aimed at promoting a business's attempts to diminish their carbon footprint and advance sustainable development. By proving to the Chinese people that they care about China's long-term goals and environmental concerns, businesses are able to brand themselves as responsible, trustworthy corporations, increase customer and employee loyalty, and boost their competitive advantage."[35]

Given the unique Chinese media systems and infrastructure, skills and experiences in media relations and informal relations building are great assets for public relations practitioners in China. Since Chinese media are still closely controlled by the government, it is important for public relations practitioners to explore and choose alternative communication channels wisely. Drobis emphasized that "a strong partnership is invaluable for developing messages, assessing language and interpretation issues, identifying appropriate communications vehicles and securing strong quanxi [*guanxi*] or connections."[36] For example, one of the major problems for foreign advertisers is the fact that some Chinese media have started to charge imported brands up to three times as much as local brands pay for ad spots. Having a strategic Chinese partner with *guanxi* can be very helpful when dealing with the media.

Drobis also warned that many companies will call upon public relations only after they are caught in a communication mess. "Their failure to properly plan for, and act upon, China's complex business environment is a crisis in the making that can destroy any chance of future success."[37] For example, in May 2008, Hollywood movie star Sharon Stone made insulting comments to the press at the Cannes Film Festival about the victims of the Sichuan earthquake. Angry Chinese started an online Sharon Stone boycott. One of their strategies was to boycott Christian Dior products, since Sharon Stone endorsed Dior cosmetics. Chinese consumers sent thousands of letters of complaint and telephone calls to Dior's headquarter and local offices in China and the United States. A Dior spokesperson in China quickly disassociated Dior from Sharon Stone's comments. Within 2 weeks, Dior China officially removed all Sharon Stone images from its advertising campaign and in-store product displays.

Communicating with Chinese Audiences: Coca-Cola's Failed Acquisition of Huiyuan Juice

Failure to get support from China's public helped defeat Coca-Cola's effort to buy China Huiyuan Juice Group. In September 2008, Coca-Cola was ready to spend US $2.4 billion to buy the Huiyan Juice Group, China's largest fruit juice company. "Coca-Cola," said Coca-Cola's chief executive officer Muhtar Kent, "enjoyed the fastest growth of business in China."[38] Coca-Cola offered 12.20 Hong Kong dollars (US$1.56) a share and Huiyan's three major stockholders seemed happy enough to sell.[39] It would have been the second-largest acquisition in the US-based company's history.[40] More importantly, in Chinese eyes it would be the largest purchase of a controlling interest in a major Chinese company.[41]

Coca-Cola was careful to say that "initially, Huiyuan will continue to function as usual, while a review of its operations and synergies are undertaken."[42] Meanwhile, Coca-Cola and Huiyuan awaited approval by the Ministry of Commerce, which oversees China's new anti-monopoly law. The law took effect in August 2008, just a month before Coca-Cola was ready to move to buy Huiyuan.

According to Mei Xinyu, a researcher at the Chinese Academy of International Trade and Economic Cooperation a government think tank under the Ministry of Commerce (MOC), the Chinese government faced two main difficulties. They were concerned that the large size of the two companies, "will raise concerns about monopolies," and that "The brand of Huiyuan is considered to be protected as a famous domestic brand."[43]

Awaiting ministry approval, Coca-Cola's main public relations strategy was to stress the investment (such as research center and infrastructure building) it would bring to China and boost the global economic development, while taking a cooperative stance toward the regulatory process by working closely with the Ministry of Commerce. Coca-Cola CEO Kent emphasized in a March, 2009 statement that as its third-largest market, China was "very important to Coca-Cola."[44]

That same month the Ministry of Commerce announced that it would not approve Coca-Cola's bid to acquire China Huiyuan Juice group because it failed to meet the country's anti-monopoly law. The Ministry added that it appreciated multinational firms such as Coca-Cola's new investment and that it demonstrated confidence in China's economy. The MOC's statement said it had communicated with Coca-Cola several times and suggested it make changes in the acquisition document so that it would not disturb market competition, but Coca-Cola has not yet satisfied the request.[45] Experts said the decision to reject Coca-Cola's acquisition will cost the world's largest soft drink maker the opportunity to increase its shares of China's juice market by more than 20 percent.[46] Coca-Cola and Huiyuan Juice simply said that they respected the MOC's decision to reject Coca-Cola's 2.4 billion US$ bid for China's largest juice maker.[47]

Zhang Junsheng, an economics professor at the University of International Business and Economics said the ministry's decision aims to maintain competition and avoid potential hostile competition.[48] For PR practitioners, however, especially those working in China, the falling out was not surprising from a communications perspective. Imagethief.com, a popular blog written by a Western PR practitioner in China, labeled the acquisition as "Coke and Huiyuan: Let the PR slanging begin."[49] The PR blogger wrote "It's a reminder that western companies trying to acquire well-known Chinese brands are almost always behind the PR eight-ball and should therefore prepare *in advance* for the backlash."[50] The theme of the public's responses could be seen in the many caricatures and cartoons on China's Internet. The graphic from China Economics Web and also spotted on *Wall Street Journal* blog[51] shows Coca-Cola trying to swallow Huiyuan.

The PR lessons that could be learned, according to PR blogger Imagethief.com, is that "If you're a large foreign firm taking over a Chinese firm, prepare to be flogged in public. And prepare for it *before* you announce your acquisition. A basic PR lesson to go along with that: Part of selling any acquisition is convincing stakeholders of the value that the acquisition will bring in terms *that make sense to them*. That last part is the detail that often gets lost."[52] In this particular case, Coca-Cola failed to make sense to the Chinese audience. It did not match their public relations strategies with the public perception of foreign acquisitions in China.

As Imagethief summarized, the general negative public perception of foreign acquisitions provides a "difficult communication challenge for any company in Coke's position,"[53] going beyond the typical capitalistic mentality of just communicating benefits to shareholders. The author further summarized that, "in communicating about a major planned acquisition in China, and knowing that both government and popular backlash are likely, leading with shareholder value might not be the ideal approach."[54] A multinational firm like Coca-Cola must also consider domestic rivals and drinks industry groups, who can easily use defensive tactics and call for government protection to protect national interests and brands.

To finalize this case from the public relations perspective, Coke and Huiyuan could have communicated the deal's benefits more effectively with its key communities, including shareholders, domestic consumers, local rivals, regulators, and other governmental officials. As the Western PR practitioner highlighted on the Imagethief.com, "Foreign companies making significant acquisitions in China should assume that the default starting communication position is 'in trouble,' and plan appropriately."[55] According to David Wolf, a corporate communications and marketing strategist who has lived and worked in Beijing since 1995, "Any acquisition of a local firm by a foreign company demands a communications effort directed at *both* the general public and the policy making elite that makes a logical, intelligent, and sensitive case for the purchase. The bigger the buy, the better you need to be at the communications."[56] This holds very true when using public relations to enhance international business communications in China.

Public Relations Associations and Professional Development

Since the setup of the first Chinese non-governmental PR organization, the Guangdong Public Relations Club, in January 1986, more than 400 other PR associations have been formed across the country. Since 1988 these organizations have held joint meetings annually, the first in Hangzhou in December 1988. At the second, in Xi'an in September 1989, a document titled "The Professional Moral Norm of Public Relations in China" was released. Since then, initiatives aimed at instilling professional ethics have been actively encouraged, with the China International Public Relations Association (CIPRA) playing a significant role. The Public Relations Society of China, which links local PR societies, holds its own ethics seminars twice a year. Managers, PR professionals, and students joined in these seminars which were supported by central and local governments.[57]

By 2003 there were more than 150 PR associations in China at local, provincial, and national levels.[58] CIPRA, located in Beijing, counted 1,000 members and aimed to enhance professionalism through case-study competitions, conferences, and surveys. The other leading national PR association is the China Public Relations Association, also located in Beijing. The biggest local PR associations are the Shanghai PR Association, Guangdong PR Association, and Beijing PR Association.

Due to the different social, political, and economic systems and unique Chinese cultural traditions, values, and morals, the goals and professional standards of Chinese public relations professionals are very different from those in Western cultures.[59] There is a strong emphasis on guest relations, especially for the low-level PR employees. There can also be problems dealing effectively with the media since relatively few Chinese PR practitioners have worked in the media prior to entering public relations. Strenski and Yue see Chinese public relations professionals facing three major challenges: First, professional standards must be better aimed at satisfying the needs of society and the market economy. Second, public relations professionals must strengthen ties with international public relations firms and become a true bridge to the entire business information industry. A third goal must be to build relationships with domestic enterprises. Chinese businesses represent the majority of the client base of public relations firms.[60] In the past, many Chinese business organizations included in-house marketing capabilities, but now most rely on outside assistance for at least some services. This is particularly true of small-to medium-sized businesses. Successful Chinese public relations firms, like their worldwide counterparts, typically find a stable, diverse client list to be indispensable.

One issue within China's public relations profession still to be addressed is workforce diversity. One survey found female PR practitioners in China reported feeling constrained by job definitions and male stereotyping. They also found themselves being required to behave as technicians but think as managers when handling guest relations.[61]

Two Chinese publications, *Public Relations Magazine* and *Public Relations News*, played a significant part in promoting professional public relations practice as the profession developed in China. *Public Relations Magazine*, started in 1989, was published every 2 months with 64 pages and a full color cover. Its paid circulation is now 160,000 with a further 40,000 controlled circulation. *Public Relations News*, a full-size weekly newspaper, has a circulation of 50,000. These two publications advocated an appreciation of public relations as a serious management discipline in China even in the early development years of the profession in China.[62]

Earlier, in November 1984, the Chinese Academy of Social Science's News Research Institute set up a project team specializing in PR. Nine months later it finished its first project, a book titled "An Introduction to Public Relations," edited by Dr. Ming Anxiang. It was the first comprehensive academic book on public relations in China.[63] Since then more than 200 others have been published, some translated from English. Additionally, more than 30 various publications report on PR activities in China. Among them are: Public Relations (bi-monthly), edited by China Public Relations Special Committee, and Public Relations Research (semi-monthly), edited by the Shanghai office of the Public Relations Society of China.

Public Relations Education

In 1983, a public relations course was included in the undergraduate curriculum of the journalism department at Xianmen University.[64] To meet the need for more systematically educated and trained young PR practitioners, PR education in China has grown rapidly. The first PR educational program started in September, 1985 at Shenzhen University.[65] By the early 1990s, there were public relations programs in over 100 Chinese universities, four of them with formal degree programs. By 1991, Shenzhen University alone had enrolled 506 PR students on its campus courses with an additional 30,000 PR students on its distance learning program. Shenzhen faculty have published 12 PR textbooks and produce a PR magazine.[66] There were also more than 20 universities and 300 colleges and institutes in China offering PR courses with some 1,000 teachers. PR courses were also offered by two of China's vocational schools, one in Beijing and one in Heilongjiang Province.[67]

By the end of the 1990s, public relations courses were being offered at leading universities including China's Institute of International Relations in Beijing, Nankai University in Tianjin, and Zhongshan University in Guangzhou. Still, the public relations workforce remained dominated by former journalists and government affairs officers.[68] In 1994, Zhongshan University set up the first public relations bachelor's degree program in China.[69] By 2007, more than 20 universities in China offered a bachelor's degree in public relations including Zhongshan University, Xiamen University, China Media University, Gonghua University, Shanghai Foreign Languages University, Shanghai Normal University, and Hunan Normal University. Graduate level public relations education started in 1994 when Zhongshan University allowed master's students in their public administration program to focus on public relations. In 2003, Fudan University set up China's first Masters Program in public relations. By 2007, more than 10 universities in China offered either a master's degree or a graduate concentration in public relations. These included Zhongshan University, Xiamen University, International Relations College, Shanghai Foreign Languages University, Fudan University, and China Media University.[70]

New Challenges and Opportunities

CIPRA's 2007 annual survey of the public relations industry in China summarized the new directions and challenges faced by PR practitioners in China in the coming years. Publicity, event planning and execution, corporate communication, marketing communication, and consulting are likely to continue to be the main services provided by PR firms and agencies. The hot topics in 2008 included the Beijing Olympics, the 2010 World Expo in Shanghai, Internet PR, event Marketing, CSR (corporate social responsibility), and sports communication.

PR scholars and professionals in China have identified these main challenges. First, the improvement of professional standards, the strengthening of ties with international PR firms and the establishment of relationships with domestic companies.[71]

Second, PR professionals need to: 1) pay more attention to economic related topics while communicating with government departments; 2) apply regional operation strategy while conducting a national campaign; and 3) be aware of public opinion and avoid any connection with foreign policy affairs.[72] The shortage of PR professional has seriously affected companies' daily operations and healthy development in the industry. The turnover rate in China's PR industry is still relatively high and most practitioners stay in the same firm for an average of only 2–3 years.[73]

Third, the "PR industry in China faces a pressing talent shortage and has a predominantly young workforce. An estimated 500,000 people are currently studying public relations in China, a dramatic expansion considering students only began informal study of the industry in the 1980s. Despite the growth of formal public relations education and the potential for future employees, PR agencies are currently finding a general lack of creativity and shortage of talent to be an obstacle in building successful campaigns"[74]

Finally, the "PR industry in China must integrate communications to keep pace with the changing marketplace. Firms must be able to operate successfully in a global environment while also providing their clients with extensive local knowledge as campaigns pinpoint more precise key audiences. This not only entails using public relations, but also requires expanding into marketing, advertising and sales promotion. In order to maintain the level of growth that the PR industry has shown in past years, practitioners have to integrate all communications to successfully brand their clients."[75]

Changes and innovations in the Chinese media landscape actually help public relations practitioners deal with media relations in an easier and more flexible way. China is a world leader in the use of new media.[76] The Chinese own 540 million mobile handsets, an increase of 7 million mobile phone handsets owned per month through July 2007. In 2007, the Chinese sent out 535 billion Short Message Service (SMS) messages in just 11 months, a 37 percent increase from 2006. By the end of 2007, there were 162 million Chinese Internet users and 30 million Chinese blogs. Even more Chinese are regular users of Internet discussion groups or bulletin boards (BBS) as a main forum for learning, self-expression, and networking.[77] Grassroots campaigns, text-message campaigns, blog PR and word-of-mouth campaigns have gained more and more weight in the tool kit of Chinese practitioners. Sina.com.cn, the leading Chinese portal website and BSP (blog services provider), has developed and marketed blog space to many celebrities including movie stars, musicians, and writers as their personal PR tool for interaction with their fans. Corporations in China have started to utilize social media as an important channel for communicating with internal and external publics. For example, bokee.net had a professional marketing site dedicated to educating corporations on how to use blogs to spread positive and credible word-of-mouth messages about a company and its products, as well as a building trusting corporate–consumer relationship. It also provides a discussion forum for individuals and organizations with PR needs in the rapidly-developing blogsphere in China.

David Zhao, managing director of Hill & Knowlton Shanghai, says "Blogs and BBS forums are powerful new platforms for both consumer opinion and consumer activism in China."[78] He gives examples of blog posts and BBS activity spreading criticisms of companies and bringing real changes: "When Volkswagen was criticized on BBS forums for its Polo advertisements on subways that BBS users felt derided subway riders, it immediately picked up on the discontent and pulled the offensive ads. A Starbucks shop in the Forbidden City closed down after bloggers stirred up a patriotic debate that spread into mainstream media about the establishment of a Starbucks inside a cultural landmark. Due to the rapid nature of communication on the Internet, online criticisms can swiftly snowball, increasing the need for timely crisis communications and broader media monitoring on the part of PR agencies."[79] Social media and new technology therefore accelerate the evolution of PR in China. This requires higher quality service and better practitioner ability and experience to capitalize on these new media.

Media and cultural climates will change rapidly alongside economic and political reforms and public relations will also continue its rapid development. There are many challenges facing the professional development and educational programs in China's public relations community. There are also an enormous number of opportunities to effectively and ethically manage communications between organizations and the public in China. Kate Wang, Director of Corporate Communications for Caterpillar, highlighted the trend and future of public relations practice in China: "There is a mixture of PR practices, ranging from being very professional to unethical or even illegal. A few years ago, PR practice was coverage driven – more concerned about the number of media articles rather than quality. The changing media environment is causing the overall profession to increase in sophistication."[80]

12

Film

An Industry versus Independents

Chinese cinema is moving toward a large industry model; but we must face our shortcomings and challenges. (Huang Jianxin, film director and executive producer)[1]

"The huge contrast between large production numbers and few box-office revenues of middle and low budget films, is an important indication of the Chinese movie market's abnormal configuration." (Rao Shuguang, Bi Xiaoyu, film critic)[2]

Mainland China's movie industry is growing rapidly but the independent filmmaking field is shrinking. In 2007 box-office revenues totaled 3.3 billion yuan (US$475 million). Movies made in China accounted for 54 percent of the income, the fifth consecutive year domestic films beat imported foreign movies the majority of which were Hollywood big-budget blockbusters. For the 2007 New Year–Spring Festival season, China's biggest holiday, box-office income was 500 million yuan (US$70 million), much more than the 300 million yuan (US$43 million) films earned in the same period in 2006.[3] During this festival Chinese and English films are shown alongside each other as can be seen in Figure 12.1. China's biggest film distribution company, China Film Group (CFG), was considering a public stock offering to become the first Chinese film company listed on a stock market.[4] An increasing number of private but larger film production and distribution companies are playing a stronger role in the Chinese film market. These companies include Huayi Brothers Films, Poly-bona Film Distribution, and Paige Media Investing Inc. They have handled most of the recent high-budget Chinese commercial movies and have also invested in some

Figure 12.1   Film festival week at a Shanghai cinema. James Bond's 007 shares billing with a film made in China.
Source: Wynne Wang

middle- and low-budget films. Smaller production companies can only finance 1.5–3 million yuan (US$200,000–400,000) low-budget films. It is difficult and costly to distribute these films to cinema audiences, so most go directly to national or local television movie channels or find their way on to the shelves of shops selling pirated DVDs.

Imbalanced Battle: Fifth Generation's New Niche vs. Cursed Still Life

Since 2001, all the domestically produced box-office hits have been made by private film companies. Feng Xiaogang's *Big Shot's Funeral* (Da Wan), a 2001 comedy co-produced by private film companies Huayi Brothers, Taihe Film and TV Investment Company, and Warner Brothers Asia had the top box office revenues for domestic movies that year, earning 30 million yuan (US$4.3 million). In 2002, in first place was Zhang Yimou's *Hero* (Ying Xiong), made by the Beijing New Pictures Distribution Company. *Hero* took in more than 250 million yuan (US$36 million). In 2003, the top film was Feng Xiaogang's *Cell Phone* (Shou Ji), a production by Huayi Brothers, and Taihe. In 2004, Zhang Yimou's marshal art epic, *House of Flying Daggers* (Shi Mian Mai Fu), was the box-office winner. In 2005 Chen Kaige's *The Promise* (Wu Ji) was top in movie receipts for Chinese domestic films. This movie was actually produced by the American company, Moonstone Entertainment.

Zhang Yimou and Chen Kaige were the two most important representatives of the internationally acclaimed Fifth Generation Chinese Filmmakers. They started their careers immediately after graduating from Beijing Film Academy in the early 1980s. Zhang Yimou was the cinematographer of Chen Kaige's first two films, *The Yellow Earth* (Huang Tu Di, 1984), and *The Big Parade* (Da Yue Bing, 1986). The two films earned Chen Kaige worldwide critical praise because of the refreshing and stylized visual approaches – noticeably different from earlier generations of Chinese film directors. In 1988, Zhang Yimou's directing debut, *Red Sorghum* (Hong Gao Liang, 1987), won the Golden Bear Award from the Berlin International Film Festival. In 1992, Zhang Yimou's *The Story of Qiu Ju* (Qiu Ju Da Guan Si, 1992) won a Golden Lion from the Venice International Film Festival. In 1993, Chen Kaige's *Farewell My Concubine* (Ba Wang Bie Ji, 1993) won top prize, Palme d'Or, at the Cannes Film Festival. The above works were regarded as the milestones of Chinese artistic films and established the two filmmakers as the most important figures of the Chinese Fifth Generation directors.

During the entire 1990s their films were shown in Chinese cinemas although sometimes with censorship troubles. Zhang Yimou's *To Live* (1994), has never been released in Chinese cinemas. Movie-goers embraced these films passionately, but they were often criticized by the Chinese reviewers for focusing on the negative side of traditional Chinese culture and for the stereotyped formulated portraits of Chinese people. Most of their films, during this stage, were set in historical times and in remote mountain or village areas in China. Sometimes, the period and region were both vague, just providing some general sense of pseudo-China for Western audiences to fit their imaginary China, showing its exotic culture and visual rituals.

During this early period, most of their films are tragedies with a sad ending that emphasizes the politically pessimistic tone of their works. Most protagonists in Zhang Yimou's films were peasants, characteristically represented by a string of village woman characters consistently and excellently performed by the famous Chinese superstar actress, Gong Li. In Chen Kaige's films, though relatively diverse, most of his characters were lower-class figures. The exceptions were those in his epic historical drama, *The Emperor and the Assassin*, (Ci Qin 1999). The film is based on a well-known historical story about the assassination of the cruel King Qin, who unified ancient China and founded the Qin Dynasty over 2,000 years ago.

Zhang Yimou and Chen Kaige's early works were strongly influenced by European Art-house filmmaking styles theory, by Freud's psychoanalysis, and by Friedrich Nietzsche and Jean-Paul Sartre's modern existentialism philosophy. Meanwhile, they also carried on the former Soviet Cinema and older generations Chinese filmmakers' realism traditions. Their early works' achievements in top European film festivals substantiated one of the basic principles of international communication. Many Chinese critics regarded Zhang Yimou's films as a very successful example of how a non-westerner can satisfy Western audiences by showing them an inferior "other" culture. Chinese critics consider this portrayal of China satisfies Western moviegoers because "a self-satisfied, on-top civilization needs a subordinated otherness figure," and "a stopped China is the denied otherness figure in the background of the progressive western cultural myth."[5]

On the visual style and storytelling tactic level, however, it is undeniable that the Fifth Generation filmmakers' early works represented by Zhang Yimou and Chen Kaige are the peak and highlight of Chinese national artistic cinema. They represent the best films made in China since the Chinese film industry was first developed in the 1930s and since the golden years of Chinese filmmaking in the 1940s.

WTO Brings New Challenges

After China joined the World Trade Organization (WTO) in 2001 more American blockbuster movies were imported and shown in Chinese cinemas nationwide, Chinese domestically produced films fell both in numbers and box office revenues. This was the turning point for Chinese cinema. While it faced huge marketing pressure from the Hollywood giants, it was also an opportunity to reestablish the once flourishing movie industry by borrowing Hollywood commercial movie-making approaches and devices. When the younger filmmakers retreated to underground film making, the Fifth Generation filmmakers, led by Zhang Yimou, took up the challenge. After making three small-budget films between 1997 and

2000, he raised US$30 million, brought together an all-star cast, and made a stunning historical martial arts drama, *Hero* (Ying Xiong, 2002). The investment, about 250 million yuan based on the exchange rate at the time, was a record for a Chinese-produced film. Everybody waited to see how Zhang Yimou, whose success was based on relatively low-budget artistic films, would handle this huge-budget martial arts movie. The film's story was a version of the assassination of China's King Qin. Zhang Yimou's rival Chen Kaige just 3 years earlier made a film based on the same story, *The Emperor and the Assassin* (Ci Qin, 1999), and it was a box office failure.

Audiences were not disappointed with Zhang's version. His Kung Fu action scenes were beautifully shot and dazzling to the audiences while his all-star cast of actors gave shining performances. Nevertheless, along with the skyrocketing box-office revenues nationwide came critical attacks. The critics mainly concentrated on the film's storytelling strategy and its superficial exhibition of traditional Chinese cultural potpourris, such as, the calligraphy, the fencing, the game of go, and the guqin, a traditional Chinese musical instrument. Critics from Taiwan were focused on its subtext of reunification and some Western reviewers "felt the film had advocated autocracy and reacted with discomfort."[6] However, "Zhang Yimou himself maintained that he had absolutely no political points to make."[7]

Hero's cinema success set the box-office record in China at 250 million yuan (about US$30,000,000). After nearly 2 years, it was released with English subtitles in the United States and the United Kingdom. In the United States "it debuted as the Number one film, achieving US$18,004,319 ($8,864 per screening) in its opening weekend. The total was the second-highest opening weekend ever for a foreign language film. Its US$53,710,019 North American box office total makes it the fourth highest earning foreign language film and fifteenth highest earning martial arts film in North American box office history. The total worldwide box office revenue was US$177,394,432."[8] It was also nominated for Best Foreign Language Film at the 2003 Academy Awards. A notable phenomenon was that *Hero*'s storytelling format, criticized by Chinese reviewers and even some Chinese audiences, was praised by both American critics and audiences. On Yahoo most moviegoers rated the film's story A or A+, nine critics' average rating for it was B+.[9]

Zhang Yimou's *Hero* is a brilliant "visual banquet" and a milestone not only for his personal aesthetic style but also for China's commercial movie production and its national movie industry. In 2002, the year of *Hero*'s release, total box-office revenue for Chinese-produced films for first time surpassed that of imported movies (mostly Hollywood blockbusters). A trend maintained for six consecutive years.[10]

The negative impact of *Hero* on Chinese filmmaking was that most of the later huge-budget commercial successes were of the historical martial arts genre, including Zhang Yimou's next two commercial hits. Among these big-money productions, Zhang Yimou's comrade and unspoken competitor Chen Kaige's reportedly 350 million Yuan movie, *The Promise* (Wu Ji, 2005), earned just 200 million yuan at the box office. The film received bad reviews and complaints from both critics and moviegoers for its terrible script and laughable performances from its Asian superstar cast. One amateur critic even became famous when he inserted some clips from *The Promise* with other television show sequences and made a satire piece titled, *A Bloody Homicide Caused by a Steamed Bun*, and put it online. It soon became the nation's hottest hit on the Internet. Director Chen Kaige threatened to sue but never did.

In 2008, Chen Kaige's updated work, *Forever Enthralled* (Mei Lan Fang), made with a 100 million yuan investment, gained Chen Kaige many positive reviews and decent box-office returns. A biographical film about the famous Beijing Opera legend, Master Mei Lanfang, it was selected and shown in the competition program at the fifty-ninth Berlin International Film Festival.

The Vanishing Independents

Meanwhile, films by independent Chinese film makers are almost vanishing from commercial mainstream cinemas. If they get into Chinese cinemas at all, most of them only can be seen at the morning or early afternoon showings. A typical and perhaps symbolic example of the imbalanced competition between big-budget commercial movies and low-budget "indie" films was Zhang Yimou's 2006 epic *Curse of the Golden Flower* (Man Cheng Jin Dai Huang Jin Jia) versus Jia Zhang Ke's 2006 *Still Life* (San Xia Hao Ren). *Still Life*, the story of two people searching for their spouses against the backdrop of the giant Three Gorges Dam, won a Golden Lion award at the Venice International Film Festival. Zhang decided to release his big budget *Curse of the Golden Flower* during the 2007 New Year–Spring Festival period; Jia told the press he would release his low-budget but prize winning *Still Life* the same week. He said he was confident audiences would make their own choices and that *Still Life* would do well. Audiences did make their choices, but overwhelmingly chose his rival's film.

After the first week *Curse of the Golden Flower* earned over 100 million yuan (US$15 million) nationwide, while *Still Life* only took in 50,000 yuan (U$7,000).[11] In Shanghai, *Still Life* had only four screenings in the holiday period and, one critic said, "so far its box office revenue may almost be ignored." The rivalry continued as Jia complained to the press that cinemas only showed his film in the morning and afternoon while saving evening show times for Zhang's movie in order to maximize their profits. Zhang, famous for his early films about Chinese peasants, struck back by saying, "You can't blame other people for your own bad harvest."[12] Meanwhile, Jia continued to produce films that pleased the critics but did not have mass audience appeal. A film about Chinese factory workers, *24 City*, opened in the United States in 2009 with the usual praise from critics but clearly appealed only to cinema fans.

Surviving a Relaxed Censorship Proves Even Harder

Chinese independent filmmakers cannot take on the big-budget movies directly if they want to survive in China's unregulated film market. Therefore, their low-budget films are more often offered to the public via DVDs sold on street corners or in small shops, rather than being screened in cinemas. Also, as independent filmmakers do not have sufficient money for promotion and distribution, sometimes they would rather sell their films directly to CCTV-6, the movie channel of China Central TV, in order to recoup their expenses. At times they advertise their films via trailers in cinemas and then quickly distribute DVD copies. One success model they hope to emulate was that of the 2007 Brazilian film *Elite Squad*. That film first became popular on DVD and was then distributed to cinemas by Universal Studios. Independent films in China are not yet dead and Chinese independent filmmakers (including those previously underground) are making more movies since censorship rules were relaxed in 2003. However, even this has caused problems.

One result of the loosened ideological control of Chinese cinema in recent years has been the surfacing of the previously banned underground "Sixth Generation" film makers. The "Sixth Generation" is the title given to a group of Chinese directors who graduated from the Beijing Film

Academy and Central Drama Institute in the late 1980s and early 1990s. These directors focused on contemporary society. Their films were at first banned by Chinese censors even though they won prestigious prizes all over the world.

Jia Zhangke is the most important representative of this group. His four early films, *Xiaoshan Returns Home* (Xiao Shan Hui Jia, 1995), *Xiaowu* (Xiao Wu, 1997), *Platform* (Zhan Tai, 2000), and *Unknown Pleasure* (Ren Xiao Yao, 2002), are still denied exhibition approval by the government. However, in 2005 Jia's first domestic film released to cinemas, *The World* (Shi Jie), encountered no significant difficulties with censors. In an interview, Jia said his reason for attempting to resurface from the underground was the relaxed environment of censorship. "Originally . . . the censorship apparatus was to a large degree restricting our freedom of choice," he said. "But now it looks like we'll have the chance to express ourselves freely, and that's why I'm willing to give it a try."[13] When he submitted his film *The World* for review by the censorship board, he said he was surprised that, with the exception of a few lines of vulgar language, the majority of the film was allowed to remain intact.[14]

Another former underground film maker, Xiaoshuai Wang, emerged in 2005. The ban on his 2001 film, *Beijing Bicycle*, which won the Silver Bear Prize at the Berlin Film Festival, was lifted. His two more recent films, *Shanghai Dream* (Qing Hong, 2005) and *In Love We Trust* (Zuo You, 2007), were approved by the Chinese film censors. Both films won prizes in foreign film festivals but had limited success in the Chinese market.

Unfortunately, most of the Sixth Generation directors' films win overseas prizes, but become box office disasters in China. Chinese audiences were curious about the Sixth Generation's underground films, especially since they were banned by the government and won prizes at heavyweight Western film festivals. So, audiences in China tried to view them through any possible route, usually as pirated DVDs or through online downloading. After the censorship bar was lifted in 2003, these films could not compete with other films and lost their audiences.

A Rating System with Chinese Characteristics

As censorship is being lifted, more sex and violence is appearing in Chinese films. Some suggest it is time to establish a rating-system for Chinese movies similar to those used for decades in the United States and many other countries. The State Administration for Radio, Film and Television (SARFT), China's equivalent to the US Federal Communications Commission (FCC), has held hearings and conferences on this issue but has not made a decision.[15] Even Chinese actress Gong Li, an international superstar, has called for a rating system.[16] However, the veteran film producer, the Vice President of Shanghai Film Group (SFG), Mr. Xu Pengle expressed his concerns about conducting a rating system, "Nowadays, it is impossible to launch a rating system and it cannot work out in China, in my opinion. Why? Because China's film market is unregulated, the film-related legislations are incomplete. When piracy is so rampant that teenagers can easily access films that even haven't been shown in theatres at every street corner, how can we conduct a rating system? . . . Only after the Chinese film market becomes clean and regulated, let's talk about it then."[17]

A transformation from hard censorship, which decides what is permitted on screens, to the soft censorship of a rating system, which does not proscribe the content of films but rather classifies them as appropriate for certain segments of the public, seems likely to come eventually to Chinese cinema. In November, 2007, the film *Lust, Caution*, which won a Golden Lion award, stirred up the rating discussion again. Since there is no rating system in China, Director Ang Lee had to personally edit a "clean" version specifically for mainland cinemas by deleting most of the sexually graphic scenes in the film. Ang Lee stated that the shortened version would be as enjoyable as the uncut version but, people still crossed into Hong Kong to see the full version where it was shown with a "III" rating, similar an "R" rating in the United States. Again, a heated discussion about bringing a proper rating system into mainland China emanated from websites. There is still no sign, from SARFT, of introducing a mainland rating system. TV journalist Qiu Luwei of Hong Kong's Phoenix TV told her audience, "Today's (Chinese) government is unexpectedly demonstrating rationality and flexibility and even openness, so I'd like to keep my optimism (on this matter)."[18]

The first signs of this transformation to more openness can be found in a document on censorship regulation issued by SARFT in September 2003. SARFT now requires film makers only to submit a 1,000-word draft script to get approval for shooting. After that, the completed film is sent not to SARFT but directly to local film censorship boards unless it touches on sensitive topics such as the Cultural Revolution, anti-Japanese sentiment, or the 1989 Tiananmen Square "incident." This dissemination of censorship power from the central government to the provinces is important to film makers. It reduces the possibility of a national ban on a completed film, thus causing a total loss. It also provides more space for different approaches and opinions on film censorship. Out of 214 films that were submitted to the censors under this new system in 2004, only one film, *Jianghu*, a Hong Kong production with violent content, was denied approval for release in mainland China.

In 2005, there was a censorship case against film maker Lou Ye and his film, *The Summer Palace* (yuan Ming yuan), which included sex scenes related to the Tiananmen Square incident. Lou finished the film without submitting it for either central or local censorship review and then sent it to the Cannes Film Festival. Like *Purple Butterfly*, his earlier film, *The Summer Palace* won no prizes. SARFT asked Lou to revise his film for the domestic market but he refused to cut even one frame from his film. At that point SARFT finally banned *The Summer Palace* release.

Just 3 days after the 2008 New Year, a prime time for new films to hit the Chinese market, a 4 million yuan (US$570,000) Chinese indie film, *Apple* (Ping Guo), was suddenly banned nationwide. In just 1 month in the cinemas *Apple* had accrued revenue of more than 17 million yuan (US$2.4 million). The public was astonished by *Apple*'s sensational sex scenes that were widely distributed via Internet clips. SARFT later said that *Apple*'s producer had tricked officials by submitting a different version of the film for review. SARFT even tried to stop its DVD distribution.[19] Nevertheless, *Apple*, *The Summer Palace*, and other banned films, can generally be found as pirated DVDs inside the country.

Until the movie market develops more balance, Chinese independent films will reach viewers mostly as pirated DVDs. This is the only positive side of the piracy problem in China. Pirated DVDs do serious damage to China's movie market, as well as to the imported Hollywood blockbusters. Pirated DVD makers are well organized and try to match their faked DVDs release time to the original premiere in the United States or Europe as closely as possible. Dubbed Hollywood films are also widely available on DVD. Examples can be seen in Figure 12.2. This may be one reason that the imported Hollywood movies box office has decreased for 5 consecutive years in the mainland market. Chinese high budget commercial movies suffer the same damage from the piracy criminals as they battle for a place in China's film market.

Figure 12.2   Dubbed Hollywood films are widely available in China on DVDs.
Source: Wynne Wang

Twin Peaks: High Budget and High Box-office

Hollywood's impact on Chinese filmmakers is not decreasing. On the contrary, Hollywood's influence is becoming more significant, most of the Chinese epic commercial movies that win large audiences are modeled after successful Hollywood films from production style to market promotion, although with smaller budgets. With more Hollywood money now involved at both production and distribution stages of Chinese-language movies, their budgets are rapidly increasing. John Woo's 2008 epic war film *Red Cliff*, which is based on a famous Chinese novel, reportedly costs 600 million yuan (US$85 million) to make. Its first half was released right before the 2008 Olympics, and earned 302 million yuan (US$47 million) in a few weeks – a box office record for a domestic Chinese movie. The producers expect *Red Cliff* to earn much more, especially when the second half is released. This kind of shoot-once-make-money-twice marketing strategy is borrowed directly from Hollywood and is expected to work well in China. John Woo, a Hong Kong trained Hollywood film maker, making an epic Chinese film adapted from one of the most famous historical Chinese novels, and using Hollywood production and promotion tactics illustrates the Americanized beefing-up of the Chinese movie industry.

It is also worth noting that the distribution company for *Red Cliff* is China's biggest film organization, China Film Group (CFG) a state-run, independently- capitalized enterprise. In early 2008, CPG successfully distributed another historical epic movie, *The Warlords* (Tou Ming Zhuang, 2007), directed by another acclaimed Hong Kong film maker, Peter Chan. Han Sanping, the CEO of CFG, said he hoped to launch his company on the stock market to raise more capital for expansion.[20] With over 200 million yuan (US$30 million) in domestic box-office receipts, *The Warlords* production pattern is as same as the one for *Red Cliff*. Film makers from Hong Kong, Taiwan, and mainland China, along with some American professionals, created the film and hit both the mainland and Hong Kong movie market. *The Warlords* also won eight Hong Kong Golden Film awards in April 2008. Han Sanping is willing to raise money in the stock market so he can bring more talents together from the three Chinese-speaking regions in order to make movies that succeed outside the Chinese-speaking market.[21] Another distribution giant, the private film company Poly-bona Film Distributions, has the same idea and its chief executive, Yu Dong, indicated that Poly-bona has already attracted international venture capital. Yu hopes Poly-bona will become the first private Chinese film company listed on an overseas stock market.[22]

Shanghai Film Studio (SFG), another veteran film production company that had been state run and had become independent, planned to be listed on the stock market as early as 1996. However, at that time China's film market was not very dynamic and promising, so the idea was finally discarded. Recently, SFG Vice President, Mr. Xu Pengle stated his willingness to do so in the near future as a long-term commitment: "Our solution is to operate with diversified investment, diversified creative and collaborative teams, and diversified marketing strategies. Overall, we believe the saying that is to make the creative marketable and to make the marketing creative."[23]

Huge investments return huge profits. More and more Chinese film makers and producers realize this film industry principle. However, in a growing and still unregulated movie market in China, seeking money to make movies is more difficult than in the United States. In the United States it is not unusual for a bank to lend money to a film company, but this rarely happens in China. By 2008 only one Chinese film maker, Feng Xiaogang, had succeeded in getting a large bank loan (50 million yuan or US$7 million) from a Chinese bank. He is sometimes referred to as China's Steven Spielberg. He had no problems with the China Merchants Bank loan repayments because of his string of box office successes with films that pleased both movie-goers and critics.

No Third-party Guarantee

After his early success in television, Feng Xiaogang directed his first film in 1994. *Lost My Love Forever* (Yong Shi Wo Ai), earned fair reviews from the critics and decent box-office returns. Since then, each of his films has made tremendous profits in mainland China's market. His later three low-budget comedies, *Party A, Party B* (Jia Fang Yi Fang, 1997), *Be There or Be Square* (Bu Jian Bu San, 1998), and *Sorry, Baby!* (Mei Wan Mei Liao, 1999), were the New Year season's domestic film box-office champions for three consecutive years. His next two films, *Big Shot's Funeral* (Da Wan, 2001), and *The Cell Phone* (Shou Ji, 2003), were also the respective year's box-office winners. Feng made these two films with a comparatively low budget of less than 10 million yuan (US$1.4 million). With his continuing success, his long time financial supporter Huayi Brothers, agreed to invest 100 million yuan (US$14 million) in his next film. Feng decided to join with other major Chinese film makers, Zhang Yimou and Chen Kaige to bring out his first historical epic film, *The Night Banquet* (Ye Yan), in 2005. Though the film was not well scripted and received weak reviews, it still earned nearly 200 million yuan (US$28 million) at the box-office. This looked good to its backers as another epic film that came out that year, *The Promise*, was a box office disaster – earning just 190 million yuan ($27 million) on a reported 350 million yuan ($50 million) investment and also received a lot of bad reviews.

Many film goers considered *The Night Banquet* a fairly well made, decently performed historical film. This didn't stop many critiques regarding it as Feng's biggest failure, with a weak story and little character development. At the same time as some critics and audiences were saying that Feng's skills were limited to making modern life comedies, he went on to make a surprising war movie, *The Assembly* (Ji Jie Hao). The film was released in December 2007, the beginning of the New Year-Spring Festival season. *The Assembly* ran against Peter Chan's big budget (280 million yuan/ US$40 million) historical war movie, *The Warlords*. Both films were smash hits, with *The Warlords* box office hitting 200 million yuan (US$28 million) and *The Assembly* bringing in about 270 million yuan (almost US$40 million). Both movies were very well received by reviewers and audiences. *The Assembly* tells a story about a Liberation Army veteran spending almost all the second half of his life searching for the evidence that could prove his 48 dead comrades were revolutionary martyrs instead of missing persons. The film's elaborately structured first half is full of cruel, bloody battle scenes; the second is the journey of the protagonist, Guzidi, as he searches to justify the 48 dead soldiers' sacrifice. In the end, Guzidi finds the proof that his dead buddies were martyrs, but the truth is more than he wanted to find: Guzidi found that along with the other 48 soldiers, who desperately hoped their platoon would retreat, they were actually sent to the battle field only as a sacrifice in the entire battle strategy. Feng's film is a very humane and symbolic portrayal of war and the individual tragedies war caused in Chinese modern history. Not only did critics praise his narrative structuring and story-telling skills, but also highly acclaimed his character development. Some critics concluded that *The Assembly* was Feng's best film so far, not only a landmark for a master film maker, but also the "Mark of the Maturity of Chinese High-Budget Commercial Films"[24]

Critic Jia Leilei noted: "Since entering the industrial era, we have talked about the harmonious balance between the commercial appeals of mainstream filmmaking and national mainstream ideology in Chinese cinema. However, successful examples are scarce . . . *The Assembly* is not only a film that is a tremendous economic achievement, but also one that is ideologically positive and lifts up the spirit; meantime, it is a film that has universal cultural values."[25]

Another critic, Zhang Yiwu, in his article "*Assembly: Visit and Ponder on the Past of Chinese History*," emphasizes the possibilities of the new imagination and narrative patterns that *The Assembly* brought to Chinese cinema. Zhang also credits a series of high-budget historical movies, starting from Zhang Yimou's 2002 *Hero*, as allowing the Chinese people to revisit and ponder the pain and hardships of twentieth century Chinese history.[26]

While critics praised the monumental contribution of *The Assembly* to Chinese history and culture, the press also noted the movie's innovative fundraising format. However, few critics realized that perhaps more significant was the willingness of a Chinese bank to be directly involved with an expensive film project. Though *The Assembly*'s 80 million yuan ($US11 million) budget was not the highest in Chinese film history and Huayi Brothers was willing to put up about one-third of the cost, Feng still needed 50 million yuan to make the picture and persuaded China Merchants Bank to lend it to him without any backer guaranteeing repayment. In unfamiliar financial territory with a bunch of movie makers instead of the usual manufacturers, the bank sent a manager to the filming sites to see what was going on with its money. "I probably am the first person from a Chinese bank who has followed the whole filming period for a high-budget commercial movie," said Zao Ke, customer manager of the Shenzhen branch of the China Merchants Bank.[27]

Film making was a risky area for CMB because of the unfamiliarity and uncontrollability during the production period. Who knows what might happen during the process of making the movie? What if the finished movie does not pass the censorship review so that it cannot be released and the investors get zero? Or suppose the movie is distributed successfully but nobody goes to see it so that the borrowers cannot repay the money? With these questions in mind, after agreeing to the loan, CMB monitored the film's progress closely: "During that period of time, we intensely monitored the crew's every move. If there was something odd, we were highly cautious," said Zao. He recalled that one time after he saw a TV report that Zhang Hanyu, the leading actor of the film, had fallen from a horse, he hurried to the shooting location to check personally on the actor's health.[28]

All worked out well, of course, especially financially. And at the twenty-ninth Hundreds of Flowers Film Awards (equivalent to the People's Choice Awards in the USA), *The Assembly* won prizes for Best Film, Best Director, Best Leading Actor, and Best Supporting Actor.[29] Hopefully, *The Assembly*'s wins at both commercial and artistic levels will build enough confidence in China's developing film industry for the large banks to lend more money not only to the established film makers like Feng Xiaogang and Zhang Yimou, but also to the so far unknown independent filmmakers.

Stardom System

The Warlords director Peter Chan said that in China it is easier to get funding for the low-budget films and the expensive blockbusters than for films budgeted around 10–20 million yuan (US$1.5–3 million). Mid-range movies are regarded as the most dangerous for investors because in China it is hard to attract a superstar within the budget. To do so a director might have to sacrifice some of the production budget or even some of the director's ideas for the film. One superstar cannot guarantee a film's success, but Chinese audiences really like to see their favorite stars on screen. This is a typical dilemma that middle-budget movies have to face. The low-budget films do not need stars to attract the small audiences needed for financial success, while high-budget films have enough funds to cast at least two superstars to secure their box-office success. Therefore, since 2001, all domestic box-office champions have featured multi-superstar rosters. Some of them were even all-star blockbusters. These included: *Hero* (2002), starring Jet Li, Tony Leung, Maggie Chang, and Zhang Ziyi; *Cell Phone* (2003), starring Zhang Guoli, Ge You, and Xu Fan; *Curse of the Golden Flower* (2006), which cast Gong Li, Chow Yun Fat, and Jay Chou; *The Warlords* (2007), with Jet Li, Andy Lau, Takeshi Kaneshiro, and Xu Jinglei; and John Woo's *Red Cliff* (2008), with Tony Leung, Takeshi Kaneshiro, Zhang Fengyi, Zhao Wei, and Chang Chen. Feng Xiaogang's *Big Shot's Funeral* (2001) even included Hollywood stars Donald Sutherland and Paul Mazursky, Rosamund Kwan from Hong Kong, and Ge You from China. Chen Kaige's *The Promise* (2005) had an Asian all-star cast including Jang Dong-gun from Korea, Hiroyuki Sanada from Japan, and Cecelia Cheung and Nicholas Tse from Hong Kong. The Chinese film *Beast Stalker* also drew large audiences because of its "homegrown stars" (see Figure 12.3).

As the list of stars grows, so do the box-office champions' budgets. *Big Shot's Funeral*'s 26 million yuan (US$3.7 million) budget in 2001 jumped to 350 million yuan (US$50 million) for *The Promise* in 2005 and then to 600 million yuan (US$85 million) in 2008 for John Woo's *Red Cliff*. Production costs for these big budget Chinese epics increase more than 20 fold in only 7 years with most of the budget increase being used on superstar payment. The extreme example is Jet Li's 100 million yuan (US$12.5 million) salary in *The Warlords*, about one-third of the total budget for that epic film.

Figure 12.3   The Chinese film *Beast Stalker* drew large audiences because of its stars from Mainland China and Hong Kong.
Source: Wynne Wang

Jet Li, Gong Li and Zhang Ziyi are three internationally famous movie stars who originated from mainland China. Jet Li gained fame as a young martial arts athlete in the early 1980s by playing a Kong Fu monk in *Shaolin Temple* (Shao Lin Si, 1982). From the late 1980s through the 1990s, he developed his movie career as a Kong Fu star in Hong Kong. In the late 1990s, he launched on the road to Hollywood by playing a cruel gangster in *Lethal Weapon 4* (1998); then he starred in a series of Kong Fu movies in Hollywood and the most recent being *The Mummy: Tomb of the Dragon Emperor* (2008), in which he played an ancient Chinese Emperor Han. During this period, he also returned to China and joined several Chinese huge-budget historical marshal art film productions, such as *Hero* (2002), *Fearless* (2006) and *The Warlords* (2007). He has become a box-office guarantee for markets both at home and abroad.

Gong Li starred in Zhang Yimou's film debut, *Red Sorghum* (Hong Gao Liang) in 1987 and began her 8-year cooperation with Zhang Yimou in seven films. The pair also co-starred in a Hong Kong made film, *A Terracotta Warrior* (Qin Yong, 1990). In the seven films on which they worked together, Gong Li mostly played village women from remote country areas. The best known, Qiuju, was a stubborn pregnant peasant who tried every way she could to make the village leader apologize to her husband, who had been attacked by the village leader as a result of a misunderstanding. This role won Gong Li the Best Actress Award at 1992 Venice International Film Festival, along with the Golden Lion Award for Best Film for Zhang Yimou. The couple became Chinese cinema's golden pair of the 1990s. After the last film they made together, *Shanghai Triad* (Yao A Yao, Yao Dao Wai Po Qiao, 1995), Gong Li tried to work with other directors (mostly Fifth Generation film makers), but none of them could inspire her to the level performance achieved with Zhang Yimou. In 2005, by co-starring with two other Chinese actresses, Zhang Ziyi, and Michele Yang in *Memoirs of a Geisha*, Gong Li established her career in Hollywood and then continued by appearing in the following Hollywood movies: *Miami Vice* (2006) and *Hannibal Rising* (2007). In 2006, Gong Li reunited with Zhang Yimou and took the role of an empress in his historical drama, *Curse of the Golden Flower* (Man Cheng Jin Dai Huang Jin Jia). The pair's reunion was certainly the biggest selling point for the movie – it became that year's Chinese box-office champion. More importantly for Gong Li, she won the following year's Hong Kong Film Award for Best Actress. It is worth noting that in recent years Jet Li; Gong Li; Zhang Ziyi and other famous Hong Kong superstars, such as Jacky Chan, Chow Yun Fat, and Michele Yang, have worked on both sides of the Pacific Ocean allowing them to maintain and develop their international celebrity status while contributing to China's movie industry development. A worry is that the superstar strategy forces Chinese film makers to focus on blockbuster epics that will be a commercial success at the expense of creativity and aesthetic value. Others say the star system is essential for China's movie industry if motion pictures are to be seen as an entertainment medium. On this issue, film director and executive producer, Huang Jianxin says the audience will decide, "If stars influence the box-office, then the stardom system is necessary. If audiences won't buy it (the stardom system), then it's unnecessary."[30] The stardom strategy has been a successful strategy in Hollywood for decades and has worked with audiences all over the world as it has with Chinese film makers and audiences. Thus, the big directors are willing to pay superstars their skyrocketing salaries and the money men are also willing to provide the funds. John Woo's 2008 *Red Cliff* with 10 major characters played by superstars from Taiwan, Hong Kong, and mainland China and a budget of 600 million yuan (US$85 million) is just the latest example. A smash hit at cinemas all over Asia, *Red Cliff* earned back that investment, in just a few months, before the second part was released.[31]

With this kind of success, the Chinese film industry is likely to focus on developing more stars to build up its "stardom system." This will require huge budgets for new films. Chinese cinema will thus focus largely on Hollywood-type "star movies" based on an industry system, replacing the long time European tradition of "auteur films" which emphasized a director's style and vision. Thus, Chinese cinema will embrace an era of industrialization.[32]

This development depends on the availability of large financial investments in the Chinese film industry. The 2008 downturn in China's stock market could slow this development. Despite some great successes, film making remains a very risky investment. Production companies that seemed eager to raise funds are now hesitating. Nonetheless, the record-high amounts of domestic movies made for the 2009 New Year-Spring Festival season and the new box-office revenue records created during the season indicate that, during maybe the worst economic crisis worldwide since the Great Depression, China's movie industry might be one the beneficiaries of this recession. This mirrors the Hollywood dream works factory's golden years prosperity boosted by the Great Depression.

Summary

There are some in China's film industry that say it is time for some regulations. They want not just a rating system but rules relating to fundraising, the stardom system and some support for independent film makers. These film makers now struggle more with the profit-driven market than with government censorship. Censorship will not disappear in the foreseeable future but there has already been a loosening as the government is unable to ban films on the accessible global stage. Without some changes to the above policies, it is predicted by some that China's independent film makers are likely to disappear.

The fast growing Chinese movie industry has faced challenges from a global economic recession, a shrinking domestic stock market, a lack of strong copyright laws for the protection of productions, comparatively limited fundraising sources, and a surge in superstar salaries. All these challenges will test Chinese movie policy makers' wisdom and courage as well as Chinese film makers' creativity and persistence.

13

English-Language Media in China

The existence of English-language media in Chinese society can be traced back almost two centuries when foreigners first began to establish their own newspapers. An English-language newspaper was set up in 1827 in Guangzhuo[1] and the first daily in English appeared in 1857. Although the official language in China is Chinese, English-language media have been part of the media industry in China since the early nineteenth century. English-language media in China were also initiated by Chinese intellectuals, mostly educated in the West, in an effort to let the world know more about a China that was then isolated from the rest of the world linguistically and culturally.

Even after the *North China Daily News* (one of the most influential foreign-owned newspapers in Shanghai) left mainland China in 1951, Radio Peking (now China Radio International or CRI) continued its services in foreign languages including English while English magazines like *Beijing Review* and *China Reconstructs* (now *China Today*) were published. English dailies and weeklies and English TV channels did not emerge in Communist China until after 1978 when China began to open up and took on a reform policy to modernize the nation. English-language media developed rapidly and grew more influential even though still limited.

Overview

The development of English-language media in China has been marked by different forms of media in different stages in the past 60 years. This chapter focuses on the three traditional media and the new medium: the

Internet. It follows the time sequence of radio–newspaper–television–Internet as they emerged in the media industry in China.

Radio Services

English radio services in China are mainly provided by China Radio International (CRI, formerly Radio Beijing) inaugurated on December 3, 1941. CRI has been the only overseas radio service available from China that targets foreign listeners all over the world. By 2008, with a daily programming of 192 hours in 43 languages and with English and Chinese broadcast globally, CRI reached about 240 million listeners in more than 200 countries and regions. CRI has 10 transmitting stations in China and eight relay stations in Europe, Africa and the Americas. In terms of the number of languages used and broadcast hours, the volume of listener letters and total transmission power, CRI ranks among the top world broadcasting services. It is one of the most influential international broadcasters in the world, especially in developing and underdeveloped countries.[2]

CRI's English Service was founded on September 11, 1947. It has been one of CRI's most important divisions and in 2008 offered more than 60 broadcast hours per day with about 60 million overseas listeners in more than 100 countries and regions. The English Service programs focus on news, features, and music. CRI's English Service is considered very effective in providing news about China as well as music and is a useful medium for English learners.[3]

As more foreign tourists visited China, from the beginning of the early 1990s, regional English radio services developed. On October 1, 1992, Shanghai Calling, the first regional English Service in the nation, was launched by Shanghai People's Radio Station. At first, Shanghai Calling broadcast for about 12 hours a day, focusing on the local news, weather, music, and services for foreigners in the area. In the same year, Radio Guangdong was started, appealing to the local audience in the Pearl Delta area in South China. On May 8, 2001, Beijing started a 3-hour English service known as "Touch English," targeting Beijing listeners with local news, Chinese cultural programs, and information about life in Beijing. "Touch English" aimed to create a better language environment for foreigners in Beijing and to help raise the English-speaking population in the capital from 15 to 30 percent by the year 2008. This was part of the bidding effort for the 2008 Olympics.[4] However, except for "Touch English," which was started especially for the 2008 Olympics, most regional English radio services have been shrinking and may not survive. Shanghai Calling ceased broadcasting in 1998 and now only relays the English broadcasts of CRI.

Magazines and Newspapers

Before 1981 when *China Daily* was launched, except for English radio services, the only other English-language media available in China were English magazines. These included *Beijing Review*, *China Today*, *China Pictorial*, and *China Women*, all sponsored by such Beijing-based organizations as the China Foreign Language Publication Administration and the All-China Women's Federation.

Perhaps because most are funded by the government, the circulation of these English magazines was never very high and most have had to go online to survive. For instance, *Beijing Review*, launched on March 5, 1958, started as the first multilingual news weekly in China and used to be published in English, Japanese, French, German, and Spanish. Since 2001 only its full-color English edition has continued as a hard copy issue with all other editions published on the Internet.[5]

Local English magazines were published in big cities like Shanghai. *Shanghai Today* is a monthly that reports on culture in Shanghai. Some specialized journals are published by professional organizations. For example, the *Chinese Medical Journal* (English edition) is published by the Chinese Medical Association.[6]

Before 1951, China had several influential English newspapers, most located in Shanghai. These included the *North China Daily News*, *Celestial Empire*, and *Shanghai Mercury*. During the next 30 years publishing an English-language newspaper in China was virtually impossible because of the continuous internal political turmoil, which isolated China from the rest of the world. In this sense, the launching of the 12-page English-language *China Daily* on June 1, 1981 had special significance. According to Zhu Yinghuang, its former editor-in-chief, the birth of *China Daily* signified that an open China was integrating itself with the world and therefore needed an English-language daily for effective international communication. The China Daily Group has since become the dominant English-language newspaper publisher in China.

As the first and only national English-language newspaper in China, *China Daily* started with financial support from government. However, after 20 years, the Daily Group grew financially independent and developed eight publications including *China Daily* Hong Kong Edition, *China Daily* web-edition, *Business Weekly*, *Shanghai Star* published in Shanghai, *Beijing Weekend*, and *Reports from China*. The group also published the *21ˢᵗ Century*, a weekly designed to promote the use of English among learners.

Regional English-language media, some published daily and some weekly, also emerged in Beijing and in the big coastal cities like Shanghai, These can be divided into three categories. The first focuses on comprehensive news and reporting in the regional areas while the second category stresses English learning. The third category, which are mostly tabloids some distributed free, concentrates on local life style and entertainment and are particularly popular among expatriates.

Shanghai Daily, *Shenzhen Daily*, and the *Guangzhou Morning Post* all fall into the first category. The 8-page *Shenzhen Daily*, inaugurated on July 1, 1997, was the only English newspaper in China's economic zones while the 12-page *Guangdong Morning Post*, which also started publication on July 1, 1997, was the first English newspaper in south China. The 8-page *Shanghai Daily*, launched on October 1, 1999, targeted English speakers in the Shanghai area. These newspapers mainly cover local news and serve foreign and Chinese speakers in their regions.

As foreign populations rose across China (Shanghai had about 150,000 foreign residents and seven million foreign tourists in 2008), regional English newspapers turned to lifestyle, fashion, and entertainment. *Beijing Weekend* and *Shanghai Star*, both sponsored by *China Daily*, were the earliest newspapers devoted to entertainment for regional foreign readership. Of course, competition became fierce as more foreign-funded English tabloids such as *City Weekend* and *Metro* began to emerge in Beijing. *Beijing Today*, an English language weekly which started publication in May 2001, added to the competition of the English tabloids in the capital.[7]

Besides the regional English newspapers, China also has a number of English tabloids that target English learners. The newspaper *21ˢᵗ Century* targets university students while *Shanghai Student's Post*, *English Weekly* and *Learning English*, all launched in the early 1980s, target primary to middle school students. Except for the *21ˢᵗ Century*, these publications focus on content that is relevant to the English textbooks used in China's primary and middle schools such as the one shown in Figure 13.1. *English Weekly*, published in Shanxi Province, claims to have 3.8 million readers who are studying for high school and university entrance exams. Despite their large circulations, the influence of these newspapers is limited to English-language learners and they are not generally known among other English speakers.

Figure 13.1 An advertisement for an English-language school for children. Many Chinese schools offer English classes starting in the third grade. Anxious parents bring babies to private English-language schools hoping they will get an early start in English.
Source: Wynne Wang

English Channels

English-language TV programs were first started in 1982 at China Central Television (CCTV) with English educational programs like "Follow Me." The program's English hostess attracted a huge following of her three-times-a-week English lessons. However, English TV services did not really come into existence until "English News" was broadcast at the end of 1986, coupled with an interview program "Focus" and more entertaining programs such as "Cultural Lounge" and "Hello Beijing." These programs gradually formed a network of English TV programs at CCTV.[8]

On September 2, 2002 this network was turned into CCTV-4, also known as CCTV International, a satellite channel in Chinese that included 4 hours of English-language programs. CCTV-4 aimed to serve Chinese citizens living overseas, foreign nationals of Chinese origin and foreign viewers who were interested in China. CCTV-4 is a general channel delivering news and current affairs, as well as economics, entertainment, sports, children's programs, movies, TV dramas, and documentaries. Since 1998 CCTV-4 has broadcast 24 hours a day in four units rotating every 6 hours. This arrangement allows audiences in different time zones to watch CCTV-4 at times most convenient to them.[9]

"Your Window on China" is the 24-hour English language channel CCTV-9 started as an experiment in 1996 and officially launched on September 25, 2000. After 2 years CCTV merged the 4 hour English programs from CCTV-4 into CCTV-9. CCTV-4 became a Chinese-language channel with global on-the-hour news coverage. Meanwhile, CCTV-9 became the only national English-language channel and even started to employ foreign anchor persons to host its English programs, a practice unprecedented in the recent history of China's media. This intends to emulate the Western TV style and also aims to communicate with English-speaking viewers more effectively, according to Jiang Heping, CCTV-9's former director and now director of CCTV-5.

Paralleling the English TV services at the central level, regional English TV services in China also experienced a boom starting in the 1980s. Shanghai Broadcasting Network (SBN) was launched on October 1, 1998, as a satellite TV service to showcase Shanghai to the world. With a mixture of English and Chinese programs, SBN was merged into a new satellite TV channel, known as Dragon TV, on October 23, 2003. On January 1, 2008, SBN was again converted into China's first regional English channel, known as International Channel Shanghai (ICS), that broadcasts 19 hours per day. The launching of ICS was largely stimulated by the 2010 Shanghai Exposition, the biggest event in China after the 2008 Beijing Olympics. Guangdong TV Station, in southern China, started a daily 2-hour English news broadcast in Guangzhou in 1988, but faced fierce competition from the "overspill" TV waves of two English channels from Hong Kong.

The development of English-language TV media echoed the development in China's media industry over the past 20 years. The media have become the fourth most profitable industry in China, with advertising volume jumping from 3.5 billion yuan (US$500 million) to 79.8 billion yuan (US$11.5 billion) from 1991 to 2006 for the four traditional media. While it is true that the media in China used to be subsidized by the government, more than 95 percent of their revenues now come from advertising.[10]

Internet Symbiosis with Traditional Media

The Internet was not available in China until April 1994, but has expanded rapidly since. By June 30, 2008, there were 253 million Internet users in China, more than in any other country. China also had, according to the twenty-second CNNIC (China Internet Network Information) Report,[11] almost two million websites, including those in English.

Although the Internet has become increasingly important for entertainment (music) and information (news) both in Chinese and English the Internet media do not tend to replace traditional English-language media. Instead, a kind of symbiosis pattern of the new medium and the traditional media has emerged. In 2002, 10 major English-language websites were nominated as key English websites, as part of efforts to enhance China's international communication with the outside world. Most of these are affiliated to major English and Chinese media, including *People's Daily*, Xinhua news agency, CCTV, Radio China International, and China Net, affiliated to the China Internet Information Office. Other affiliations included Dragon News Net, supported by all the local news media in Beijing, Eastday Net, supported by all the media in Shanghai, and Nanfang Net, supported by *Nanfang Daily* in south China. As they are supported by leading Chinese and English-language media and government organizations, these English websites soon became as influential and authoritative as their affiliated traditional media organizations.

Development Patterns

As noted earlier, in 1981 China had only one English-language radio station and a couple of English magazines. Since then the media industry has been booming, including English-language media. The English media shows two development patterns.

First, compared with Chinese-language media, the development of English-language media was relatively slow and stable, and hardly affected by politics in China. This was mainly because: (1) they are theoretically targeting overseas or foreign audiences and are not at the center of Chinese politics; (2) their influence may still be limited compared to Chinese media; and (3) government control over media content may be weakened to some degree simply because the content is in English and most government officials do not fully understand them.

Second, English-language media were centralized at first but then began to appear in regional centers. China Radio International, *China Daily*, CCTV-9 and most early English websites were based in Beijing, demonstrating this early centralization pattern. However, since the late 1980s, regional centers such as Shanghai and Guangdong have launched their own English-language media. Though they may not be as professional as the national English-language media, they are certainly playing roles that cannot be replaced by central-level media in a country as geographically large as China.

Of course, like the central-level English media, English-language media at regional centers have also followed a development sequence of radio-newspaper-television-Internet as each new medium matured and got more involved in its English services. For instance, in Shanghai and Guangdong, English-language media all started with radio, with Shanghai Calling in Shanghai and Radio Guangdong in Guangzhou. The English media then gradually began to be available in print with *Shanghai Daily* in Shanghai, *Guangzhou Morning Post* in Guangzhou and *Shenzhen Daily* in Shenzhen. When ICS was launched in Shanghai on January 1, 2008, that English TV channel and the developing websites in English were also following the development pattern at the regional level.

Despite the decentralization tendency in the 1990s, the political nature of international communication in China has always reinforced the dominance of the centrally-based English-language media. Of course, if the central dominance is a result of political considerations, the prosperity of English-language media in China's business capital of Shanghai may be related to its colonial tradition of foreign-run English-language newspapers – the situation before 1949.[12] Even though not as influential as the capital city of Beijing, Shanghai, with its historical experience of English-language newspapers and with its strong economic momentum, can still be considered the largest regional center of English-language media in mainland China. Shanghai was the first city to start English radio (Shanghai Calling) and English TV (Shanghai Broadcasting Network). Shanghai is also the only regional city with an English-language daily (*Shanghai Daily*) and an English-language TV channel (ICS) specifically aimed at a regional audience.

Three Roles

Three roles can be identified for the English-language media in the Chinese environment. These are the elite role, language role and bridging role. They can be distinguished in a particular period of social development or may simply exist throughout the social development of China that commenced in 1949.

Elite role

The elite role of English-language media was most obvious from the 1950s to the 1980s, when China was in an enclosed social environment and was totally separated from the outside world. To some degree, English-language media became the only channel for China to communicate with the rest of the world, which enhanced its elite status in the Chinese society.

As they targeted only the foreign audience outside China (at that time, there were almost no foreigners inside China), English-language media looked noble, lofty, and even mysterious and unknown to most Chinese. Their international influence far exceeded their influence within China, where their role was quite limited and, of course, elite-oriented.

During this period of social development, English-language media in China had the following three features:

- English-language media were basically part of the state propaganda machine and the tools for its overseas propaganda, which was very much politically-oriented;
- the communicative pattern was one-way communication and self-centered, with almost no attention paid to communication effects as the media contents were political in nature; and
- their operations were funded by the government with no need for advertising. Professionals in these English media organizations were often considered elite people as they were usually drawn from state cadres and were not journalists or editors. This has remained the case for most people working in the English-language media, at least at the national and central levels.

Language role

Starting in the early 1980s, English-language media in China took on another role – the language role. English-language media were used as tools for English-language learning among people who were eager to speak English in order to succeed professionally.

The language role of English-language media emerged in this social stage because of the open and reform policy adopted by the Government in the early 1980s. This called for a large number of people who could speak English, a popular "world language," to communicate internationally and to be engaged in all kinds of internationally-oriented activities. This role has remained important.

In order to learn English well, it is first of all imperative for learners to obtain good and up-to-date English materials. These were non-existent before the 1980s as English-learning could be considered a kind of "capitalist tail" in the Cultural Revolution (1967–76). Therefore, it was natural for English learners in China to turn to English-language media that were updating English content daily. As a result, many people started to listen to English news programs and read news reports in English, to find material for their English learning and to improve their English proficiency quickly rather than for the news value. Many adverts such as that shown in Figure 13.2 are bilingual and thus support both languages.

Three audience surveys of English-language media in China have supported this analysis. Since 1990 the Chinese audience has contained a very high percentage of English-language media users, sometimes even higher than that of the international audience.[13] The huge social demand for English learning materials had led to the creation of many English-learning tabloids such as the *21ˢᵗ Century* by the China Daily Group and *Shanghai Students Post* by the Jiefang Daily Group who also publish the party newspaper in Shanghai. These papers tried to satisfy the needs of the growing number of English learners, ranging from primary school students to adults.

Even Chinese newspapers opened up bilingual columns and pages for English learners as a way to promote their publications. Sometimes, the language role of the English-language media in China has been played up to such a degree that some media professionals have expressed doubts about the overall professionalism of these publications and thereby about the elite role of English-language media in China. According to Jiang Heping, former director of CCTV-9, English-learning newspapers are

Figure 13.2   A city bus advertises a toothpaste brand in Chinese and English.
Source: Wynne Wang

normally so language-oriented that they sometimes just provide English-learning materials and little in the way of information.

Many fear that the language role of English-language media in China may negate their professionalism and even weaken their ultimate goal of international communication. The language role in fact has acquired some distinctive features of its own:

- It is embedded in a social trend of a particular social period and is driven by a huge educational market. It is mostly limited to English-language newspapers, which are, to a degree, suitable as English readers and textbooks.
- It is complementary to the elite role, because both roles perform different social functions for English-language media in China and cannot replace each other in terms of their separate audiences; and
- Although it creates a large number of loyal readers and raises profits, their social influence is not comparable to the elite English-language media. In fact, some English-learning newspapers are simply being used to support financially weak elite publications, as in the case of *China Daily* and its *21st Century*.

Bridging role

In the early 1990s, English-language media started to develop a bridging role. These media increasingly became platforms for China's international communication. This role has been made possible through the development of the global information village. Technology made international communication much easier and efficient and the global public opinion environment much more diversified and transparent. The changing world public opinion environment demanded that English-language media in China employ a more effective communication model and abandon the propaganda model inherited from the past. The social structure of China has also undergone dramatic changes that call for fair, objective, and professional English news media, rather than propagandist media.

The bridging role provides a niche for the English-language media to reposition themselves in a new social environment and to change or reform their past propaganda style and model. The bridging role maintains a good balance of English-language media's party-line (elite and party functions to promote China's national interest) and bottom-line (professional and language functions to exchange information and seek understanding and trust.)

To a degree, the bridging role is an inevitable choice in this era of globalization and also the result of China's current social environment. The bridging role can be considered a combination of the elite and professional roles at a higher level, which may promote the professional development of English-language media in China. Furthermore, the bridging role of English-language media also demonstrates that these media bridge mostly in terms of political functions. In other words, their very bridging role itself shows English-language media have not yet fully merged with Chinese society. Although they are now mainstream politically they are still marginalized in terms of their social functions and their position in the media industry and in terms of their limited influence.[14]

Marginal Elite

Despite the recent increasing changing nature and number of English-language media, they remain a kind of marginal elite or elite minority in terms of circulation and influence in Chinese society.

Their marginality is well demonstrated in the fact that China still has only two English-language TV channels (CCTV-9 in Beijing and ICS in Shanghai), one English radio service (part of China Radio International, CRI), nine English-language dailies and weeklies and about 10 English magazines as well as a dozen English-language websites. In contrast, there are 1,900 Chinese radio and TV stations, 1,931 Chinese newspapers, 9,468 periodicals as of 2007 as well as nearly two million Chinese websites.[15] Further reasons can be identified for the current status.

First, English-language media exist in a Chinese environment where the majority of the population speaks and uses Chinese as the official language. English penetration has been very obvious in Chinese society and China has attracted an increasing number of English-speaking foreigners in the past three decades, particularly to big cities like Beijing and Shanghai. To a degree, English-language media are still popular among most foreign residents and visitors due to linguistic availability. Most Chinese turn to English-language media only when it is necessary, for example to communicate with their foreign colleagues. Even those Chinese who are fluent English speaker, readers, use Chinese when conversing with other Chinese even in an English-language environment. English-language media in China still lack a mature English environment for further development.

Second, as China enjoys a close relationship between its media system and politics, some local governments simply regard English-language media as a kind of ceremonial media (for demonstration purpose). They want to establish an English newspaper or English TV channel in their administrative region, but they may not pay much attention to the overall operations and may even ignore their usefulness for communicating with some audiences. The bureaucratic attitudes towards English-language media in China have, to some degree, contributed to English-language media's marginality in China.

Third, despite dramatic economic changes in the past three decades, media reforms in China (often considered part of political reforms) have been slow and have swung back and forth. In most cases these reforms have been limited to Chinese-language media. English-language media are usually outside the scope of the reforms unless there is a special reason such as the 2008 Beijing Olympics or 2010 Shanghai Exposition. As a result, despite dramatic changes in media consumption patterns and professional practices, private ownership of English-language media in China, as is the case for most media in China, is still a taboo. There was a break-through in 2003 when *Shanghai Daily* allowed foreign ownership. The otherwise unchanged status of English-language media ownership may affect their development and operational status in a commercial marketplace. This has thus placed them in the awkward position of a marginal media elite with only a marginal role in the Chinese society.

Future Trends

This chapter has predicted three trends for English-language media development in China in the near future.

First, English-language media in China will continue to make efforts to operate as commercial media instead of just tools of propaganda for the government, even though they are partially or fully funded by the government. They will continue to merge with the media industry within China as a whole.

However, English-language media will also continue to be a marginal elite even though they perform a variety of social roles. In other words, the English-language media's identity will continue to be an issue that will remain when it faces more direct competition from some "illegal" tabloids. For example, *That's Shanghai*, is a free publication available to foreign expatriates in Shanghai hotels, but considered illegal because it is registered by a local government in nearby Jiangsu Province. Like the *Wall Street Journal*, *That's Shanghai* is not supposed to be freely distributed in China.

Second, English-language media will continue to be centered in big cities like Beijing, Shanghai, and Guangzhou and have even formed their own respective models known as the Beijing Model, Shanghai Model and Guangzhou Model. English-language media under the Beijing Model are normally at the central level, with a focus on politics and the economy and have a more aggressive attitude and a higher level of professionalism. English-language media under the Shanghai Model concentrate more on the economy and lifestyle. The Shanghai Model is considered next to the Beijing Model in terms of its professionalism and overall operations because Shanghai has its colonial tradition of English-language publications. The Guangzhou Model's concentration on lifestyle and local flavor is facing fierce competition from non-Chinese English media from Hong Kong and overseas.

Third, Internet technology will continue to exert its influence as it allows free and uncontrolled exchange of information, at least technologically, between Chinese society and the outside world. This has forced English-language media to try to become more professional and market oriented. Thus, they have experienced the two-sided sword of globalization much earlier than the Chinese-language media. While the Internet effect has only begun to emerge, English-language media will inevitably have to address this technological issue.

Of course, it may also provide an opportunity to experiment with creating real English-language media in the Chinese-dominated society the Chinese way. In other words, they may be able to establish an English-language media in a Chinese environment that can effectively communicate with the rest of the world and also fit professionally into its roles in China.

14

Overseas Media Serve Chinese Diaspora

Numerous media systems, based on the Chinese language, are scattered throughout several nations in South Asia. Wherever there are significant numbers of ethnic Chinese living and working, there are also found media in Mandarin, or Cantonese – or English.

Today, Chinese people are dispersed in almost all parts of the world. A large number of Chinese are found in Southeast Asia, North America, and Europe, with fewer in South America, Africa, and Near Asia. In all there are an estimated 40 million Chinese in 130 other countries. About half of all Chinese overseas live in Southeast Asia. Where Chinese populations dominate, as in Hong Kong, Taiwan, and Singapore – all called the "Asian tigers" because of their economic success – or where Chinese constitute sometimes unpopular minorities as in Thailand, Malaysia, and Indonesia, there will be news and entertainment in the Chinese-language media.

The current media juggernaut of Communist China looms over and influences their ethnic brothers in cultural, political, and economic ways. These "overseas " Chinese all have similar media systems – traditional print and broadcasting making way for the new high-speed digital computers, cell phones, satellite broadcasting, text messaging so favored by today's youth the world over. The media in the Asian Tiger states, as in Beijing, operate under greater or lesser authoritarianism. In each nation, these media chafe under government restrictions but also generally support their nations and nudge them toward more democratic and open societies.

China's biggest state-controlled news organizations plan to spend billions of dollars to expand overseas as part of government efforts to improve the nation's image abroad and to create respected international news organizations.[1]

Hong Kong

This teeming, commercially vibrant island of 6.9 million would appear today to be an integral part of mainland China. Well, it is but it isn't. In 1842, China ceded Hong Kong to Britain. The free-wheeling British colony over time became an economic and financial powerhouse – mixing Chinese and Western influences. An outspoken press and lively populace developed a taste for press freedom and democracy. Hong Kong became a special administrative region of China in 1997.

Operating under the principle of "one country, two systems," China agreed to permit the island a high degree of autonomy and to preserve its economic and social systems for the next 50 years. China controls Hong Kong's foreign and defense policies but the territory has its own currency and customs controls. This uneasy relationship has continued for over 10 years. With British rule came unusual economic freedom and Hong Kong flourished and prospered. Media also enjoyed unusual freedom to report and criticize mainland China.

Since the 1997 return, the media have been more muted but Hong Kong is still home to many of Asia's biggest media players. In 2007, the international press group, Reporters Without Borders, noted that Hong Kong enjoyed real press freedom but said political and financial pressures from Beijing were on the rise.

Hong Kong has one of the largest film industries in China and is a major regional center for broadcasting and publishing. There are scores of Chinese language newspapers and a handful of dailies including the renowned *South China Morning Post* and an influential business paper, *The Standard*. Hong Kong is still a favorite place for foreign news organizations to locate their news bureaus.

During the 1989 riots in Tiananmen Square, the most outspoken public and media support for the demonstrators came from Hong Kong, then under British control. Only in Hong Kong could publisher Jimmy Lai's Next Media Inc. publications continue to defy Chinese authorities by agitating for press and political freedoms in China by pairing two unlikely subjects – democracy and sex. His financial success has triggered his competitors, including the top-selling *Oriental Daily News*, to imitate his publications' risqué, celebrity-centered style. Readers flock to his *Apple Daily* (*Ping Kuo Jih Pao*), which is second in the Hong Kong newspaper readership ratings, and his top-selling magazines. His US$600 million stake in Next Media Inc. makes him the wealthiest media owner in greater China. He sees no contradictions in his paparazzi journalism. "Just because we promote democracy doesn't mean we have to be puritan," he told the *Wall Street Journal* in October 1997. Lai's public battles make him an awkward liability to some democracy advocates and journalists who worry that his excesses may spark a government backlash in Hong Kong's relative oasis of free speech.[2]

Since the 1997 handover to Chinese rule, Hong Kong's press has so far avoided the government crackdown on its freedom that some had feared. Most of Hong Kong's publications are owned by companies or families with ties to Beijing or have aspirations to expand their businesses to the booming mainland. (Jimmy Lai even publishes an *Apple Daily* edition in Taiwan.) Some journalists see a creeping self censorship practiced by publications in order to curry favor with Beijing and advertisers. A recent survey of Hong Kong's journalists from the city's 15 Chinese language papers found that 31 percent had practiced self censorship or have observed the practice.

For the burgeoning Chinese film industry, Hong Kong's more open and tolerant environment has proved a boon. In late 2007, the ranks of mainland visitors to Hong Kong were swelled with many movie goers who flocked to see the full, uncut version of Director Ang Lee's film *Lust, Caution* about love and betrayal in Shanghai during World War II. On the mainland, the racy and explicit film had been heavily censored. This film reflected the rise of a class of affluent urbanites in China's eastern cities who are accustomed to having more choice in their lives. Many in the Chinese film industry support the idea of introducing a ratings system, like that in America, which advocates say would lessen the need for outright censorship. Movie people say the fact that a censored *Lust, Caution* was available at all in mainland China demonstrated how far the parameters of the acceptable had broadened since the beginning of China's reform era three decades ago. Movie makers in China well understand the censorship reality that may sometimes prevent the making of good movies, but they feel that the environment in Chinese cinema is becoming more and more relaxed.

Taiwan (Republic of China)

When Mao's army defeated the forces of Chiang Kai-Shek in 1949, the Nationalist army and followers fled to Taiwan (Formosa), an island of 13,885 square miles. Sixty years later Taiwan, with its estimated (2007) population of 20,546,500, has become another Asian economic success story. Beijing has long considered Taiwan an integral part of China but in recent years tensions have eased somewhat while economic exchanges and interdependency have increased. Even direct scheduled air service began between Taiwan and the mainland in late 2008, avoiding the circuitous route via Hong Kong air space that had previously been required. Taiwan has been evolving from a military authoritarianism toward an increasingly open and democratic society. This evolution has been aided by an increasingly independent media system replete with all the new media found in the other "Tiger" states.[3]

In 1987, President Chiang Ching-Kuo lifted martial law in Taiwan and encouraged the liberal forces that have brought about rapid change. Newspapers and other media played a major role, overcoming major taboos and expanding media freedom. Taboo subjects like criticism of government and its leaders, reportage about mainland China, and information about defense spending are now permitted. The military no longer controls the media and a law requiring the registration of newspapers has been lifted.

The public has a choice of a dozen daily papers and over 150 radio stations. Taiwan has five terrestrial TV stations competing with 70 cable systems. Currently 16 domestic Taiwanese communication satellite stations offer 94 satellite channels and 16 foreign communication satellite broadcasters offer 31 channels.

Taiwanese citizens travel to mainland China and many local companies have invested in mainland enterprises. As much of the population becomes better educated and more affluent, the Taiwan media have in turn become much more informative, offering more outspoken news and comment.[4]

Singapore

Singapore was an early success story in economic growth and media development but one achieved without press freedom or representative democracy. Admittedly Singapore is a special case – a small city state without multitudes of rural peasants. With 4.4 million people crowded on a small island of only 255 square miles at the southern tip of the Malay peninsula it was one of most dramatic examples of economic development in the post-WWII world. This collection of poor, fractured, and contentious communities of mostly Chinese (77 percent), plus Malays (16 percent) and

Indians (6 percent) evolved into a prosperous society of highly educated, well-housed, gainfully employed citizens enjoying a per capita income of US$27,490 (source: World Bank, 2006). Currently its economy is driven by electronics manufacturing and financial services. Economic success has turned the state into a place where telephones (and electronics) work, streets are clean, the air is clear, and water is pure. Mandarin and English are the main languages. However, Singapore has always had its critics; one wag called it Disneyland with the death penalty.

Singapore has been ruled in an autocratic manner since 1951 by Lee Kwan Yew and his People's Action Party (PAP). Even his many enemies have conceded that Lee and his arbitrary actions made Singapore what it is today. Prime Minister Lee yielded to his protégée Goh Chok Tong in 1991. His son, Lee Hsien Loong, took over in August 2004 without an election as part of a planned takeover of power. The elder Lee, though retired still enjoys great influence. The elder Lee has long and often intervened in most aspects of public affairs, especially the press. Singapore's media are highly regulated; censorship is common. Internet access is regulated, and private ownership of satellite receivers is not allowed. Government officials, and mainly the elder Lee, acquired a long record of winning defamation suits against foreign publications. The media watchdog group, Reporters Without Borders, has charged that the domestic press is in the grip of a rigorous self censorship over its coverage of domestic politics. In response Prime Minister Lee Hsien Loong charged that international media were trying to impose "their norms and their standards" in the area of freedom of expression. He said that Asian countries that got "the best financial results were those whose media was less aggressive."[5]

Two organizations dominate the media. Singapore Press Holdings, which maintains close ties with the ruling party, has a virtual monopoly of the newspapers. Media Corp, owned by a state investment agency, operates radio and television stations. Political debate has found an outlet on the Internet. However those who post political material are expected to register with the authorities. Hence, political dissidents are quickly identified and intimidated. Singapore Press Holdings (SPH) publishes 15 newspapers and six magazines plus the *Straits Times*, a long-standing well-known regional newspaper. With its control of all local media, Lee and the PAP eliminated all challenges to Lee's authoritarian control of what is ostensibly a parliamentary democracy.

Tiny Singapore has quarreled with and harassed the Western press more than any other nation in South Asia. *Time*, *Newsweek*, *Financial Times*, and

The Economist have all had run-ins with Singapore's government. The most difficulties were faced by the *Asian Wall Street Journal*, a daily, and the *Far Eastern Economic Review*, a weekly, because they both maintained resident correspondents in Singapore. Penalties administered were rather novel – *Wall Street Journal*'s local circulation of 10,000 was restricted to 500 copies. Singapore has shown that if economic and social opportunities for development are present, then an authoritarian political atmosphere does not preclude media growth. However, a direct result of Lee's "Singapore Inc." is the lack of diversity and meaningful discussion of public affairs. Singapore has adopted the rhetoric and precepts of capitalism: investment, saving, free trade, global economy productivity, etc., but the Singaporean government has shown little concern for free speech, press freedom, or political pluralism. In fact, Lee has often argued that Singapore is a special situation and cannot afford the luxury of free expression.

Among the Asian Tigers, Singapore has clearly won the admiration of Beijing with its successful combination of economic prosperity with authoritarian control over the media and many other aspects of life.[6] Singapore rather than Taiwan or Hong Kong may be the most attractive role model for mainland China to follow – for today, but perhaps not for the long term.

There are some large Chinese communities in English-speaking countries outside Asia, and, of course, there are Chinese-language media there to serve them. Some of the media targeting these Chinese communities are in English, reaching out to the generations that have lost cultural attachments to China. These media have helped the Chinese communities outside China develop "a distinct and practical way of being Chinese".[7] The United States has about three million people defined by the US census as Chinese. There are four US TV networks with at least some programming in the Chinese language plus more than a dozen Chinese TV stations. There are a dozen radio stations and an equal number of daily newspapers in Chinese circulating in the United States. Also, targeting the United States Chinese language community are dozens of weeklies, monthlies, and special interest publications in Chinese. Some of these media mix English and Chinese programs and articles.[8]

Canada has two TV networks for its Chinese communities along with radio stations and publications. Australia's 24-hour Chinese-language radio station 3CW in Melbourne became a business success as well as a highly influential community voice. It has an English and Chinese website. New Zealand's small population of Chinese includes about 25,000 first generation immigrants. Its Chinese media are mainly in English. The United Kingdom's 250,000 Chinese, mostly immigrants from Hong Kong and Southeast Asia, do not have an extensive media to serve them. They do, however, have DimSum, an English-language Internet site that provides the dispersed Chinese community with news and has been used to rally members to protest against perceived discrimination.[9]

The long-term future of the Chinese language media in these English-speaking countries is possibly showcased by DimSum. Separated geographically from their homeland, these Chinese may not need these media after the immigrant generation passes on.

Unfettered News Into China

China's impressive capability to communicate throughout Asia and indeed the whole world implies that the People's Republic will be on the receiving end of messages, some of which it disapproves of and would censor if it could. Chinese authorities have periodically jammed incoming transmissions of the BBC, Voice of America (VOA), and the US-funded Radio Free Asia. China also continues to block websites it regards as politically sensitive.

When the government blocked news of the 1989 Tiananmen Square riots, many millions in rural China learned about it from short wave radio broadcasts in Mandarin from the BBC and VOA. It has been estimated that more than 50 million people in mainland China tune in to foreign radio stations for information they cannot get from Chinese sources. Chinese authorities are active in blocking these broadcasts.

Recently, a small media empire based outside China has enabled dissidents supporting Falun Gong, a spiritual and meditation movement banned by Beijing as an "evil cult," to speak out against the suppressions. One organization, the New Tang Dynasty Television, has been sending satellite broadcasts to China from North America since 2002. Viewers can tune in via satellite or via the Internet. The Chinese government has banned individual satellite dishes, but illegal ownership is widespread. New Tang has been extended to Asia, Europe, and Australia with 24-hour broadcasts in Chinese and English plus interactive websites in a number of languages. Its supporters say that it allows an opposition viewpoint to be heard.

Other media and cultural groups funded by Falun Gong followers include the Sound of Hope Network which originated in local Chinese radio operations in San Francisco in 2001. Now it broadcasts in five languages in 11 countries in North America, Asia, and Europe. It is also available online and can be found on short wave and satellite radio beamed into China. Another important dissenting voice comes from old media, *The Epoch Times*, a Chinese newspaper with online editions from New York City. Since 2003, the paper has been printed in 10 languages and distributed in 29 nations of North and South America, Europe, and Asia with 17 languages on the Internet.[10]

Through its embassies and legations abroad the Chinese government is well aware of these overseas media groups. In November 2007, the Canadian Broadcasting Corporation (CBC) cancelled a documentary about the Falun Gong 24 hours before its scheduled broadcasting. The CBC said its decision was influenced by phone calls from Chinese diplomats in Canada and the fact that the CBC was scheduled to broadcast the Beijing Olympics to Canada several months later.

Impact of Out Migration

A recent wave of Chinese diaspora may create new media markets as some of the newly affluent Chinese emigrate to South East Asia, North America, and Europe. Many of China's younger generation – well educated and affluent – are moving their families abroad but still working in China. Around the world, some large cities have minority populations of 300,000 to 400,000 Chinese. As mentioned, the total expatriate population has been estimated at 40 million with most living in Southeast Asia.

Mass Chinese migration in the modern era began as early as the nineteenth century but what is different now is that the new emigrants are more affluent and better educated. According to a 2006 UN report, mainland China had a net emigration of nearly 400,000 each year between 2000 and 2005.

Media Chinese International, created in 2008 from a merger controlled by Malaysian tycoon Tiong Hiew King, claims to be the largest Chinese-language publisher outside greater China. The group includes the Hong Kong-based *Ming Pao Daily*, Malaysia's Sin Chew media and Nanyang Press Holdings, and about 30 magazines. It distributes to Hong Kong, Canada, the US, Malaysia, and Indonesia.[11]

Also, as mentioned above, Beijing's state controlled media are planning overseas expansions aimed at migrant Chinese and the world at large. They are trying to acquire international media assets as they want to open more international news bureaus and to publish and broadcast more broadly in English and other languages. Some Chinese media have announced plans to hire English-speaking Chinese and foreign media specialists. The plan, first announced on January 15, 2009 in the *South China Morning Post*, includes the creation of a 24-hour news channel modeled on Al Jazeera, the Arabic-language news network, with correspondents around the world. The media outlets planning to expand overseas include China Central Television (CCTV;) Xinhua, the state-run news agency; *People's Daily*, the news organ of the Communist Party; and the Shanghai Media Group.[12]

CCTV, China's biggest and richest television network, already broadcasts in English, Spanish, and French. No decisions have been made on the media expansion but the aim is to improve China's image abroad and to gain more respect for its international news organizations with, possibly, less control from Beijing. Some China experts believe China has been concerned with its image overseas and does not like the way that China is portrayed by the international news media. So, one way to deal with this difficulty would be to set up a 24-hour news channel that could reach the US, Europe, and other parts of the world. There is a felt need to match China's communication status with its global economic status. For such an expansion into international news communication, China certainly has the financial resources and capable, trained journalists to achieve these goals – if the central government can refrain from interfering with journalists and imposing controls on the news. Otherwise these global voices will lack credibility with the 40 million Chinese overseas as well as the rest of the world.

15

Conclusion

Within a 30-year period China has developed an extensive and highly advanced system of mass communication based on electronic satellite communication, Internet computers, cell phones, and other digital systems.

These sophisticated ways of sharing information and spreading ideas, news, trends, and lifestyles have subtly shaped public opinion and discourse for many millions of educated and increasingly affluent city dwellers. As a result, many Chinese are enjoying greater freedom of thought and expression. Multitudes of Chinese – chatting and listening over cell phones and computers – cannot be silenced or persuaded and controlled as they were when Mao led China.

As the previous chapters explained, China today enjoys complex and highly advanced media through its newspapers, magazines, radio and television broadcasting, and cinema accompanied by the necessary ancillary services of advertising and public relations. In the cities advertisements vie for attention (see Figure 15.1). These media and services, while technically still "owned" by the ruling Communist Party, are in fact influenced strongly by market and financial forces and are constantly evolving. These media must become and remain profitable or they will wither and die.

Electronic communication in China is rapidly changing attitudes and perceptions as has been the case in Western nations. Flux and change permeate mass media everywhere. Many millions of poor rural peasants, however, are not reached by mass media and that is important.

A careful reader of this book may be surprised and impressed by how well media are established and institutionalized in China today. A Western traveler in Shanghai cannot escape the feeling that much in modern China is "just like us." Maybe so but beyond the technology and

Figure 15.1 A Western ice cream brand, a Turkish restaurant, and the Goodyear blimp compete for attention in a city area.
Source: Wynne Wang

images, mass communication is of course very Chinese in its cultural and social content.

China's commitment to journalism and communication education and training reflects the government's intention to keep up with and even surpass other nations. According to Professor Guo Ke, China in 2009 had a total of 650 undergraduate communication programs in 360 colleges and universities. These include 250 advertising programs, 180 journalism programs, 128 broadcasting (radio and television) programs, 50 editing and publishing programs, as well as 20 in communication.

At the graduate level, Chinese universities have 123 master's programs in journalism and mass communication with 60 journalism masters programs and 19 masters programs and 19 doctoral programs – 10 for journalism and 9 for communication.[1]

For universities in general, during 2009, 6.1 million students will graduate – nearly six times as many as in 2000. For the following year, 2010, the total is expected to rise to about 7 million. Where will they all go? Will jobless students create problems for campus stability?[2]

Billions were spent by China in the preparation and hosting of the 2008 Olympics at Beijing and then more to promote China's image as a great global power. However, other efforts such as arresting potential political dissidents may have proved to be counter productive in burnishing China's worldwide image. Official statistics on security crackdowns related to the Olympics reported that in the first 11 months of 2008 1,100 people had been indicted in the Western region of Xinjiang on suspicion of "endangering state security." This was considered an extraordinarily large number for the indictments which cover inciting separatism and can carry the death penalty.[3] Despite the negative images, the Chinese government persists in suppressions of political rights of minority groups.

Greater Threats Loom

In December 2008 the ruling Communist Party celebrated the thirtieth anniversary of the reform era that transformed China into a global economic power and, in so doing, changed the world. President Hu Jintao invoked the name of Deng Xiaoping who consolidated power in 1978 and began "reform and opening." "Only development makes sense," said Hu quoting Deng. Beyond the oratory, Hu and other Chinese leaders were then facing a new era in which Deng's export-led economic model as well as his tight political control faced unprecedented challenges. In the incipient global recession world demand for Chinese goods slumped and unrest was on the rise in the industrial heartland as China began scrambling for a new formula to preserve stability and to ensure economic growth. The economic turndown was so swift that exports fell for the first time in 7 years and Beijing was being forced to abruptly shift its priorities. Factories were closing, many jobs were lost and fears increased about possible strikes and political unrest.

The government had shifted from its promises to curb rampant pollution and income inequality and instead focused on restoring tax breaks for exporters and pushing down the value of Chinese currency to encourage exports. Politically, Chinese reformers had hoped that, after the Olympics, some measure of political reform to address official corruption and help in the diffusion of social tension would be imposed.

As Beijing worried about strikes and mass layoffs, it seemed that official intolerance of political dissent had narrowed.[4] Public security administrator Meng Jianzhu warned leading officers in Beijing in early January 2009 that "The present situation of maintaining national security and social stability is grave. China faces economic pains, sensitive anniversaries."[5] In the months that followed, China's economy rebounded and appeared to lead Europe and America out of the recession.

This was indeed a challenge for China's serious news media. Obviously media will try to explain and ameliorate the nation's woes but at the same time the media may face dangers to its own freedoms as it deals with an increasingly arbitrary government. Yet, a freer and more independent press would help the nation cope with its deepening troubles.

In April 2009, China attended a world economic summit in London with a sense of momentum and an economy that seemed to be prospering while most of the world still suffered. With US$2 trillion in exchange reserves, China was viewed as a savior to an ailing economy.[6] Even with all its financial resources, China still must deal with factors threatening its growth: widespread poverty; authoritarian rule; a culture shrouded by decades of isolation; and poorly understood intentions. China, it has been argued, will not realize its global ambitions until it resolves these problems. While megacities boom and China's coast becomes the world's factory, 800 million of the nation's 1.3 billion people remain farmers with many mired in poverty. So China remains a developing country, still vying for first world status.

Such reservations about China's future have been echoed by John Pomfret long time China expert for the Washington Post. Despite its impressive economic gains, Pomfret doubts China is destined to become another superpower.[7] Pomfret believes there are four big constraints that darken China's future: 1. dire demographics; 2. an over-rated economy; 3. an environment under siege; and 4. an ideology that doesn't travel well.

First, demographics – a rapidly aging China may become the first nation to become old before it becomes rich. As a result of the one-child-per-family policy, the average number of children born to a Chinese woman has dropped to 1.8 today, below the ratio of 2 : 1 needed to stabilize the population. Additionally, life expectancy has increased from 35 in 1949 to more than 73 today. So, as the working population shrinks labor costs rise. Ominously, China's elderly will pose a great crisis: their numbers will balloon from 100 million people aged over 60 today to 334 million by 2050, including 100 million aged 80 or older. This has been called a slow motion humanitarian tragedy in the making.

As for the economy, Pomfret says that with 1.3 billion people, China should have a big economy. However, on a per capita basis, the economy sits in one-hundred-and-ninth position on the World Economic Outlook Database, right between Swaziland and Morocco. The economy is large but its average living standard is low and will stay that way for a long time.[8]

China leads the world in environmental woes. In 2008, it surpassed the United States as the world's number 1 emitter of greenhouse gases and it's the largest polluter of the Pacific Ocean. Pomfret points out that China has 16 of the world's 20 most polluted cities. By 2030, China will face a water shortage equal to the amount that it consumes today. To sum up Pomfret points to another weakness in the view about China's inevitable rise: "The place remains an authoritarian state run by a party that limits the free flow of information, stifles ingenuity, and doesn't know how to self-correct."[9]

Publicly, at least, Chinese leaders reject such criticism. China's number 2 Communist Party official recently issued a terse and complete disavowal of interest in Western democracy. Wu Bangguo said China would never adopt a multiparty political system, separation of powers, a bicameral legislature, or an independent judiciary.[10] The comments established a hard line against political reform when the leadership was worried about political protests. The previous December more than 300 intellectuals and dissidents had demanded that China abandon Communist rule and move toward a more democratic system. Without a single Communist Party in control, Wu said, a nation "as large as China would be torn by strife and incapable of accomplishing anything."[11]

Western Media Look To India

After years of deal making and lobbying in China, American media companies feel they have not accomplished a great deal and appear to be shifting their attention instead to India. US media executives still think Chinese audiences are receptive to Western culture but many are pulling back out of frustration over censorship, piracy, strict restrictions on foreign investments, and the glacial pace of Chinese bureaucracy. [12] America Online (AOL) closed down Chinese operations for the second time. Warner Bros., the movie studio aligned with AOL Time Warner, had plans as of 2006 to open more than 200 retail stores in China with a local partner, but has now shelved the plans. The focus is now on India with its growing economy and few impediments for foreign media investments. This is a stark reversal. For US media companies frustrations, in China, have been growing. For several years now, China has restricted the number of foreign films that can be shown in cinemas to 20. In November 2008, Warner became the first studio to say it would make new movies available in China over a video-on-demand at prices low enough – 60 cents to US$1 – to compete with pirated versions. That service is still not underway. Even with access, only a tiny portion of the Chinese populace can be reached. In China, CNN International is available only in hotels that cater for foreign business travelers and in embassies. Viacom has MTV China but only reaches about 14 million homes in the area around Guangdong near the coast.

Despite his strenuous efforts to expand in China media magnate Rupert Murdoch has had only limited success. Besides his MySpace China, a joint operation by the News Corporation, there is only his Star TV, a Pan Asian Satellite service, which has channels in China but reaches only a small presence on mainland China. The company has significantly cut its staff in recent years.

In time, China (and the world) will emerge from the current global recession. The news media will become, if permitted, a more effective agent for stability as well as change if political and social changes arrive in the Middle Kingdom. Greater autonomy for the media will make possible more and meaningful debates about public issues and opportunities to discuss politics. For that to happen, the Chinese people must able to elect their own public officials and to enjoy an honest and even-handed judicial system, in effect to establish the rule of law.

The crux of China's deep problem concerning press freedom and freedom of expression was well stated by Xin Xin who wrote: "China's media are regulated mainly by administrative order, rather than by a well-established legal system. China does not have media law. This enables the central government to change policy and regulation more flexibly."[13]

In the years ahead, China faces such endemic problems as water shortages, a widely polluted environment, and the time bomb of a rapidly aging population plus a myriad of other social and economic challenges. However, by late 2009, China's economy was roaring back[14] – just eight months after Chinese workers had rioted outside of factories closed by the global downturn. Many factories reopened and rehiring began. Even the hardest hit – those depending on exports to the US and Europe were starting to rehire workers.

A more vigorous and free press would greatly help China deal with such challenges.

Notes

Introduction

1 Yin, Jing and Hall, Bradford J. (2002) "Talking Cultures: A Comparative Analysis of Chinese and American Stories about Human Rights," in *Chinese Communication Studies: Contexts and Comparisons*, eds. Xing Lu, Wenshan Jia and D. Ray Heisey, Westport, CT: Ablex Publishing, 210.

2 Yuhui, Fu (2007) "A Summary of Internet and Online Media Research in 2006 in China," *Journal of International Communication*, 147, January, Beijing: Renmin University School of Journalism, 21–4.

3 Nuo, You (2007) "We need investigative journalists," *China Daily*, June 18, 4.

4 Barboza, David "Pushing (and Toeing) the Line in China," *New York Times*, April 18, C3.

5 Surveys conducted by one of the editors in two classes at Fudan University and Shanghai International Studies University in Shanghai, China, in May 2007. Other surveys of students have found the same interests at other schools. Graduate students tend to be more professionally focused.

6 Tau-fu, Zhang (2006) "The Reconstruction of the Social Function for China's Media," *China Media Research*, 2, 3, July.

7 French, Howard W. (2005) "Fashion Magazines Rush to Mold China's Sense of Style," *New York Times*, October 3, A10.

8 Griffiths, Dan (2005) "China's Breakneck Media Revolution," BBC News, August 19; "China's Media: Back on the Leash," *The Economist*, August 18, 2005, 50.

Chapter 1

1 Nicholas Kristof, (2008) "A Not So Fine Romance," *New York Times*, April 8, A23.

2   "Chinese students, Canadians Protests against Tibetan rioters, Media Distortions," *People's Daily*, March 30, 2008.

3   Lee, Chin-Chuan (2003), "The Global and the National of the Chinese Media: Discourses, Market Technology, and Ideology," in *Chinese Media, Global Contexts*, ed. Chin-Chuan Lee, London: Routledge/Curzon, 1–31.

4   "Police Tighten grip; China says Olympics won't be Disrupted," Associated Press, March 19, 2008.

5   Fan, Maureen (2008) "Chinese Media Take Firm Stand On Openness About Earthquake," *Washington Post*, May 18, A18.

6   "Days of Disaster," *The Economist*, May 17, 2008, 51.

7   Jacobs, Andrew (2008) "To the Rescue, Uncensored," *New York Times*, May 14, A1.

8   French, Howard W. (2008) "Earthquake Opens Gap in Control on Media," *New York Times*, May 18, Y6.

9   Nicholas Zamiska, (2008) "Quake Quiets the Critics of China's Human-Rights Record," *Wall Street Journal*, May 20, A8.

10 Dyer, Geoff and Dickie, Mure (2008) "The Caring Face of China," *Financial Times*, May 17, 9.

11 Mitchell, Tom (2008) "Beijing Tells Media to Rein in Quake Coverage," *Financial Times*, June 2, 21.

12 Areddy, James T. (2008) "China Stifles Parents' Complaints about Collapsed Schools," *Wall Street Journal*, June 18, A10.

13 Anderlini, James (2008) "New Spirit of Citizen Activism Unsettles Beijing," *Financial Times*, August 4, 3; Hooker, Jake (2008) "Voice Seeking Answers for Parents About a School Collapse Is Silenced," *New York Times*, July 11, A5.

14 Eimer, David (2009) "Sichuan Earthquake Anniversary: Parents of Victims Told Not to Hold Memorials," Telegraph.co.uk (online version), May 12.

15 "School House Safety Under Check Nationwide," *China Daily*, May 12, 2009.

16 Eimer, op. cit.

17 Barboza, David (2009) "Artist Defies Web Censors in a Rebuke of China," *New York Times*, March 20, A6.

18 Rich, Frank (2008) "Last Call for Change We Can Believe In," *New York Times*, August 24, wk 9.

19 "Global Media Coverage of Beijing Olympics Avoids Politics," University of Maryland, September 17, 2008.

20 Fowler, Geoffrey A. and Meichtry, Stacy (2008) "China Counts Cost of Hosting the Olympics," *Wall Street Journal*, July 16, A12.

21 Lin-Liu, Jen (2008) "Beijing Under Wraps," *New York Times*, August 4, A21.

22 "Uneasy Relations: China and Foreign Press," AP Reports, August 13 2008; Bradsher, Keith (2008) "China is Said to Restore Blocks on Web Sites," *New York Times*, December 16.

23 Blumenstein, Rebecca, Batson, Andrew and Fowler, Geoffrey A. (2008) "China Takes a More Open Stance With Foreign Press," *Wall Street Journal*, August 1–3, A5; Bradsher, Keith (2008) "China is Said to Restore Blocks on Web Sites," *New York Times*, December 16.

24 Wong, Edward (2008) "Would-Be Protesters Find the Olympics Failed to Expand Free Speech in Beijing," *New York Times*, September 12, A6.

25 Venter, Nick (2008) "China – Orwell's Dream Come True," *Dominion Post* (New Zealand), August 25.

26 Bradsher, Keith (2008) "China Lists Dos and Don'ts for Olympics," *New York Times*, June 3, A6.

27 Kristof, Nicholas D. (2008) "Terrorism and the Olympics," *New York Times*, May 29, A27.

28 Barboza, David (2008) "Chinese TV Hits Jackpot with Games," *New York Times*, August 22, C1.

29 Pan, Philip P. (2008) *Out of Mao's Shadow*, New York: Simon & Schuster, 320.

30 Kristof, Nicholas D. (2008) "Malcontents Need Not Apply," *New York Times*, August 16.

31 *The Guardian*, July 1, 2009, 4.

32 Personal communication to Anne Cooper-Chen, November 4, 2008.

33 Cui, Xiaohuo (2008) "China's Journalists 'An Unhealthy Lot,'" *China Daily*, November 8–9, 1.

Chapter 2

1 Robert L. Bishop, (1989) *Qui Lai: Mobilizing One Billion Chinese: The Chinese Communication System*, Ames: Iowa State University Press, 29. Professor Bishop's pioneering work was very useful for this study.

2 Roswell Britton, (1933) *The Chinese Periodical Press, 1800–1912*, Shanghai: Kelly and Walsh, 1–2, quoted in Bishop, op. cit., 41.

3 Roswell Britton, op. cit., 2, quoted in Bishop, op. cit., 42.

4 Philip P. Pan, (2008) *Out of Mao's Shadow*, New York: Simon & Schuster, xiv.

5 Ibid.

6 Ibid, xvi.

7 Michael B. Hinner, (2006) "An Attempt to Harmonize the Conflicting Images of China," *China Media Research*, 2, 3, July, 31–42.

8 Brian Knowlton, (2008) "Economy Helps Make Chinese Lead in Optimism," *New York Times*, July 23, A8.

Chapter 3

1 Blogcount.com December 1, 2008.

2 Anti, Michael (2007) "The End of the Golden Age of Blogs in China," November 27.

3 Anderlini, Jamil (2005) "Blog Founder Seeks Success Writ Large," *South China Morning Post*, July 12, www.asiamedia..ucla.edu/eastasia.asp

4 Rein, Shaun (2006) "China's New Obsession with Blogs and How Companies Can Benefit," *China Stocks*, July 11.

5 Lee, Chin-Chuan (2000) "Chinese Communication: Prisms, Trajectories and Modes of Understanding," in *Power, Money and Media: Communication Patterns and Bureaucratic Control in Cultural China*, ed. Chin-Chuan Lee, Evanston, IL: Northwestern University Press, 10.

6 Zhao, Y. (1998) *Media, Markets and Democracy in China*, Urbana, IL: University of Illinois Press, 182.

7 "Q&A: China's New Internet Restrictions," *New York Times*, September 29, 2005.

8 Yardley, Jim (2003) "Internet Column on Sex Thrills, and Inflames, China," *New York Times*, November 30.

9 Weifeng, Liu (2007) "Long Way to Go to Win 'People's War,'" *China Daily*, June 5, 5; Zhao, J. (2008) "A Snapshot of Internet Regulations in Contemporary China: Censorship, Profitability and Responsibility," *China Media Research*, 4, 3, 37–42.

10 Ibid.

11 Barboza, David (2008) "The Wild Web of China," *New York Times*, May 7, A1.

12 French, Howard W. (2006) "Mob Rule on China's Internet: The Keyboard as Weapon," *The International Herald Tribune*, June 1, 1.

13 French, Howard W. (2006) "As Chinese Students Go Online, Little Sister is Watching," *New York Times*, May 9, A2.

14 Zhang, Lena L. (2006), "Behind the 'Great Firewall:' Decoding China's Internet Policies from the Inside," *The International Journal of Research into New Media Policies*, 12, 3, 271–91.

15 Chadwick, Andrew (2006) *Internet Politics*, New York: Oxford University Press, 281.

16 Benjamin Bates, (2008) "Implications of Digital Network Economy for Chinese Media," Panel presentation at the Convention of Association for Education in Journalism and Mass Communication, Chicago, August.

17 "Are Firewalls Burning?" *China Digital Times*, March 18, 2008.

18 Xiaobing, Jin (2006) "The Vanishing of Internet Anonymity" *China Media Reports*, October, 17.

19 Pan, Zhongdang (2000) "Improvising Reform Actvities," in *Power, Money and Media: Communication Patterns and Bureaucratic Control in Cultural China*, Chin-Chuan Lee, ed., Evanston, IL: Northwestern University Press, 73.

20 Hua, Tan (2007) "Media Power and Rural Society." *China Media Report*, 22, 2, February, 95–104; Suxia, Zheng (2007) "Territorial Differences of Internet Diffusion in Mainland China," *Journal of International Communication*, Renmin University, 148, February, 55–9.

21 Fung, Anthony Y.H. (2008) *Global Capital, Local Culture: Transnational Media Corporations in China*, New York: Peter Lang, 158.

22 Zhong, Wu (2006) "Chinese Newspapers Mull Internet Boycott," *Asia Times*, June 13.

23 Hille, Kathrin (2008) "Mass Legal Challenge to Baidu." *Financial Times*, December 1, 17.

24 "Major News Websites Back Internet Self-censorship." Xinhua, April 12, 2006.

25 Rosen, Jeffrey (2008) "Google's Gatekeepers," *New York Times Magazine*, November 30, 55.

26 Markoff, John (2008) "Skype Text is Monitored by China," *New York Times*, October 2, C1.

27 www.07908.com/viewthread.php?tid=3325

28 Ha, Louisa S. and Ganahl III, Richard J. (2007) *Webcasting Worldwide*, Mahwah, NJ: Lawrence Erlbaum Associates, 273.

29 Niholas Ning, (2007) "Baidu Team Up with Video Share Site," *Shanghai Daily*, June 9–10, B3.

30 LaFraniere, Sharon (2009) "China's Students Feel a Faint Tug from the Ghosts of Tiananmen," *New York Times*, May 22, A1.

31 "Be Patriotic? First Be Cool!" *China Digital Times*, November 20, 2008.

32 Wu, Xu (2007) *Chinese Cyber Nationalism*, London: Rowman & Littlefield, 54–5.

33 Kim, Louisa (2008) "Podcasters Push the Limits in China," *All Things Considered* (National Public Radio), March 8.

34 French, Howard W. (2007) "Homeowner Stares Down Wreckers, at Least for a While," *New York Times*, March 27, A4.

35 "China's First Blogger: Isaac Mao," *Guardian* online version, August 8, 2008.

36 Kinsley, Michael (2008) "Too Much Information," *Time*, December 1, 84.

37 "Oh Grow up! Blogging is No Longer What it Was Because it has Entered the Mainstream," *The Economist*, November 8–14, 2008, 82.

38 Anti op. cit.

39 Yuhui, Fu (2007) "A Summary of Internet and Online Media Research in 2006 in China," *Journal of International Communication*, Renmin University, 147, January, 21–4.

40 Jia, Wenshan, Lu, Xing and Heisey, D. Ray (eds.) (2002) *Chinese Communication Theory and Research*, Westport, CT: Ablex Publishing, 37, 235; Wu, Xu op. cit., 108.

41 Habermas, Jürgen, (1989) *The Structural Transformation of the Public Sphere*, Cambridge, MA: MIT Press.

42 Jia, op. cit., 231–2.

43 Donald, Stephanie H. and Keane, Michael (2002) "Media in China-New Convergences, New Approaches," in *Media in China: Consumption, Content and Crisis*, eds. Stephanie Hemelnyk Donald, Michael Keane and Yin Hong, New York: RoutledgeCurzon, 4.

44 Macartney, Jane (2006) "China's Web Censors are Losing the Battle," *New York Times*, February 16.

45 Dickie, Mure (2007) "China President Urges Party Officials to 'Purify' the Internet," *Financial Times*, January 26, 1.

46 Lee, Chin-Chuan (2003) "The Global and the National of the Chinese Media: Discourses, Markets, Technology and Ideology," in *Chinese Media, Global Contexts*, ed. Chin Chuan Lee, London: Routledge/Curzon, 14.

47 "China: Censors Bar Mythical Creature," *New York Times*, March 20, 2009, A10.

48 "Trying to Evade the Censors," *New York Times*, June 4, 2009, A10.

49 "China Rounds Up Dissidents, Blocks Twitter," *Associated Press*, June 2, 2009.

50 Wines, Michael and Jacobs, Andrew (2009) "To Shut Off Tiananmen Talk, China Blocks Sites," *New York Times*, June 2.

Chapter 4

1 Hu, Huang (2001) *Development History of Journalism Industry in China*, Shanghai: Fudan University Publishing House, 23.

2 Jiang, Ling and Yuming, Feng (eds.) (2007) *The Development Report of China's Newspaper Industry*, Beijing: Social Sciences Academic Press, 43–5.

3 Streitmatter, Roger (1994) "The Americanization of Chinese Journalism," unpublished observations.

4 Lee, P.S. (1994) "Mass Communication and National Development in China: Media Roles Reconsidered," *Journal of Communication*, 44, 22–37.

5 Ning, Zhang (2007) "Government and Social Power Structures as Represented in the Media Landscape," unpublished PhD dissertation, Fudan University.

6 Jiang, Ling and Yuming, Feng op. cit., 33–7.

7 Dianyuan, Zhang (2007) *Innovation of the Chinese Newspaper Media System*, Guangzhou: Nanfang Daily Press, 2.

8 Jiang, Ling and Yuming, Feng op. cit., 107.

9 Cited from the annual report available at http://library.corporate-ir.net/ library/84/846/84662/items/233865/06AnnualReport.pdf

10 Jiang, Ling and Yuming, Feng op. cit., 35.

11 The survey was carried out in November 2005 by a research group of the People's University in Beijing, China.

12 In 2005, China published three central party newspapers, 41 provincial party newspapers and 391 local party newspapers, figures from the 2007 Development Report of China's Newspaper Industry.

13 Professional newspapers refer to newspapers that target readership in a particular area such as real estate, technology, agriculture, English or Chinese learning, world news, economy etc.

14 Jiang, Ling and Yuming, Feng op. cit., 43.

15 Liangrong, Li (2003) "On the Dual-Track Media Systems in China," *Modern Communication*, 4th ed.

16 Zhao, Yuezhi (1998) *Media, Market, and Democracy in China*, Chicago and Urbana: University of Illinois Press, 5.

17 They are Chengdu Commerce Daily, Jiefang Daily Group, Beijing Youth Daily, People's Daily Group, and *China Computer Daily*.

18 In fact, due to severe competition from the Internet and TV industry, in 2006 *Beijing Youth Daily* only made use of 3 percent of the investment that it gained from the stock market in 2004 and its operating revenues were down almost 8 percent in 2006 compared with 2005.

19 Taken from a report on the China Journalism & Communication Review website, on January 4, 2008.

20 These political campaigns include the Campaign against Spiritual Pollution in 1984 and the Campaign against Bourgeois Liberalization in 1986 and the Campaign against Peaceful Evolution in 1989 after the Tiananmen event in Beijing.

21 Liancheng, Duan (1998) *How to Help Foreigners to Know China: Principles and Skills of Communication*, Beijing: China Reconstructs Press, 159.

Chapter 5

1 This is based on a figure quoted by Cui Baoguo and Zhang Xiaoqun in their article "2008: China's Media Entering the World," in *Report on Development of China's Media Industry*, ed. Cui Baoguo, (2008) p. 21 from www.ctrmi.com. It shows that in 2006, TV, newspapers, magazines, radio, and Internet accounts for 28.8, 19.9, 1.5, 3.6, and 2.9 percent respectively of total advertising. However, magazine advertising revenue increased dramatically in 2007, from 2.41 billion yuan in 2006 to 8 billion yuan (US$1.15 billion).

2 Quanzhong, Guo (2007) "An Overview of the Development of China's Magazine Industry," *Youth Journalist*, 3&4, 70.

3 Leping, Wu (2002) "A Review of China's Recent Five Years' Magazine Advertising Market," *A Vast View on Publishing*, 3, 19.

4 Feng, Wu (2008) "2007–2008: An Overview of the Development of China's Magazine Industry," *Media Today*, June, 29.

5 Xuanyi, Fan (2005) "The Managing Strategies of International Fashion Magazines' Chinese Edition," *The Journalist Monthly*, August, 66.

6 Cui Bapguo, Professor at Journalism School of Tsinghua University, personal communication, November 8, 2008, Beijing.

7 This is based on a data from Li Pin, (ed.) (2007) *Report on the Development of the Magazine Industry in China (No. 2)*, Beijing: Social Sciences Academic Press, 124; In 2005, *Stories* had a profit of more than 35 million yuan (U\$5 million), while *Elle China's* profit was 12 million yuan (US\$1.7 million*).

8 Li Pin, (ed.) (2007) *Report on the Development of the Magazine Industry in China (No. 2)*, Beijing: Social Sciences Academic Press, 57.

9 Ibid., 51.

10 Feng, Wu op. cit., 30.

11 Li Pin op. cit., 10.

12 Chao, Wei (2007) "Magazine Advertising Market in China in 2006," in *Report on the Development of the Magazine Industry in China (No. 2)*, ed. Li Pin, Beijing: Social Sciences Academic Press, 285.

13 Zeqing, Zhang (2006) "Nine Phenomena of 2005 China Periodicals," *Media*, February, 60.

14 Qiuqing, Shang Guan (2007) "A Review of Market Performance of Women Magazines," *China Book Business Report*, January 5.

15 Jian, Zheng (2007) "Analysis on the Main Trend of News Periodicals and Social Identity," *Press Circles*, 6, December, 43.

16 Ibid., 44.

17 *Caijing Magazine* was ranked ninth in advertising revenue in the first half of 2006. All the other nine magazines in the top 10 advertising revenue list are fashion magazines. This is quoted by Feng Wu (2007) in "Review and Outlook of China Periodical Industry in 2006–2007," in *Report on Development of China's Industry* ed. Cui Baoguo, Beijing, Social Science Academic Press, 123.

18 www.caijing.com.cn accessed September 4, 2008.

19 Xiaoyan, Zhu (2008) "e-Magazine – A New Medium in Web2.0 Times," *Science & Technology for Development*, 39, March, 1–3.

20 Kun, Ma (2006) "The Rise of E-magazines and the Industry," *Shenzhen Special Economic Zone Science and Technology, New Industry Monthly*, April, 30–31.

21 Feng, Wu (2008), "The Retrospect of China's Periodical Industry in 2007," in *Report on Development of China's Media Industry (2007–2008)*, ed. Cui Baoguo, Beijing: Social Sciences Academic Press, 107.

22 iResearch Group, (2006) *Report of China E-magazines*.

23 Gang, Chen, Jinchao, Chen, Wenjie, Song and Zhao, Zhou (2008) "Research on the Readers of e-Magazines," *New View of Advertising*, February, 24.

24 Guoming, Yu (2007) "China's Magazine Industry: An Industry to be Booming," in *Report on the Development of the Magazine Industry in China (No. 2)*, ed. Li Pin, Beijing: Social Sciences Academic Press, 4–5.

25 Gang, Chen, op. cit., 26.

26 Jianhong, Shen (2008) "Opportunity and Strategy-an Analysis of Digital Magazine Advertisement," *Media*, May, 65.

27 Quanzhong, Guo (2007) "A Look at China's Magazine Industry," *Media*, March, 13.

Chapter 6

1 Lubing, Fang (2004) *25 Years in China's Advertising*, Beijing: China's Encyclopedia Press, 2–3.

2 Shenmin, Huang and Junshen, Ding (2001) *Research on the Integration of China's Broadcasting Media*, Beijing: Chinese Price Press, 6.

3 Hong, Xu (2003) *An Analysis of Beijing's Traffic Program*, Beijing: Beijing University Press, 4.

4 Chenghou, Jiang (2004) "China's Radio Develops Rapidly," *China Radio & TV Academic Journal*, November, 80.

5 Lanzhu, Wang (2008) "An Analysis of TV and Radio Audience of China," in *Report on Development of China's Media Industry (2007–2008)* ed. Cui Baoguo, Beijing: Social Science Academic Press, 361.

6 Ibid.

7 Yun, Liu, Hui, Liu and Weiliang, Li (2008) "A Summary of the Development of China's Broadcasting Industry," in *Report on Development of China's Media Industry (2007–2008)* ed. Cui Baoguo, Beijing: Social Science Academic Press, 115.

8 Lanzhu, Wang op. cit.

9 Yaojie, Lei and Yu, Wang (2004) "The Strategy of China's Radio Development," *The Innovation and Development of Radio*, Beijing: Beijing Broadcast Institute Press, 52.

10 Shengmin, Huang and Junshen, Ding (2001) *Research on the Integration of China's Broadcasting Media*, Beijing: Chinese Price Press, 13.

11 Yanqiu, Ha and Shan, Zhao (2004) "A Study of 2003: The Year of Radio Development," *Modern Communication*, March, 31–3.

12 Lu, Cao and Jinghua, Huang (2005) "The Expansion of Radio in its Management," *China Radio & TV Academic Journal*, January, 14–16.

13 Qiannian, Chen (2004) *Climbing: Works by Chen Qiannian*, Shanghai: Shanghai People's Press, 19.

14 Lingying, Xu (2004) "2004 Key Words for China's Radio: Industrialization," *China Broadcasts*, April, 12.

15 Chen Qiannian, vice president of Shanghai Media Group. Interview on April 28, 2005.

16 Xinxin, Deng (2004) "Program Formats and Online Broadcasts", in *The Innovation and Development of Radio*, ed. Hu Zhengrong, Beijing: Beijing Broadcast Institute Press, 204.

17 Lu, Cao and Jinghua, Huang, op. cit., 14.

18 Ibid.

19 Yun, Liu, Hui, Liu and Weiliang, Li op. cit., 117.

20 Ling, Lin (2005) "A Feasibility Study of Setting up Radio Stations in the Countryside," *Xin Wen Zhi Shi*, March, 36.

21 "Statistics on the Development of Radio Website in China," *China Broadcasts*, August 2004, 42.

Chapter 7

1 Fong, Mei, "CCTV Tower: Beijing's Rising Ambitions," *Wall Street Journal*, November 7, 2008, 34.

2 These figures and most of those in this chapter come from research reports released by the State Administration of Radio, Film and Television (SARFT) and CSM Media Research, China's largest professional TV-rating data provider.

3 Weber, Ian (2003) "Localizing the Global: Successful Strategies for Selling Television Programmes to China," *Gazette* 65, 3, 273–90.

4 Cooper-Chen, Anne (2003) "Entertainment East and West: A Comparison of Prime-time U.S. and Asian TV Content Using the Methodology of the National Television Violence Study," paper presented to the Association for Education in Journalism and Mass Communication, Kansas City, July 30–August 2.

5 Zhu, Ying (2008) *Television in Post-reform China: Serial Dramas, Leadership and the Global Television Market*, New York: Routledge, 29; The sections on TV dramas draw upon Zhu (2008).

6 Ibid, 50.

7 Ibid, 91.

8 Chen, Yubo (2008) "Analysis of Sino-Japanese Animation," unpublished paper, Beijing, 2.

9 Fallows, James (2007) "Win in China!" *Atlantic Monthly*, April, 72; The section on reality shows draws on Fallows (2007).

10 Ibid., 78.

11 Cooper-Chen, Anne (1994) *Games in the Global Village*, Bowling Green, OH: Popular Press.

12 Zhu op. cit., 141.

13 Macartney, Jane (2005) "TV Talent Contest 'Too Democratic' for China's Censors," *The Times*, August 29.

14 Stelter, Brian and Stone, Brad (2009) "New Wave of Pirates Plunders Hollywood," *International Herald Tribune*, February 6, 2009, 11.

15 Weihua, Chen (2008) "Parody is a Norm of Life, Accept It," *China Daily*, December 27–28, 8.

16 Don Lee (2009) "China Limits on Entertainment Imports Violate Free Trade practices, WTO Rules", *Los Angeles Times*, September 2.

Chapter 8

1 Spiegel, Peter (2009) "China's CCTV Network Gets Little Sympathy After Hotel Fire," *Los Angeles Times*, February 11.

2 "Netizens Ridicule CCTV," *China Digital Times*, February 12, 2009.

3 "China TV faces propaganda charge," *BBC News*, January 12, 2009.

4 Reynolds, James (2007) "China Ethics Plea after Fake Buns," *BBC News*, July 24; "Tough Times for Staff at CCTV," *China Media News*, November 7, 2008.

5 "China TV faces Propaganda Charge," op. cit.

6 O'Brien, Chris (2009) "Obama's Address Censored in China," *The Washington Times*, January 21.

7 "CCTV News Edges toward Reform," *China.org.cn*, June 17, 2006.

8 Yinbo, Li (2002) "How Chinese Television and New Media Presented the U.S. 9/11 Tragedy: A Comparative Study of Sina.com, CCTV, and PhoenixTV." *Television & New Media*, 3, 223.

9 Ibid.

10 Ibid.

11 Fung, Anthony Y.H. (2008), *Global Capital, Local Culture: Transnational Media Corporations in China*. New York: Peter Lang, 128.

12 Ibid., 133.

13 Wang, Siwen (2009) "Strategies Used by Phoenix TV in Its News Commentary Programs" April 28, unpublished paper, Marquette University.

14 Zha, Jianying (1995) *China Pop*, New York: The New Press, 170.

15 "Newspeak and the Chinese Media," *The Digital Age*, May 10, 2009.

16 "CCTV Reporter's Arrest Causes a Stir," *Wall Street Journal*, December 9, 2008.

17 "Senior Leader Stresses Media Supervision in Corruption Fight," *China View*, Xinhua, May 29, 2009.

18 "TV Made Me Do It," *The Economist*, October 14, 1989.

19 "CCTV News Edges toward Reform," op. cit.

20 Ibid.

21 Chang, Jung (1995), *Wild Swans: Three Daughters of China*, New York: Simon & Schuster, 226–34.

22 Martinsen, Joel (2007) "Everybody Loves CCTV," *Danwei*, December 21.
23 Barboza, David (2008) "Chinese TV Hits Jackpot with Games," *New York Times*, August 22, C6.
24 Ibid.
25 Chang, T.K. (2002). *China's Window on the World: TV News, Social Knowledge and International Spectacles*, Cresskill, NJ: Hampton Press, 259.
26 Ibid.
27 Wang, Siwen op. cit.; Zhao, Yuezhi (2008), *Communication in China: Political Economy, Power and Conflict*, Lanham, MD: Rowman & Littlefield, 253.
28 Houghton, Kate (2009) "Subverting Journalists: Reporters and the CIA," Committee to Protect Journalists.
29 Chang (2002), op. cit., 259.
30 Ibid.
31 Cooper-Chen, Anne (2006) "The World According to *Xinwen Lianbo*, 2005: China's 900-milion-viewer "News-zilla," AEJMC annual meeting, San Francisco, August.
32 Stevenson, Robert (1988) *Communication, Development and the Third World*, White Plains, NY: Longman, 146.
33 Zhang, W. (1997) *Politics and Freedom of the Press*, Sydney: Australian Centre for Independent Journalism.
34 Hao, X.M. and Huang, X.Y. (2005). "Party Journalism vs. Market Journalism: The Coverage of SARS by Chinese Newspapers" International Communication Association, New York.
35 Barboza, op. cit.
36 Zhang, 1997, op. cit.; Y.Z. Zhao, (1998). *Media, Market and Democracy in China: Between the Party Line and Bottom Line*, Urbana: University of Illinois Press.
37 Jirik, John (2004) "China's News Media and the Case of CCTV-9," in *International News in the 21ˢᵗ Century*, C. Paterson and A. Sreberny, eds., Eastleigh, UK: John Libbey/Luton Press, 133.
38 Cooper Chen, Anne (2006). "The World of China's News: Topics and Frames on CCTV-9, 2005." International Association for Mass Communication Research, Cairo, Egypt, July 23–8.
39 Dong, Dong and Chang, Tsan-Kuo (2006) "Foreign News and Views on Television in China: The Decline of the Cold War News Frame," International Communication Association, Dresden, Germany, February 5.
40 Scotton, James F. (2002) "Atlanta, Beijing and London Present the News," Shanghai International Studies University, April.
41 Ibid.
42 Chang, T.K. op. cit., 238.
43 Tunstall, Jeremy (2008). *The Media Were American*, London: Oxford University Press, 194.

44 Glionna, John M. (2007) "China's Man at the Anchor Desk," *Los Angeles Times*, December 4.

45 Ibid.

46 MacLeod, Calum (2009) "China Plans a Media Empire to Boost Image," *USA Today*, February 19.

47 Ford, Peter (2009) "Beijing Launching a Chinese CNN to Burnish Image Abroad," *Christian Science Monitor*, February 5, 2009.

48 Barboza, David (2009) "News Media Run by China Look Abroad for Growth," *New York Times*, January 15, A6.

49 Ford, op. cit.

50 Ibid.

51 Fung, op. cit., 128–9.

Chapter 9

1   Xinhua website, May 2009; Associated Press website, May 2009.

2   Reporters without Borders, "The World's Biggest Propaganda Agency," 2005 special report.

3   Strupp, Joe (2000) "More Windows on the World: Nouveau Foreign Correspondents' Tastes Range from Wine to War," ASM Communications, Inc., *Editor & Publisher*.

4   Reporters without Borders, op. cit.

5   Zhao, Yuezhi (2008) *Communication in China: Political Economy, Power and Conflict*, Lanham, MD: Rowman & Littlefield, 29.

6   Ibid., 25.

7   Chang, Tsan-Kuo (2002), *China's Window on the World: TV News, Social Knowledge and International Spectacles*, Cresskill, NJ: Hampton Press, 108–9.

8   Zhao, op. cit., 324.

9   "Blowin' in the Wind" website, Xinhua.com, May 17, 2009.

10 Elliott, Charles W. (2000), "Flows of New from the Middle Kingdom: An Analysis of International News Releases from Xinhua," in *The Global Dynamics of News: Studies in International News Coverage and News Agenda*, eds. Abbas Malek and Anandam P. Kavoori, Stamford, CT: Ablex Publishing, 343–88.

11 *China View*, May 17, 2009.

12 Ibid.

13 Fung, Anthony Y.H. (2008), *Global Capital, Local Culture: Transnational Media Corporations in China*, New York: Peter Lang, 134.

14 Brief Introduction to Xinhua News Agency, May 2009.

15 Reporters Without Borders, op. cit.

16 Mulligan, William A. (1985) "Remnants of the Cultural the Revolution in Chinese Journalism of the 1980s," *Journalism Quarterly*, 65, 1, 20, 21.

17 Xin, Xin (2006) "A Developing Market in News: Xinhua News Agency and Chinese Newspapers," *Media Culture & Society*, 28, 1, 49.
18 Ibid., 48.
19 Tunstall, Jeremy (2007), *The Media Were American*, New York: Oxford University Press, 202.
20 Robert Bishop (1989), *Qi! Lai!*, Ames, IA: Iowa State University Press, 126.
21 Lee, Chin-Chuan (2000), "The Paradox of Political Economy: Media Structure, Press Freedom and Regime Change in Hong Kong," in *Power, Money and Media: Communication Patterns and Bureaucratic Controls in Cultural China*, ed. Chin-Chuan Lee, Evanston, IL: Northwestern University Press, 288–336.
22 Chu, Yik-yi (1999) "Overt and Covert Functions of the Hong Kong Branch of the Xinhua News Agency, 1947–84," *The Historian*, 62, 1, September, 31–46.
23 Lu, Ning (1997), *The Dynamics of Foreign Policy Decision Making in China*, Boulder, CO: Westview Press, 119.
24 Bishop, op. cit., 126.
25 Lu, op. cit., 203.
26 Elliott, op. cit., 357.
27 Hachten, William A. and Scotton, James F. (2007), *The World News Prism*, Malden, MA: Blackwell Publishing, 94.
28 Brief Introduction to Xinhua News Agency, xinhua.com.
29 Xin, Xin (2008) "Structural Change and Journalism Practice: Xinhua News Agency in the Early 2000s," *Journalism Practice*, 2, 1, 46.
30 Jon Swan, (1996) "I Was a 'Polisher' in a Chinese News Factory," *Columbia Journalism Review*, March/April, 33–8.
31 "Xinhua," China Media Guide, Danwei, May 17, 2009.
32 Zhao, op. cit., 105–6.
33 Chang, op. cit., 259.
34 Zhao, op. cit., 105–6.
35 Ibid., 101.
36 Elliott, op. cit., 348.
37 Xin, 2008, 52–3.
38 Mulligan, op. cit.
39 Elliott, op. cit., 348.
40 Reporters without Border, op. cit.
41 Xin, 2006, 55–6.
42 Chin-Chuan Lee, op. cit., 35.
43 Xin (2006), 50–1.
44 Chang, op. cit., 108–9.
45 Xin (2006), 53.
46 Ibid., 55–7.
47 Swan, op. cit., 33.

48 Xin (2008), 52.
49 Swan, op. cit., 34.
50 Pan, Zhongdang (2000) "Improvising Reform Activities: The Changing Reality of Journalism Practice in China, in *Power, Money and Media: Communication Patterns and Bureaucratic Controls in Cultural China*, ed. Chin-Chuan Lee, Evanston, IL: Northwestern University Press, 68–111.
51 Reporters without Borders, op. cit.
52 Xin (2008), 51.
53 Xin (2006), 62, n.10.
54 Xin (2008), 51.
55 Reporters without Borders, op. cit.
56 Xin (2008), 55.
57 Ibid., 56.
58 Ibid., 57.
59 Reporters without Borders, op. cit.
60 Ibid.
61 Elliott, op. cit., 363, 372.
62 Xin (2006), 60.
63 Peter Ford, (2009) "Beijing Launching a Chinese CNN to Burnish Image Abroad," *Christian Science Monitor*, February 5, 2009.
64 Barboza, David (2009) "News Media Run by China Look Abroad for Growth," *New York Times*, January 15, A6.
65 Lieshan, Yan (2009) "When in Rome . . . – A Few Thoughts on 'External Propaganda'," *China Digital Times*, March 20.
66 Zhao, op. cit., 102.

Chapter 10

1 Cheng, Hong (1996) "Advertising in China: A Socialist Experiment," in *Advertising in Asia: Communication, Culture, and Consumption*, ed. K.T. Frith, Ames, IA: Iowa State University Press, 73–102; Cheng, Hong (2000) "China: Advertising Yesterday and Today," in *International Advertising: Realities and Myths*, ed. J.P. Jones, Thousand Oaks, CA: Sage Publications, 255–84; Yu, Hong and Deng, Zhenqiang (2000) *A History of Contemporary Advertising in China*, Changsha: Human Science and Technology Press; Xu, Baiyi (1990) *Marketing to China: One Billion New Customers*, Lincolnwood, IL: NTC Business Books.
2 Madden, Normandy (2006) "China's $30 Billion Ad Market," *AdAge China*, March 1, http://adage.com/china/ accessed September 8, 2008; Zimei Fu, "China's Advertising Revenue in 2006 Reached RMB157.3 Billion," *People's Daily*, May 21, 2007 MediaChina.net, accessed September 12, 2008; Li, Yushi

"Chinese Advertising Industry Leaps to the Second Place in the World," *International Finance News* MediaChina.net, accessed September 12, 2008.

3   Zhang, Jinhai (2008) "An Examination of Chinese Advertising Growth in 30 Years," accessed December 3, 2008 http://www.mediach.com/html/51/n-27351.html

4   "A New Era for China's Advertising Industry," 2008, accessed December 3, 2008 http://english.maad.com.cn/content.asp?articleid=100

5   Zhang, op. cit.

6   Ibid.

7   Ibid.

8   Madden, Normandy (2008) "China and India: Are They Shelters in a Global Storm?" *Ad Age China*, September 17, http://adage.com/china/article?article-id=131046

9   Xu Lin, (2008) "Beijing Olympics Inspire an Ad Boom, Report from the Beijing 4Nshow 2008," *International Market News*, July 4, MediaChina.net, accessed December 3, 2008.

10   Madden, (2008) op. cit.

11   Fan, Lubin (2004) *Twenty-five Years in China's Advertising*, Beijing: China Encyclopedia Press, 94–116.

12   "China's Economic Conditions, CRS Report for Congress," March 1, 2008, http://www.accessmylibrary.com/coms2/summary_0286-34510480_ITM, accessed December 3, 2008.

13   Sanders, L., Madden, N., and Wentz, L., (2005) "Agency Holding Companies Rush to Stake Claims in China and India," September 19, *Advertising Age*, 76, 38, 1.

14   Adler, Roy D. (2008) "Counting on the Middle Class," November 4, http://www.miller-mccune.com/article/counting-on-the-middle-class,   accessed December 3, 2008.

15   Hung, Kineta, Gu, Flora Fang and Tse, Davis (2005) "Improving Media Decisions in China: A Targetability and Cost-Benefit Analysis," *Journal of Advertising*, 34, 1, 50.

16   World Trade Organization (WTO) (2008) "Members and Observers," http://www.wto.org/english/thewto_e/whatis_e/tif_e/org6_e.htm,   accessed December 3, 2008.

17   Hung, Gu, and Tse, op. cit.

18   Zhang, op. cit.

19   Ibid.

20   Ibid.

21   Cheng, (1996) op. cit., 86.

22   Fan, op. cit., 94–105.

23   Cui, Baoguo, Lu, Jinxhu and Li, Feng (2006) "Innovation and Transition – 2006 Chinese Media Industry Development Final Report," in B. Cui, ed., *Report*

on Development of China's Media Industry, Beijing: Social Sciences Academic Press, 18.

24 Huang, Shengmin and Shao, Huadong (2006), "Reforms and Conflicts-Analysis of Advertising Market and Its Trends in 2005," in *Report on Development of China's Media Industry*, ed. B. Cui, Beijing: Social Sciences Academic Press, 423.

25 Zhao, Shuguang (2006) "Blueprint of the Integration of Newspaper Advertising Management," in *Report on Development of China's Media Industry*, ed. B. Cui, Beijing: Social Sciences Academic Press, 123.

26 Ibid.

27 Yao, Lin (2006) "An Analysis of Chinese Newspaper Advertising Market in 2005," in *Report on Development of China's Media Industry*, ed. B. Cui, Beijing: Social Sciences Academic Press, 132–4.

28 Shen, Ying and Deng, Shiyong (2006) "Overview of Chinese Magazine Readership and Future Development, 2005–2006," in in *Report on Development of China's Media Industry*, ed. B. Cui, Beijing: Social Sciences Academic Press, 181.

29 Ibid.

30 Ibid., 183.

31 Yao, Lin and Zhang, Xiaohu "An Analysis of Chinese Periodical Advertising Market in 2005," in *Report on Development of China's Media Industry*, ed. B. Cui, Beijing: Social Sciences Academic Press, 169.

32 "The Gift behind the Glossy Circulation" *China Daily* Hong Kong Edition, November 10, 2005, 4.

33 Hung, Gu, and Tse, op. cit., 49–63.

34 Keane, M. and Spurgeon, C. (2004) "Advertising Industry and Culture in Post-WTO China," *Media International Australia*, 11, 104–17.

35 Zhan, Zhengmao, Xiong, Yan and Chen, Xiaoqing (2006) "A Study of Magazine Advertising Price: A Case Study of Fashion Magazines," in *Report on Development of China's Media Industry*, ed. B. Cui, Beijing: Social Sciences Academic Press, 157.

36 Xie, Gengyun and Tang, He (2008) "Chinese Television Advertising in 2007," *China Journalism Review*, http://cjr.zjol.com.cn/05cjr/system/2007/01/09/008095098.shtml, accessed September 28, 2008.

37 Ibid.

38 Chang, Tsan-Kuo (2002) *China's Window on the World: TV News, Social Knowledge and International Spectacles*, Cresskill, NJ: Hampton Press.

39 Yang, Ting "CCTV Advertising Revenue in 2007 Topped RMB10 Billion," *China Economics News*, MediaChina.net, accessed September 13, 2008.

40 Li, Benjamin (2008) "All About . . . The CCTV Auction," November 8, http://www.brandrepublic.asia/Media/newsarticle/2008_11/All-About-The-CCTV-auction/33502, accessed December 3, 2008.

41   Ibid.
42   Coonan, Clifford (2008) "CCTV Advertising Auction Shows Solid Growth,"
     November 20, http://www.varietyasiaonline.com/content/view/7527/1/, accessed
     December 3, 2008).
43   Li, op. cit.
44   China Central Television (CCTV), (2008) "9.2567 Billion [Yuan]: An Con-
     fidence Indictor," November 21, http://ad.cctv.com/20081121/106617.shtml,
     accessed December 3, 2008.
45   Li, op. cit.
46   Coonan, op. cit.
47   Landreth, Jonathan (2008) "CCTV Expects to Weather Downturn Broadcaster
     Facing Lower Fourth Quarter after Olympics," November 18, https://secure.
     vnuemedia.com/hr/content_display/finance/news/e3i2dd2f2ead332946a2a36
     a6676762637b, accessed December 3, 2008.
48   China Central Television (CCTV), op. cit.
49   Wang, Jing (2008) *Brand New China: Advertising, Media, and Commercial
     Culture*, Cambridge: Harvard University Press, 259.
50   Ibid., 247.
51   Zheng, Yangpeng (2008) "Ad Auction Bucks the Trend," *China Daily*,
     December 1, http://www.chinadaily.com.cn/bizchina/2008-12/01/content_
     7257327.htm, accessed December 3, 2008.
52   Landreth, op. cit.
53   Xie and Tang, op. cit.; There are 34 provincial-level administrative units
     in China, including 4 municipalities, 22 provinces, 5 autonomous regions,
     2 special districts, and Taiwan, which Beijing considers a province but is not
     actually under the administration of the People's Republic of China.
54   Li, Xiuzhong (2006) "One Radio Station Makes RMB 300 Million from
     Advertising; Radio Becomes a 'Strong' Medium," *Finance News*, September
     9, MediaChina.net, accessed December 3, 2008).
55   Sun, Shufeng and Wang, Quanjie (2006) "Reform and Development of Chinese
     Radio Industry," in *Report on Development of China's Media Industry*, ed.
     B. Cui, Beijing: Social Sciences Academic Press, 293.
56   Ibid.
57   Li, op. cit.
58   Huang, Shengmin and Shao, Huadong (2006), "Reforms and Conflicts-
     Analysis of Advertising Market and Its Trends in 2005," in *Report on Develop-
     ment of China's Media Industry*, ed. B. Cui, Beijing: Social Sciences Academic
     Press, 429.
59   Xu, Shenglan (2008) "Olympics Fuel China's Internet Ads," *China Daily*,
     August 20, MediaChina.net, accessed December 3, 2008; "Online Advertising
     in China: The Olympic Year," *eMarketer*, September 14, 2008, MediaChina.net,
     accessed December 3, 2008.

60   "Online Ad Revenues 2008: U.S. vs. China," *Trinetizen*, MediaChina.net accessed December 3, 2008.

61   Hou, Tao (2006) "Keywords of Chinese Internet Advertising Industry in 2005," in *Report on Development of China's Media Industry*, ed. B. Cui, Beijing: Social Sciences Academic Press, 427.

62   "Putting RMB 600 Million in Its Pocket, CCTV Was the Biggest New Media Winner during the Olympics," *Century Finance News*, MediaChina.net, accessed December 3, 2008.

63   "RMB 600 Million Reaped; CCTV Online the Largest Olympic New Medium," *The 21st Century Economic News*, 2008, http://finance.jrj.com.cn/olympic/2008/09/041351849107.shtml, accessed December 3, 2008.

64   "Online Advertising in China: The Olympic Year," op. cit.

65   Jin, Yafen "Internet Advertising Revenue in 2008 Expected to Top RMB17 Billion," *China Journalism Publishing News*, MediaChina.net, accessed December 3, 2008.

66   Ling, Huishan "Internet Advertising Revenue to Top RMB50 Billion in Three Years," *Information Times*, MediaChina.net, accessed December 3, 2008.

67   CTR Market Research, (2008) "A History of Success," http://www.ctrchina.cn/ctrchina/en/WeAretCTR-Success.html, accessed December 3, 2008.

68   Zheng, op. cit. 1.

69   Steel, Emily (2008) "Nielsen Forms China Web Venture," *Wall Street Journal*, October 10, http://online.wsj.com/article/SB122357907789819935.html#printMode, accessed December 3, 2008.

70   Xu, op. cit.

71   "Learn about the China Airport Advertising Industry, 2007," Reuters, January 9, 2008, accessed September 12, 2008.

72   Zheng, op. cit.

Chapter 11

1   Chunhui Hi and Jing Xie (2009) "Thirty Years' Development of Public Relations in Mainland China," *China Media Research*, 5, 3, July.

2   Yu, Yun (1991) "Public Relations in China – A Decade of Rapid Growth," *Communication World*, October.

3   Ibid.

4   Black, Sam (1990) "Public Relations in China Today," *Public Relations Quarterly*, 35, 4, Winter, 29.

5   Strenski, James B. and Yue, Kung (1998) "China: The World's Next Public Relations Superpower," *Public Relations Quarterly*, 43, 2, Summer, 24.

6   Yu, op. cit.

7   www.china-embassy.org/eng/gyzg/t259626.htm

8　Ibid.

9　Strenski and Yue, op. cit.

10　Wu, Youfu (2007) *20-Year Development Report of China's Public Relations*, Shanghai: Foreign Learning Education Press, 522–4.

11　Wu, Xu (2002) "Doing PR in China: A 2001 Version – Concepts, Practices, and Some Misperceptions," *Public Relations Quarterly*, 47, 2, Summer, 10.

12　Chen, Ni and Culbertson, Hugh M. (1992) "Two Contrasting Approaches of Government Public Relations in Mainland China," *Public Relations Quarterly*, 37.n.3, Fall, 36.

13　Ibid.

14　Ibid.

15　Ibid.

16　Ibid.

17　Chen, Ni and Culbertson, Hugh M. (2003) "Public Relations in Mainland China: An Adolescent with Growing Pains," in *The Global Public Relations Handbook: Theory, Research, and Practice* (Lea's Communication) eds. Krishnamurthy Sriramesh and Dejan Vercic, Mahwah, NJ: Lawrence Erlbaum.

18　Yu, op. cit.

19　Translated by the author. The original Chinese version was retrieved on April 14, 2008 from www.cipra.org.cn/guidance/ShowArticle.asp?ArticleID=660

20　Black, op. cit.

21　Xu Wu, op. cit.

22　Ibid.

23　Hackley, Carol Ann and Dong, Qingwen (2001) "American Public Relations Networking Encounters China's Guanxi," *Public Relations Quarterly*, 46, 2, Summer, 16.

24　Xu Wu, op. cit.

25　Chen, Ni (2003) "From Propaganda to Public Relations Evolutionary Change in the Chinese Government," *Asian Journal of Communication*, 13, 2, 96–121.

26　Drobis, David (1996) "Chinese Consumers: The Riches Beyond the Wall," *Public Relations Quarterly* 41.n.1, Spring, 23.

27　Xu Wu, op. cit.

28　Ibid.

29　Chen and Culbertson, 2003, op. cit.

30　Hackley and Dong, op. cit., 16.

31　Ritchey, David, (2000) "The Changing Face of Public Relations in China and Hong Kong," *Public Relations Quarterly*, 45, 4, 2000, 7.

32　Ibid.

33　Chen, op. cit.

34　Bernhardt, Jay M. (2008) "China – The New Health Marketing Frontier," March 6, www.cdc.gov/HealthMarketing/blog.htm

35 David Zhao, (2008) "2008 PR Industry Overview," March 31, retrieved from: http://blogs.hillandknowlton.com/blogs/ampersand/articles/10492.aspx

36 David Drobis (1996) "Chinese Consumers: The Riches Beyond the Wall," *Public Relations Quarterly*, 41, Spring, 23.

37 Ibid.

38 "Coca-Cola to Invest More Than $2 bn in China over Next Three Years," Xinhua, March 3, 2007.

39 Ibid.

40 "Coke Offer for China's Huiyuan Could Face Difficulties Winning Approval," Xinhua, September 3, 2008.

41 "Coke and Huiyuan: Let the PR Slanging Begin," imagethief.com, September 11, 2008.

42 "Coke Offer for China's Huiyuan Could Face Difficulties Winning Approval," op. cit.

43 Ibid.

44 "Coca-Cola to Invest More Than $2 bln in China over Next Three Years," op. cit.

45 "Coca-Cola's Purchase of China's Huiyuan Fails to Pass Antimonopoly Review," Xinhua, March 18, 2009.

46 Ibid.

47 Ibid.

48 Ibid.

49 "Coke and Huiyuan: Let the PR Slanging Begin," op. cit.

50 Ibid.

51 "Coke-Huiyuan's Chinese Media Battle," *Wall Street Journal*, September 10, 2008.

52 "Coke, Huiyuan and the Audiences that Matter," imagethief.com, April 1, 2009.

53 Ibid.

54 Ibid.

55 Ibid.

56 "Seven Reasons for the Coke-Huiyuan Epic Fail," siliconhutong.typepad.com, March 18, 2009.

57 Black, Sam (1992) "Chinese Update," *Public Relations Quarterly*, 37.n.3, Fall, 41.

58 Chen and Culbertson op. cit.

59 Culbertson, Hugh M. and Chen, Ni (1996) *International Public Relations: A Comparative Analysis*, Mahwah, NJ: Lawrence Erlbaum Associates.

60 Strenski and Yue, op. cit.

61 Culbertson and Chen, op. cit.

62 Youfu Wu, op. cit.

63 Black, 1990, op. cit.

64 Youfu Wu, op. cit.

65 Black, 1990, op. cit.
66 Ibid.
67 Ibid.
68 Strenski and Yue, 1998.
69 Youfu Wu, op. cit.
70 Xu Wu, op. cit.
71 Strenski and Yue, op. cit.
72 Xu Wu, op. cit.
73 Chunhui Hi and Jing Xie op. cit.
74 Zhao, op. cit.
75 Ibid.
76 Bernhardt, op. cit.
77 CNNIC (China Internet Network Information Center) retrieved from http://cnnic.cn
78 Zhao, op. cit.
79 Ibid.
80 Personal communication, September 25, 2008.

Chapter 12

1 Lin, Jinxi (2008) "Industrialization, Industrialization System, Stars. An Interview with Huang Jianxin," *Contemporary Cinema*, 7, 148, 7.
2 Shuguang Rao and Bi, Xiaoyu (2008) "The Predicament and Strategy," *Contemporary Cinema*, 6, 147, 9.
3 Yang, Guoqiang (2008) "China Film Group Makes Effort to Do its IPO first in Movie Industry," *CBNews Daily*, January 14, C1.
4 Ibid.
5 Zhou, Ning (2000), *Forever Utopia: China's Image in the West.* Wuhan: Hubei Education Press, 157.
6 http://en.wikipedia.org/wiki/Hero_(movie) accessed May 19, 2009.
7 http://en.wikipedia.org/wiki/Hero_(movie), originally cited from "I'm not interested in politics," Interviews, guardian.co.uk/Film, accessed May 19, 2009.
8 http://en.wikipedia.org/wiki/Hero_(movie) accessed May 19, 2009.
9 http://movies.yahoo.com/shop?d=hv&cf=info&id=1808404384 accessed May 20, 2009.
10 http://www.gov.cn/jrzg/2009-01/09/content_1201105.htm accessed May 20, 2009.
11 *Guangzhou Daily*, December 25, 2006.
12 http://yule/sohu.com/20061227/n247291438.shtml, accessed September 9, 2008.

13 Jaffre, Valerie (2004) "An Interview with Jia Zhangk," *Senses of Cinema*. June, http://www.sensesofcinea.com/contents/04/32/chinese_underground_film_html

14 Hou, Ningning (2005) "Jia Zhangke Doesn't Expect High Box-office Revenue," *Beijing Morning News*, April 9.

15 Ling, Zhan (2005) "Film Officials Learn How to Rate Films," *Judicial Evening News*, April 19.

16 Hu, Qiming (2008) "Rating Impossible, but Really Important," *Southern Weekend*, January 3, 4.

17 Translated from Yong Liu's interview with Xu Pengle on September 16, 2008. Liu translated the interview transcripts from Chinese to English.

18 Hu, op. cit.

19 Liang, Zhenpeng (2008) "Poly-bona Hits a Rock, Hot Apple Halts for Violation," *CBNews Daily*, January 4, C3.

20 Yang, op. cit.

21 Ibid.

22 Liang, op. cit.

23 Based on Liu interview with Xu, op. cit.

24 *Contemporary Cinema*, 2008, 3, 144, 4.

25 Jia, Leilei (2008) "As an Event Film," *Contemporary Cinema*, 3, 144, 5.

26 Zhang, Yiwu (2008) "Assembly: Visit and Ponder on the Past of China," *Contemporary Cinema*, 3, 144, 5.

27 Wang, Chunxia (2008) "CMB Describes Details about *The Assembly*'s 50 Million RMB Loan without Guarantor," *CBNews Daily*, January 8, 2008, B8.

28 Ibid.

29 http://www.news365.com.cn/yw/200809/t20080914_20225792.htm, accessed September 14, 2008.

30 Lin, Jianxi (2008) "Industrialization, Industrialization System, Stars-An Interview with Huang Jianxin," *Contemporary Cinema*, 7, 148, 7.

31 http://ent.qq.com/a/20080813/000031.htm, accessed September 12, 2008.

32 Wan, Chuanfa and Zhu, Feng (2008) "The Star and the Star System in Film Industrialization," *Contemporary Cinema*, 7, 148, 12–16.

Chapter 13

1 H. Huang, (2001) *The Development History of the Media Industry in China*, Shanghai: Fudan University Publishing House, 278.

2 Cited in CRI pamphlet.

3 Cited on http://gb.cri.cn/

4 Cited on http://www.sina.com

5 Cited on http://www.chinanet.com

6 Cited on http://www.medicaljournal.com

7 Cited on http://www.sina.com

8 Yang, R. (1993) "On the Strategic Position of English TV Service in China's International Communication," unpublished manuscript.

9 Cited on http://www.cctv.com website

10 Baoguo, Cui (ed.) (2007) *Report on Development of China's Media Industry* Beijing: Social Sciences Academic Press.

11 The 22nd CNNIC Internet Report available at: http://www.cnnic.net.cn/uploadfiles/pdf/2008/7/23/170516.pdf

12 H. Huang, op. cit., 21.

13 Guo, Ke (1999) "Liberalization and Conservatism as reflected in media development in China since 1978," *Journal of Development Communication*, Malaysia, 58.

14 Chan, Y.Y. (2000) "The English-language media in Hong Kong," *World Englishes*, 323–34.

15 Baoguo, Cui (ed.) (2007) *Report on Development of China's Media Industry, 2007*, Beijing: Social Sciences Academic Press.

Chapter 14

1 Barboza, David (2009) "News Media Run by China look abroad for Growth" New York Times, Jan. 16, A1.

2 Fowler, Geoffrey A. and Change, Jonathan (2007) "News Magnate Baits Beijing by Pairing Politics and Sex," *Wall Street Journal*, October 23, A1.

3 Wei, Ran (2000) "Mainland China News in Taiwan's Press: The Interplay of Press Ideology, Organizational Strategies, and News Structure," in *Power, Money and Media*, ed. Chin-Chuan Lee, Evanston, IL: Northwestern University Press, 337–65.

4 Dafydd Fell (2008), *Politics of Modern Taiwan*, New York: Routledge; Peter Kuo, (1993) "Taiwan's New Media," *World Affairs*, 15.

5 Reporters without Borders, *2007 Singapore Annual Report*.

6 Chin-Chuan Lee (2000) "Chinese Communication: Prisms, Trajectories, and Modes of Understanding," in *Power, Money and Media*, ed. Chin-Chuan Lee, Evanston, IL: Northwestern University Press, 21.

7 Sun, Wanning (2006) *Media and the Chinese Diaspora*, New York: Routledge, 47.

8 Zhou, Min, Chen, Wenhong, and Cai, Guoxuon (2006) "Chinese-language Media and Immigrant Life in the United States and Canada" in *Media and the Chinese Diaspora*, ed. Wanning Sun, New York: Routledge, 42–74.

9 Casciani, Dominic "Chinese Britain: How a *Second Generation Wants* the Voice of its Community Heard," BBC News Online.

10 Chen, Kathy (2007) "Chinese Dissidents Take On Beijing via Media Empire," *Wall Street Journal*, November 15, A1.

11 Kwong, Robin (2008) "Media Chinese Targets Surge in Expatriates", *Financial Times*, June 23, 1.

12 Barboza, op. cit.

Chapter 15

1 The Steering Committee of the Journalism Discipline affiliated to the Ministry of Education.

2 "Where Will the Students Go?" *The Economist*, April 11, 2009, 40.

3 Wong, Edward (2009) "China Releases Report on Pre-Olympics Crackdown," New York Times, January 6, 10.

4 Yardley, Jim (2008) "After 30 Years Economics Perils on China's Path," New York Times, December 19, A1.

5 Bodeen, Christopher (2009) The Associated Press, January 18, (retrieved from the Internet).

6 Wines, Michael and Wong, Edward (2009) "China Takes Stage as World Economic Power," *The New York Times*, April 2, A12.

7 Pomfret, John (2008) "A Long Wait at the Gate to Greatness," Washington Post, July 27, B1.

8 Pomfret, op. cit.

9 Ibid.

10 Wines, Michael (2009) "In China, No Plans to Emulate West's Ways," *The New York Times*, March 10, 2009, A5.

11 Wines, op. cit.

12 Arango, Tim (2009) "U.S. Media See a Path to India over China's Snub," New York Times, May 4, A1.

13 Xin, Xin (2006) "Xinhua News Agency and Globalization: Negotiating between the Global, the Local and the National" in *Communications Media, Globalization and Empire*, ed. Oliver Boyd-Barrett, Eastleigh, UK: John Libbey Publishing, 118.

14 Keith Bradsher (2009) "China's Economy is Roaring Back," *New York Times*, September 18, A1.

Bibliography

Baoguo, Cui (2007) *Report on Development of China's Media Industry*, Beijing: Social Sciences Academic Press.

Bishop, Robert (1989) *Qi lai! Mobilizing One Billion Chinese: The Communication System*, Ames: Iowa State University Press.

Chadwick, Andrew (2006) *Internet Politics: States, Citizens, and New Communication Technologies*, New York: Oxford University Press.

Chan, Joseph Man, Pan, Zhongdang, and Lee, C.C. (2002) *Global Media Spectacle: News War over Hong Kong*, Albany: State University of New York Press.

Chang, Tsan Kuo (2002) *China's Window on the World: TV News, Social Knowledge and International Spectacles*, Cresskill, NJ: Hampton Press.

Chang, Won Ho (1989) *Mass Media in China: The History and the Future*, Ames: Iowa State University Press.

Culbertson, Hugh M. and Chen, Ni (1996) *International Public Relations: A Comparative Analysis*, Mahwah, NJ: Lawrence Erlbaum Associates.

Curran, James, and Park, Myung-Jin (eds.) (2000) *De-Westernizing Media Studies*, New York: Routledge.

Curtin, Michael (2007) *Playing to the World's Largest Audience: The Globalization of Chinese Film and TV*, Berkeley: University of California Press.

Donald, Stephanie, Keane, Michael, and Hong, Yin (eds.) (2002) *Media in China: Consumption, Content and Crisis*, New York: RoutledgeCurzon.

Fung, Anthony Y.H. (2008) *Global Capital, Local Culture: Transnational Media Corporations in China*, New York: Peter Lang.

Guo, Ke (2003) *International Communication in China: Analysis on English-language Media in China*, Shanghai: Fudan University Press.

Ha, Louisa and Ganahl III, Richard J. (2007) *Webcasting Worldwide*, Mahwah, NJ: Lawrence Erlbaum.

Hachten, William (1993) *The Growth of Media in the Third World: African Failures, Asian Successes*, Ames: Iowa State University Press.

Hachten, William and Scotton, James F. (2007) *World News Prism*, 7th ed., Malden, MA: Blackwell.

Hong, Junhao (1998) *The Internationalization of Television*, Westport, CT: Praeger.

Hu, Huang (2001) *Development History of the Journalism Industry in China*, Shanghai: Fudan University Press.

Jia, Wenshan, Xing Lu and Heisey, D. Ray (eds.) (2002) *Chinese Communication Theory and Research*, Westport, CT: Ablex Publishing.

Jiang, Ling and Yuming, Feng (eds.) (2007) *The Development Report of China's Newspaper Industry*, Beijing: Social Sciences Academic Press.

Lee, C.C. (1990) *Voices of China: The Interplay of Politics and Journalism*, New York: Guilford Press.

Lee, C.C. (ed.) (2000) *Power, Money and Media: Communication Patterns and Bureaucratic Control in Cultural China*, Evanston, IL: Northwestern University Press.

Lee, C.C. (ed.) (2003) *Chinese Media: Global Contexts*, (Routledge Studies in Asia's Transformations), New York: Routledge.

Lynch, Daniel C. (1999) *After the Propaganda State: Media Politics and "Thought Work" in Reformed China*, Stanford, CA: Stanford University Press.

Malek, Abbas and Kavoori, Anandam P. (eds.) (2000) *The Global Dynamics of News: Studies in International News Coverage and News Agenda*, Stamford, CT: Ablex Publishing.

Meyer, Michael (2008) *The Last Days of Old Beijing*, New York; Walker.

Pan, Philip (2008) *Out of Mao's Shadow*, New York: Simon and Schuster.

Polumbaum, Judy (2008) *China Ink*, Lanham, MD: Rowman and Littlefield.

Sun, Wanning (2006) *Media and the Chinese Diaspora*, New York: Routledge.

Tam , Kwok-kan and Dissanayake, Wimal (1998) *New Chinese Cinema: Images of Asia*, New York: Oxford University Press.

Terrill, Ross (2003) *The New Chinese Empire: And What It Means for the United States*, New York: Basic Books.

Wang, Jian (2000) *Foreign Advertising in China: Becoming Global, Becoming Local*, Boston, MA: Wiley-Blackwell.

Wang, Jing (2008) *Brand New China: Advertising, Media and Commercial Culture*, Cambridge: Harvard University Press.

Wu, Xu (2007) *Chinese Cyber Nationalism: Evolution, Characteristics, and Implications*, Lanham, MD: Lexington Books.

Xing, Lu, Jia, Wenshan and Heisey, D. Ray (eds.) (2002) *Chinese Communication Studies: Contexts and Comparisons*, Westport, CT: Ablex.

Ying, Zhu. (2008) *Television in Post-Reform China*, New York: Routledge.

Yu, Frederick T.C. (1964) *Mass Persuasion in Communist China*, New York: Praeger.

Zha, Jianying (1995) *China Pop*, New York: The New Press.

Zhang, Dianyuan (2007) *Innovation of Chinese Media Systems*, Guangzhou: Nanfang Daily Press.

Zhao, Yuezhi (1990) *Media, Market and Democracy in China: Between the Party Line and the Bottom Line*, Urbana, IL: University of Illinois Press.

Zhao, Yuezhi (2008) *Communication in China: Political Economy, Power and Conflict*, New York: Rowman and Littlefield.

Zhu, Ying (2008) *Television in Post-reform China: Serial Dramas, Leadership and the Global Television Market*, New York: Routledge.

Index

advertising
  and economic development, 128
  competition, 131
  government regulation, 131
  media segmentation, 138
  Olympics, 136–7
Apple Daily, 199
Associated Press, 115
Authoritarian Capitalism, 23–4

Baidu (Chinese Google), 33–4
BBC, 100, 110, 114, 116, 125, 127
Beijing Evening News, 46–7
Beijing Radio, 136
Beijing Review, 183
Beijing Youth, 123
Belgrade, Chinese embassy bombing, 146
bloggers, 28, 30

CCTV
  9/11 attack, 99–101
  advertising, 134–5
  audience size, 104
  Barack Obama, 99
  headquarters fire, 98
  local governments, 102, 105
  Mao Zedong, 118
  overseas audiences, 107–11
  protocol news, 107
  "Super Girl", 95

Xiawen Lianbo, 100, 102, 104–7
  Xinhua, 111, 116
cell phones,
  censorship, 37
  growth, 36
  mobilization tool, 37
China Daily, 15, 185, 186
China Internet Network Information
  Center (CNNIC), 32
China News Service, 117
China Radio International, 183
China Today, 183, 185
Chinese Academy of Social Science,
  158
Chinese Journalist, 127
CNN, 100, 110, 113, 114, 116, 125,
  127
Coca-Cola, 155–7
Confucius, Analects of, 145–6
CPC (Communist Party), 88

Dalai Lama, 42
Deng Xiaoping, 144
diaspora, Chinese people, 198
  media and people abroad, 203–4
  outmigration, 205

earthquake in Sichuan, 12–14
Economic Daily, 142
education for journalism and
  communication, 208

English channels on TV, 187, 188
English media roles,
    bridging, 194,
    elite, 191
    future trends, 196
    language, 192
Elle China, 62, 134

Falun Gong, 29, 204–5

GAPP (General Agency of the Press),
    116
geography of China, 19–20
Google and Yahoo, cooperation with
    Chinese government, 34–5
Great Leap Forward, 118
Guangdong, Radio, 136

Han, Han, 98
Hong Kong, 117, 118, 141, 199–200
    film industry, 199
    press freedom, 200
    relations with UK and China, 199
Hu Jintao, 15, 41, 144, 152
Huang Jianxin, 163

India, western media look to, 211–12
Internet services, 189

Kai-Shek, Chiang, 200
Kristof, Nicholas, 12

Lee, C.C., 12
Lee, Kwan Yew, 202–3
Li, Gong, 179, 180
"Long March", 117

Macau, 116, 117
magazines,
    digital, 71–2
    in English, 185–7
    fashion, 66–9

four categories, 63
    general interest, 64–6
    joint ventures, 63
    news, financial, 69–71
    totals, circulations, 61, 62
Maher, Ed, 111, 112
major problems, demographics, poverty,
    pollution, ideology, 209–11
metropolitan dailies, 120, 121
motion pictures,
    decline of independents, 168–9
    domestic films, 164–6
    earnings, audiences, 163–4
    Hollywood influences, 173–5
    rating of films, 170–2
    relaxed film censorship, 169–70
    role of stars, 178
    WTO effects on films, 166–7

Netease, 136
Newspapers,
    changing roles, 46
    Chinese perspective, 58–60
    dual roles, 50–2
    in English, 185–7
    history, 43
    newspaper groups, 52–3
    party organs, 44
    readership, 49
    served elites, 44
    total revenues, 49
North China Daily News, 183, 185
NWIO (New World Information
    Order), 118

Olympics, 2008 in Beijing, 16–18
Oriental Daily News, 199

People's Daily, 16, 107, 116, 118, 121,
    122, 142
Pew Research Center,
    survey of attitudes to China, 113

Phoenix TV, 99, 100,
   and 9/11 attacks, 99, 100
   and mainland audience, 101
   and Xinhua, 101
Politburo, 116
press,
   cultural differences, 24–5
   Leninist theory, 22
   modern history, 20, 21
   relations with government, 25–6
Public Relations,
   Analects of Confucius, 145–6
   and Deng Xiaoping, 144
   and Hu Jintao, 144, 152
   and national economy, 142
   and SARS crisis, 153
   and Wen Jiabao, 144, 160
   Beijing Olympics, 160
   Chinese definition, 147–8
   Chinese Public Relations
      Association, 157
   foreign firms, 151
   Miss PR drama, 141
   Public Relations News, 158

QQ, 136

Radio broadcasting,
   boom times, 75
   decline, 75–6
   deregulation and revival, 76, 78
   early radio, 74–5
   English language learning, 77
   online radio stations, 81
radio services in English, (CRI), 184
Red China News Agency, 117
Reference News, 117, 119
Reporters Without Borders, 199, 202

SARFT (State Admin. For Radio,
   Film, and TV), 88, 96, 116, 120,
   171, 172

SARS epidemic, 124, 153
satires and protests, 38–9, 40
Shanghai Media Group (SMG), 136
Shanghai Radio, 136
Shanghai Style, 134
Shuguang, Rao, 163
Sichuan earthquake, 121, 154
Sina.com, 100, 116, 136
Singapore, 201, 202
Sohu.com, 136
South Morning China Post, 42, 199
Southern Weekend, 14, 127
Southern Metropolis, 114
Standard (Hong Kong), 199
Starbucks, 161
State Council, 116, 121
Stone, Sharon, 154
support of government, 26–7

Tatzebao (big character posters), 20
Tiananmen Square, 21, 41, 123, 124, 199
Tibet, protests in, 11–12
television entertainment,
   foreign influences, 91–2
   game shows, 93
   history, 85
   Olympics, 84
   reality shows, 93
   regulation, 87
   revenues, ratings, 87
   TV imports, 89–90

UNESCO, 118
USA Today, 49

Wall Street Journal, 156
webcasting, 35
Wen Jiabao, 13, 144, 152
West Germany, 118
Wild Swans, 103
WTO (World Trade Organization),
   120, 131

Xinhua,
    and CCTV, 101, 116, 120, 122
    and city newspapers, 122
    as Third World agency, 118
    auxiliary enterprise, 119–20
    diplomatic role, 118
    international plans, 126
    local governments, 124

party newspapers, 122
positive news emphasis, 121
Tibet protests, 12
Xinhuanet, 116, 121, 124

Zedong, Mao, 12, 118
Zhao, Ziyang, 124